27-672

| AUTHOR | CLASS No. |
|---|---|
| CARTER, G.A. | E02 |
| TITLE | BOOK No. |
| Warrington & the Mid-Mersey Valley | 08559973 |

# WARRINGTON
## and
# THE
# MID-MERSEY VALLEY

by

## G. A. CARTER, F.L.A.

Illustrated from drawings, paintings, and photographs,
including many original photographs by the author.

E. J. MORTEN, DIDSBURY.

1971

08559973   01900627

L000122629

© G. A. Carter, F.L.A., 1971.
Published By E.J. Morten. (Publishers)
Warburton St., Didsbury, Manchester 20.
SBN: 901598 259

Written For Joy, Janet, Michael

Printed By The Acorn Press, 10 Pall Mall, Liverpool, L3 6HJ.

The articles in this book were originally published in *'The Warrington Guardian'* from February 9, 1969 to November 27, 1970 as *"What's in a Name?"*; *"The Street Where You Live"* and *"Your Church"*.

The title *"What's in a Name?"* was suggested by the Editor, Mr. Gordon Bennett.

The first two articles *"The Mid-Mersey Valley"* and *"Digging up the past in Lancashire and Cheshire"* have not been published previously.

A Bibliography has also been added.

(Written for Joy, Janet and Michael.)

The author wishes to acknowledge the help he has received from many people in the compilation of these articles, especially from those associated with the Churches described, and in general from Mrs. Shirley Pargeter, A.L.A., Local History Librarian in the Warrington Municipal Library.

The River Mersey flows from Stockport to Liverpool and has almost always served both as a boundary and a barrier. In modern times it was the boundary between Lancashire and Cheshire until the Manchester Ship Canal was cut at the end of the nineteenth century when the Canal became the County boundary for part of its length instead of the Mersey. Even after this change occurred, however, the Mersey was retained as an ecclesiastical boundary, in the vicinity of Warrington, between the dioceses of Liverpool and Chester.

Between the departure of the Romans from England in the fifth century and the arrival of the Normans in the eleventh century, the Mersey was a boundary between the ancient English kingdoms of Northumbria and Mercia and as such was fortified by Edward the Elder and his sister Ethelfleda in the tenth century. A clear cut distinction also occurs in the Domesday Survey between the County of Chester and the land lying between the Ribble and the Mersey, indicating that the Mersey remained as a boundary before Lancashire became a County. The name Mersey, indeed, is derived from the two old English elements, the second of which *ea* means 'river'. The first element, according to Ekwall, offers some difficulties and is connected with the O.E. *(ge) maere* meaning boundary. He says that the formation *Maeres-ea* has examples of an analogous kind and it is evident that the name is derived from Old English words meaning 'boundary river'.

The fortification along the River Mersey in the Mid-Mersey Valley between Runcorn and Manchester by Edward the Elder and his sister Ethelfleda are described in the Anglo-Saxon Chronicle. Edward and his sister were intent upon conquering the Danelaw and in particular upon fortifying the northern boundary of Mercia (The River Mersey) in order to secure Mercia from any infiltration by the Danes. The entries in the Anglo-Saxon Chronicle are brief and present a number of interesting puzzles to the historian. After recording that Ethelfleda fortified Tamworth in the year 913 the Chronicle then records under the year 915 "Then – (was built) that fortress at Chirbury (Shropshire) . . . and in this same year before Christmas that at Runcorn (Cheshire)" and under the year 923 it states that "In this year, in late Autumn, King Edward went with his levies to Thelwall, and had the fortress built, settled and garrisoned. Whilst he was encamped there he ordered other levies, also drawn from Mercia, to occupy Manchester in Northumbria, and had it repaired and garrisoned."

Thus the Chronicle records the fortifying of three points on a twenty-five mile stretch, mainly of river boundary. At the western extremity it is easy to understand the fortification at Runcorn where the Mersey narrows considerably before widening again between Runcorn and Warrington. At the eastern extremity it also is easy to understand that because no river barrier

1

existed and because a number of well trodden roads led to Manchester a fortification was necessary at that point. What is difficult to understand is the selection of Thelwall as the intermediary fortification of this network, since the modern village of Thelwall had no established road crossing of the river until the modern Thelwall viaduct was constructed to carry the M6 across the River and the Manchester Ship Canal. Indeed a tenth century fortification within the modern boundaries of Thelwall appears to be particularly pointless since it would have been situated some three miles to the east of a well established road crossing of the river in Warrington by means of an ancient ford used by the Romans who had erected a station to guard the point which was crossed by the Roman roads from the South to the North. Either side of this point for several miles east and west the crossing of the river was rendered almost impossible by marsh and bog land over which no roads were constructed until modern times. A solution to the problem seems to be offered by a study of maps which show that the boundaries of Thelwall once extended into what is now the County Borough of Warrington and that a part of Thelwall once lay in an 'eye' of the River next to the ancient ford across the River. Indeed it is probable that Edward travelled northwards through Mercia along the old Roman road that would have led him directly to this ancient ford and he would then have found himself in Thelwall. Clearly it is more logical to suppose that this well established crossing of the Mersey was the site of Edward's fortification than the modern village of Thelwall which one modern writer says he could not find when exploring the neighbourhood and was told by a policeman that:- "It's a dodgy sort of place is Thelwall, and I've heard that some folks find it harder to find on Saturday nights."

The barrier presented by the Mersey to the traveller is scarcely appreciated in modern times as railway traffic moves across high level bridges with ease and road traffic crosses the river either on modern motorways or by the old established road route across Warrington Bridge. For centuries the crossing of the Mersey between Liverpool and Manchester was effected by ford and ferry and the most convenient ford was at Warrington. A bridge across the river near to this ford is first mentioned in 1305 and this was rebuilt in 1364. This second bridge had disappeared by the year 1453 when William Booth, Archbishop of York, together with the Bishops of Durham and Carlisle granted an indulgence to all Christian people who should: "Graciously contribute . . . or in any other manner extend a helping hand towards the great and costly work of building and erecting anew at Weryngton, in the diocese of Lichfield and Coventry, the bridge over the great and rapid water which was commonly called The Merce, which flows in a swift course to and from the sea, and which, both for the inhabitants and strangers who had occasion to travel that way, was troublesome and dangerous to cross."

A survey of the year 1465 also refers to a "burgage (in Warrington) . . .

upon the North shore of the sea of Mersee" and as late as the year 1845 a Warrington diarist recorded that "The river being flooded the view from Walton and from Wilderspool was most remarkable. The Arpley Meadows were nearly covered and the river rose in white surges like the fury of a sea."

Floods caused by exceptional tides on the river have now been reduced to negligible proportions through modern drainage and also the construction of the Manchester Ship Canal in which the river was used. Indeed the Canal is connected to the river at Warrington and a short distance beyond Latchford Locks the river and canal are coincident from Warburton to Irlam.

The apparently inpenetrable bog of Chat Moss on the Lancashire side of the Mersey between Warrington and Manchester was mastered by George Stephenson in the construction of the Liverpool and Manchester Railway and with the advent of railways and the more recent motorways the modern traveller is scarcely aware of a river crossing in the Mid-Mersey Valley. The river, however, can still prove a nuisance to the motorist, for with the steady increase in road traffic any accident on a road approach to existing road bridges quickly causes long queues of road traffic and makes abundently clear that more bridges are necessary to facilitate an easy passage across the centuries old barrier between Cheshire and Lancashire.

## DIGGING UP THE PAST IN LANCASHIRE & CHESHIRE

The bibliography at the end of this book contains the books and manuscripts consulted in writing the book. These books and manuscripts consists of a considerable variety of material, from complete County histories like the 'Victoria County History of the County of Lancaster' and compact village histories like William Beamont's 'History of Latchford' to sale catalogues of individual estates, Ordnance Survey maps and individual wills.

Books, manuscripts, and maps, photographs, prints, and drawings, as well as inscriptions on buildings are all material from which the history of any parish or township may be written. In the case of the Mid-Mersey Valley it is fortunate that much of the material is collected together in one Local History Library in the Warrington Central Library. There are, however, considerable collections of local history material in other towns and respositories throughout the counties of Lancashire and Cheshire. County Record Offices are situated in Preston (The Lancashire County Record Office at Sessions House) and at Chester (The Cheshire County Record Office, in The Castle). A large collection of Lancashire and Cheshire family papers together with many other court rolls, surveys and invaluable local history material is to be found in the John Rylands Library, Deansgate, Manchester, whilst substantial collections are also preserved in the Liverpool Record Office of the Liverpool City Libraries and in the Local History Library in the Manchester Central

3

Library. In addition most Lancashire and Cheshire public libraries have good collections of local history material relating to their own locality as well as printed publications like the county histories, county directories and the proceedings of a variety of historic societies giving an extensive range of material relating to both counties.

Printed guides to the material in some of these collections are also available and can save time when a preliminary survey is being made of the material likely to be useful in compiling the history of any particular locality. A 'Guide to the Lancashire Record Office' was published in 1962 and lists of Accessions have appeared subsequently. The John Rylands Library has issued a number of printed lists of local history material many of which are still available and one of these, particularly useful, was "Court rolls, rentals, surveys, and analagous documents in the John Rylands Library, 1948". A book list entitled 'Digging up the past in Warrington and District' was issued by Warrington Municipal Library in 1964. The first part of a new Lancashire Bibliography consisting of a list of Lancashire Directories 1684-1957 and indicating the libraries containing these directories was published in 1968, and this was followed by a second volume listing Lancashire Acts of Parliament 1266-1957.

The first step, therefore, in studying or writing the history of any locality is a careful survey of the material available:— are there any accounts of any archaeological discoveries — pre-historic and roman?; is there any record of Anglo-Saxon or Danish influence?; was the locality described in the Domesday Survey?; do any subsequent manorial or family papers exist?; what parish records and court rolls have survived?; what maps of the locality have been preserved?; are there any individual diaries, wills or other information relating to notable personalities?; do any buildings have useful inscriptions or dates?; are there any drawings, prints or photographs of the locality; is any material — personal, industrial or institutional in private possession likely to be available?

All this may appear to be formidable but others will probably have studied or written about the area previously and many questions will be answered by reference to the work of other local historians, always remembering that no one is infallible and many printed histories contain errors that tend to be repeated because three simple rules of the French historian F. V. A. Aulard are too often ignored namely:—

1. Always go to the sources.
2. Say nothing which you do not know from an original source.
3. Write nothing without giving your references.

Nevertheless the best starting point for the history of any Lancashire or Cheshire locality is always the County History: in the case of Lancashire, the Victoria County History and in the case of Cheshire, Ormerod's History. Both these major histories give accounts of every place in each county and the information contained in them can soon be supplemented with additional facts, often as a result of pursuing bibliographical information and footnotes contained in these histories. Much material has been published and made available, however, since both of these histories were published and it is necessary next to ascertain the extent of this additional material.

Certainly the most practical method of doing this is to examine the catalogue of the local history collection in the nearest public library to the locality being studied. Next examine the indexes to the various Lancashire and Cheshire historic society publications viz:—

The Chetham Society 1844 to date

The Record Society 1878 to date

The Lancashire and Cheshire Antiquarian Society 1883 to date

The Historic Society of Lancashire and Cheshire 1849 to date

The Lancashire Parish Register Society 1898 to date

It is also possible that a purely local history society may exist and has issued publications of local interest.

The name of each locality is a matter of considerable interest and Lancashire Place Names were dealt with by E. Ekwall in volume 81 of the Chetham Society Series and also in "The Place-Names of Lancashire", *Manchester U.P.*, 1922 whilst a survey of Cheshire Place Names was made by S. Potter and published in volume 106 of the Historic Society of Lancashire and Cheshire, 1954. A general guide to the Place Names of England is contained in Ekwall's 'Concise Oxford Dictionary of English Place-Names', *Oxford*, 1960. The first of a five volume survey of Cheshire place names was published by the English Place-Name Society in 1970.

The printed maps of both counties were described in two publications by H. Whitaker, published by the Chetham Society in 1938 and 1942. Many sale catalogues of large estates also contain useful maps.

Finally the County and local directories should be examined as much useful information can be obtained from the facts contained in such directories.

Fieldwork is also of considerable importance as buildings are constantly changing and observations made at first hand can often add usefully to the material to be included in any history and may also lead to sources of printed and manuscript material in private possession. Clearly every new history should contain new material if possible, and if not should avoid the repetition of obvious inaccuracies besides making an attempt to present accuracy with a freshness that illuminates the past to the interest and delight of readers.

## PENKETH

In Lancashire, 43 places between the Ribble and Mersey have British names. All these places, therefore, were named by the people living in

Lancashire possibly before the Romans came, but most certainly before the Anglo-Saxons added their quota of names to the area a few centuries later.

Of these 43 places, only seven have compound names of which both elements are British. One of the seven is Penketh and in consequence the name of Penketh might be older than that of Warrington.

Penketh is a compound of the Celtic words "Pen" meaning "end" or "edge" or "top" and "coed" meaning wood. The name is common in Wales and is also found in Cornwall and Brittany and means "the end (or edge) of the wood."

In the case of Penketh, near Warrington, the wood was Burtonwood which in mediaeval times was a substantial forest used for hunting and from which the seventh lord of the Manor of Warrington was permitted to take windfallen timber for his "Castle" in Warrington.

The lords of the Manor of Warrington from 1176 until 1586 were named Boteler but a family named Penketh were resident in Penketh from about 1216 until 1624 when the family mansion of Penketh Hall and the estates belonging to the family were sold by Richard Penketh to Thomas Ashton.

This family was not undistinguished, for the family pedigree was entered at the herald's visitations and Richard Penketh certainly produced the pedigree before the herald, William Flower, Norroy king of arms, on a visitation of Lancashire in 1567.

The coat of arms belonging to the family – "Argent, three popinjays Azure, sometimes with a chevron between them" – were recorded as having existed in a window of the Warrington Friary and certainly the most distinguished member of the family, Thomas Penketh who died in 1487, was not only a Friar, at the Warrington Friary but was twice the Provincial or Head of the Hermit Friars of St Augustine in England. He edited an early printed edition of the works of the mediaeval philosopher Duns Scotus in 1474 and his fame was sufficient to ensure that a mention was made of him by William Shakespeare for his part in a conspiracy with Sir Edmund Shaw to usurp the English throne in favour of Richard, Duke of Gloucester.

Thomas Penketh was the only member of the family to earn a place in the "Dictionary of National Biography" and no one named Penketh now appears in "Who's who." There are, nevertheless a number of residents of Warrington still bearing this ancient name. Fourteen individuals named Penketh still appear in the "Post Office Telephone Directory for Liverpool" but none of them appear to live in Penketh itself.

Footnote: *Penkethman is a personal name associated with Penketh but it means the man or servant of one named Penketh, and only those bearing the name of Penketh have taken their name from the place.*

Warrington Academy, Bridge Foot

Bewsey Hall

Appleton Cross

# SANKEY

Sankey is a name so old that its meaning defies definition. The first part of the name is possibly derived from a personal name and the second part means "water", "stream" or "river".

Most authorities agree, therefore, that the village of Sankey took its name from the brook which, under a more popular but less appealing name, still flows through the district and into the Mersey.

Sankey Brook was not always as unpopular, nor as polluted as it has become in modern times and once was the source of power required to drive the lord of the manor's water mill, described in 1308 as the "new mill" and to which for centuries many local people had to carry their corn to be ground. The site of this water mill may be traced upon nineteenth century maps and gives the name of "Mill Lane" which leads from "Sankey Green. "Sankey Street" is found in local deeds as early as 1390 under an earlier spelling of "Sonky" Street.

Sankey Brook formed a boundary between Great Sankey to the West and Little Sankey to the East and the division of Sankey into these two parts dates at least from 1325. Such terms as "Great" and "Little" were applied to a variety of place names in order that more specific reference could be made to any locality.

Families named Sankey are to be found throughout the British Isles and in many other parts of the world but it is intriguing to notice that the first person to be encountered in local archives and bearing the name of Sankey is described as a carpenter (this was Gerard de Sanchi who was granted a carucate of land in Sankey by Paganus de Vilars sometime between the years 1120 and 1156) while today a local firm of cabinet makers in Church Street has Mr Edward Sankey as the proprietor.

Members of the Sankey family lived at Little Sankey Hall during the same centuries that the Boteler family lived at Bewsey but the last of the Sankeys of Sankey was an Edward Sankey who, at the outset of the Civil War in 1642 enrolled in a Cheshire regiment of horse and had a commission to command a company. One branch of the family had grants of land in the reign of Mary I at Ballylarkin, Ireland, which they called Sankey Town and a descendant of this branch, also named Edward Sankey, became Lord Mayor of Dublin in 1760.

# WALTON

More than 60 places in England are either named Walton or have Walton as part of their name. And as there are at least three different meanings of the name, the true meaning of any particular Walton has to be assessed from its situation. The three meanings of Walton are:— 1. the tun where the Britons live; 2. the tun by a wall; 3. the tun in a wood or on a wold.

Remembering that Walton Cheshire was next to the walled Roman Station of Wilderspool it seems possible that its name is derived either from the fact that inhabitants who were British were living there and continued to do so until the Anglo Saxons arrived and named the place because it was a dwelling place of the British; or, it was so named simply because it was next to a walled Roman Station. Certainly the first man to explore Wilderspool systematically, Thomas May, considered that some of the names stamped upon the Roman pottery made there were the names of local British inhabitants.

People named Walton are mentioned in local charters as early as the end of the twelfth century. A Randle de Walton is mentioned in 1190 and a William de Walton in 1210.

To most Warringtonians, however, Walton is now a pleasant suburb containing Walton Hall and its beautiful surroundings. From 1836 the Hall was the home of Gilbert Greenall who was created a baronet in 1876. He had built on his estate the Church of St. John the Evangelist in 1885 at a cost of £10,000. Sir Gilbert died in 1894 and was succeeded by his son who was created 1st Baron Daresbury in 1927. Lord Daresbury died in 1938 and in 1941 Walton Hall was sold to the Warrington Corporation when Frances, Lady Daresbury resided at Walton Old Hall.

Perhaps the most distinguished Englishman to bear the name of Walton, however, was Isaak Walton whose book "The Compleat Angler" was first published in 1653. Izaak Walton had one interesting connection with Warrington and District . . . he contributed a prefatory letter to another book on angling written by Robert Venables of Antrobus and published in 1662. Robert Venables was one of Oliver Cromwell's generals and is described by Isaak Walton as his "ingenious friend".


## LYMM


Lymm in Cheshire possesses great natural beauty and contains many attractive features of considerable antiquity. Some writers claim that one or two of these features are unique and certainly the name of Lymm itself appears to be undisputably unique, at any rate in the British Isles, for no other place bearing this name is listed in Bartholomew's "Gazeteer of the British Isles".

It was Samuel Johnson who laid down the principle that: "The name is exhausted by what we see. We have no occasion to go a distance for what we can pick up under our feet . . . it turns out to be a mere physiological name". And the meaning of the name of Lymm, according to the "Concise Oxford Dictionary of English Place Names" is related to the fact that Lymm is

9

Lymm Hall

Walton Hall

10

situated on a stream. The Dictionary says: "Lymm is on a stream, which may have been OE Hlimme, 'roaring brook', formed from hlimman to 'resound, roar'."

No individual named Lymm has apparently been sufficiently distinguished to appear in "The Dictionary of National Bibliography", but those individuals bearing this unique name have never been numerous. A Gilbert de Limme was living in the reign of King John and a family bearing this name resided in Lymm until the end of the reign of Edward the third.

Lymm Hall passed from the last Gilbert de Limme to the Dumvyle or Domville family and a member of this family probably rebuilt the Hall in the reign of Queen Elizabeth. In the middle of the 19th century the Hall, then the residence of James Barrett, was standing within the remains of a moat on an eminence not far from Lymm Cross.

A former Rector of Lymm used to assert that St. Paul might have preached from the steps at Lymm Cross, but unfortunately historians have left little information on the subject.

It is somewhat difficult to classify this type of cross but it is thought that from the nondescript style of the present erection, it can hardly be later than 17th century work.

At the end of the 17th century William Domville was a benefactor of Lymm Grammar School, but the school had evidently been in existence at least for a century before this, since a Ralph Taylor appears as a master of the school in 1592 and one of the few individuals bearing the name of Lymm, a John Lymm, was master of the school in 1682.

Lymm Church was recorded in the Domesday Survey where Lymm was spelt "Lime". When the steeple of the Church was rebuilt in 1521 the founder of the Warrington Grammar School, Sir Thomas Boteler, was a contributor to "the steeple of stone then in building at Limme Church".

## BURTONWOOD

In the last 25 years the name of Burtonwood has been carried by thousands of American Servicemen to countries all over the world so that, although like Lymm it is the only place in the British Isles to bear this name, it is possible that it is known at the present time more widely than Warrington, to which it was originally a subservient manor.

Probably the original name of Burtonwood was simply "Burton" which means the "tun" by a burh or fortified manor. The burh could have been the borough of Warrington. The wood, however, was a real and extensive royal forest early in the 13th century and the name had become Burtonwood by this time so that the addition of "wood" to "Burton" gives the full meaning of Burtonwood as the wood by the tun, or farmstead, near a fortified place or burh.

11

The earliest mention of Burtonwood occurs in a charter of King John dated October 10, 1199, whereby the town of Pendleton was granted to Yarforth de Hulton in exchange for Burtonwood and Kersall wood which John had given him while he was Count of Mortain. Henry I placed Burtonwood in his forest between Ribble and Mersey and in 1228 it was perambulated in accordance with the charter of the forest of 1224-25.

The manor was sold to William Boteler, seventh lord of the Manor of Warrington, about 1264 and the Boteler family then settled at Bewsey in Burtonwood until the last of the Botelers, Edward Boteler, alienated the manor to Richard Bold of Bold in 1580.

The Chapel of Burtonwood was founded by Sir Thomas Bold in 1605 when Burtonwood was part of the Parish of Warrington but during the Commonwealth it became a separate parish, and it must have excited many of the Americans who came to Burtonwood in World War II to discover than an early incumbent of the Church, the Rev Samuel Mather, had sailed to America with his father, the Rev Richard Mather, to join the Pilgrim Fathers, in 1635. Samuel returned to this country and became Vicar of Burtonwood – and probably the first American at Burtonwood!

The Registers of Burtonwood have been published for the years 1668-1837 but do not contain any individual named Burtonwood. The only person of this name to appear in local records was John Burtonwood, who was described in 1622 as "lecturer" at St. Helen's chapel.

Although the small community of Burtonwood depended on agriculture for centuries, it is noticeable from the registers that other trades, especially watchmaking, begin to form a moderate proportion of the trades and skills supporting the inhabitants of the parish in the 18th century.


## DALLAM

Iron and steel, smoke and steam are all more likely to spring to the mind of any Warringtonian at the mention of the name of Dallam, than a vision of a place filled with meadow and the home of a family associated with music.

This is scarcely surprising since the first railway to enter Warrington was the Warrington to Newton branch line from the Manchester to Liverpool Railway. This railway link from Warrington was opened on July 25, 1831, and ran along Dallam Lane from its Warrington terminus. Dallam is still a hive of railway industry but where railway sheds and locomotives now stand were once pleasant fields. Indeed, a Survey written in the year 1587 records that "Dallam fields is arable land of the Lord's desmesne extending from . . . Warrington heath . . . unto Bewsey brook". It has been suggested that the name of Dallam means "valley meadow" and the same Survey of 1587 not only describes Dallam fields, but also Dallam meadow.

Small and obscure as the hamlet of Dallam must have been in the reign of the first Queen Elizabeth it nevertheless produced a man bearing the name of Dallam who not only undertook an important mission for the Queen but also founded a family of organ builders so famous that the names of four members are recorded in the Dictionary of National Biography.

"Thomas Dallam", says the author of a book entitled "An Organ for the Sultan", "was a little Lancashireman, an organ builder by trade . . . he constructed a highly ingenious organ (which Elizabeth sent to the Sultan of Turkey in the hope of securing further concession for English trade and the help of a Turkish fleet against Spain)". Dallam travelled with the organ to the Sultan, demonstrated it and wrote a journal describing his adventures. After his return to England, Dallam was commissioned to build an organ for Kings College Chapel, Cambridge, and also for the Chapel Royal at Holyrood House, Edinburgh. His sons Robert and Ralph built organs in St. Paul's Cathedral, York Minster, Canterbury Cathedral and St. George's Chapel, Windsor, as well as in other places. Perhaps, one day, an organ worthy of representing such a distinguished family will be erected in some church or hall situated in that part of Warrington still known as Dallam.

To-day, of course, Lancashire Steel spreads along Dallam Lane where the Dallam Forge, established in 1840, once rolled rods for Rylands Bros.

At the Warrington end of Dallam Lane stands the public house known as the Three Pigeons which, it is said, was the original booking office for the Warrington to Newton Railway and certainly the terminal of this railway lay in Dallam Lane just beyond this public house. The Railway Company in 1831 owned three locomotives built by Stephenson and Co.: The Warrington, The Newton and The Vulcan. What a pity that one was not called The Dallam.

## ORFORD

A spectacular fire at Orford Tannery recently attracted hundreds of sightseers because the tannery, once fairly. isolated, had become almost the centre of the largest post-war urban development in Warrington. Orford is now, in fact, the home of more than 15,000 Warringtonians although it was formerly but a small manor attached, at the time of the Domesday Survey, to the capital manor of Warrington.

Brooks running through the north of the town made travel to the north more difficult centuries ago, and there were fords at Longford and Orford. A manuscript of 1465 contains the name of Orford constantly spelt "Overforthe" which simply means "upper ford".

Orford Hall stood, until recent years, in Orford Park and the various families associated with the Hall have been commemorated in the naming of streets and public houses in the locality. Norris Street is named after Robert le Norris the first possessor of Orford until 1595 when the heiress of Thomas Norris married Thomas Tildesley and during their lifetime Orford Hall was rebuilt. The next possessors of Orford Hall were members of the Blackburne family from the middle of the 17th century until 1812.

This family's long connection with Orford is to be noted in the existence of the Blackburne Arms at Orford Green. Perhaps the most distinguished occupant of the Hall, however, was William Beamont, the first Mayor of Warrington and a great benefactor of the town. He built Orford Village School in 1861 and the school was also used for church services before St. Margaret's, Orford, was built in 1906.

In the present century a vicar of Orford achieved a national reputation as the author of a book entitled "The Life Beyond the Veil", the title-page of which continues: "Spirit messages received and writted down by the Rev G. Vale Owen, Vicar of Orford, Lancashire. With an appreciation by Lord Northcliffe and an introduction by Sir Arthur Conan Doyle."

Only a few years earlier, in 1916, Alderman Arthur Bennet was responsible for acquiring Orford Hall, together with 18 acres, as a gift to the town from a number of local gentlemen in memory "of the valour of the lads of Warrington in the Great War" and it became a public park. The Hall, however, was demolished in 1935.

Individuals named Orford are to be found in "The Dictionary of National Biography" as well as the local telphone directories but there are three places also called Orford in the British Isles.

## WARBURTON

A Directory of Cheshire for 1850 states that: "The inhabitants of Warburton are exempt from serving on juries, and are not liable to tolls at any of the fairs or markets in Cheshire." Today there exists in Warburton the only road in a wide area where travellers have to pay toll, and this in order to gain access from Cheshire to the high level crossing of the Manchester Ship Canal known as Warburton Bridge. These circumstances are curiously odd but this straggling parish, still scarcely touched by modern urban development, cannot fail to excite the curiosity of any visitor.

It has two churches . . . one built in 1885 by Mr R.E. Egerton-Warburton and in regular use; the other quaint, ancient and deserted but standing pleasantly in a romantic churchyard filled with the tombstones of the village departed and shaded with venerable trees.

The ancient church is dedicated to Saint Werburgh, daughter of King Wulfhere of Mercia, whose body was enshrined at Chester. Warburton takes its name from this Saint — Waerburg's tun — and the name appeared in the

Domesday Survey as "Warburgetone". A church evidently existed here before the Norman Conquest and for a few years after the time of the Domesday Survey there also existed a priory since a 12th century grant of land was made to "God and the Blessed Mary and Saint Werburga and the Prior and Brothers serving God". Other grants describe the brothers as Canons of the Premonstratensian Order [an order of White Canons originating at Premontre near Laon in France]. A field in the vicinity of the old church is known as the Abbey Croft.

Ormerod's History of Cheshire 1882 says: "The hall of Warburton has long ceased to be the family residence. Its moated site lies to the east side of the church and village, and the adjacent field retains the name of Warburton Park." Nevertheless the Warburton family have had an unbroken connection with the village from the time when Sir Peter de Dutton, fourth lord of the manor of Warburton at the end of the 13th century, assumed the name of Warburton.

Five of the ,33 known rectors of Warburton have borne the name Warburton, the earliest rector of the name being William de Warburton in 1328 and the last being Geoffrey Egerton-Warburton in 1872.

Members of this ancient family have had a number of distinguished connections with Warrington. In 1364, Geoffrey de Werbeton, John le Botiller and Mathew de Rixton were given royal protection by Edward III while they were engaged in building a new bridge over the River Mersey at Warrington; and in 1602, Sir Peter Warburton, who had married Elizabeth Boteler, took steps to compel the appointment of new Trustees of the Boteler Grammar School resulting in a re-foundation of the School in 1608.

In the 19th century when the residents of many local parishes established friendly societies and burial clubs to care for their sick and bereaved members, the residents of Warburton originated a "Cow Club" the object of which club was to provide benefits for members whose cows should fall sick or die. The "Articles to be observed by the Warburton Cow Club" were printed in Warrington in 1842. Thus in the 12th century there was a priory in Warburton, but in the 19th century priorities were somewhat different!

## APPLETON

The recent discovery of a Roman road in Appleton running in a different direction from the long-established road to the south from Wilderspool through the township of Appleton is but one indication of the wide extent of this large township.

Until the 19th century Appleton embraced both Stockton Heath and Wilderspool to the north and extended from Walton in the west to Bradley in the east.

Appearing in the Domesday Survey as "Epeltune" it was described in a deed dated before the year 1189 as "Appleton and Hull" and this description was still to be found in Kelly's Directory of Cheshire in 1939. Appleton simply means the "Tun where the apples grew" and "Hull", according to the *Concise Oxford Dictionary of English Place Names* is identical with Hoole, Lancashire, and is derived from an Old English word "hulu" meaning "hut" or "hovel". Today the northern boundary of Appleton is the Bridgewater Canal and has been since Stockton Heath was created a separate civil parish in 1867, but Appleton still includes Hill Cliffe and the Corporation reservoir in the west and extends to Grappenhall in the east.

The Domesday Survey stated that Appleton "was and is waste" and coupled with meaning of "Hull" as a "hovel" a somewhat depressing picture of the district 900 years ago is created, contrasting completely with the delightful countryside of the 20th century which contains the plushiest residential estates of the Warrington areas as well as one of the finest golf courses in the North West of England.

Warrington has every reason to be grateful to Appleton for water supplies lasting for more than 100 years. The Appleton Reservoir was, in fact, the original source of water when Warrington became a Municipal Borough in 1847 and water was supplied by the Warrington Waterworks Co. Other sources of supply have been added subsequently but in recent years Hill Cliffe and the golf course in Appleton have been used for the construction of large storage tanks for water by the Warrington Corporation.

The first person to really appreciate the delights of Appleton as a residential area was Thomas Lyon who during the 19th century, became the most substantial landowner of the area and built Appleton Hall, subsequently destined to become a Home Office Approved School.

At the centre of this extensive township is Appleton Church, erected in 1887, and nearby stands the recently replanted Appleton Thorn Tree. A song to be sung when the tree is bawmed, or decorated, was composed by Mr R.E. Egerton-Warburton when in 1880, a new thorn tree was planted by Mrs Piers Warburton on the occasion of her marriage. This tree survived until 1965 when it was blown down and a replacement soon withered and died.

The latest thorn tree, planted in October 1967, was brought as a cutting from the original Glastonbury thorn and it will be cared for by Appleton W.I.

Not very far from Pepper Street, which surely must be connected with the recently discovered Roman road, stands the remains of Appleton Cross. This is one of the many wayside crosses to be found in the locality and stands appropriately at a road junction where it is a reminder of the days when in 1365 Friar Richard de Apulton of the Warrington Friary was ordained sub-deacon at Colwich.

16

Warburton Old Church

Station Road Padgate in 1902

Culcheth Hall

# PADGATE

It would be difficult to find among the many parishes and districts of the neighbourhood of Warrington, two which were such complete contrasts as Warburton and Padgate, situated on opposite sides of the River Mersey. While Warburton remains almost isolated, untouched and ancient, Padgate is of modern origin, has been subjected to considerable modern urban development and is known throughout the British Isles as a result of institutions, encampments and industry within its borders.

Strangely, Padgate as the name of a place did not exist before the 19th century when, in 1838, an ecclesiastical parish was formed from the civil parish of Warrington and called Padgate. Before that the name of Padgate was the name of the road from Warrington to Bolton and with the erection of Christ Church in 1838 the name of the road was given to the newly-formed ecclesiastical district. "Pad" is a north country word for path, and a "Padgate" is a well-trodden path.

Certainly many paths in Padgate were well trodden during World War II when recruits to the RAF arrived at up to 500 each day, so that more than a million men experienced their first taste of Service life at Padgate between 1939 and 1953. Today this former RAF camp is being used for housing development by Warrington Corporation and since so many ex-airmen remember the friendliness of Warringtonians it is probably fitting that the camp site should now provide permanent homes for the people who befriended so many temporary visitors.

Memories of Padgate now belong to men and women trained there for pursuits differing widely from those of the war-time airmen. Since Padgate Training College was first established at Fearnhead in 1949, hundreds of newly trained teachers have carried the name of Padgate to schools throughout Great Britain.

Britain's post-war development of roads and motorways, almost as vigorous as post-war educational development, has been considerably assisted by the enterprise of the Padgate firm of A. Monk and Co. Ltd. The name of this firm, together with the name of Padgate, has been seen in recent years by all those who have travelled along the A.1 and other roads where major developments have taken place.

Perhaps confined to a smaller area will be those who cherish memories of Padgate as a result of spending their childhood at Padgate Cottage Homes. Originally built in 1884 by the Board of Guardians as an industrial home, it was taken over by the Public Assistance Board in 1930. It was re-named Padgate Hall in 1949 and ceased to be a children's home in 1954.

Fondness of Padgate prompted a former Mayor of Warrington, Alderman Arthur Bennett, to place land for a recreation ground at the disposal of the Parish Council and memorial gates to the memory of the Alderman were subsequently erected at the entrance to the Bennet Memorial Ground, which is near the railway station.

## CULCHETH

Culcheth is one of the 43 places between the Ribble and the Mersey, which, like Penketh, possesses a British name. While Penketh means "the end, or edge, of a wood", the name of Culcheth means "backwood" or "a retreat in a wood". Certainly, Culcheth has for centuries been situated in a "backwoods" position so far as its relationship with Warrington and the immediate neighbourhood of Warrington is concerned, because while it is geographically much closer to Leigh than Warrington, it was in mediaeval times a manor of the Barony of Warrington and also a part of the Parish of Winwick.

Although Culcheth is not mentioned in the Domesday Survey, it is mentioned in a Survey of the year 1212 when it was stated that Hugh son of Gilbert of Culcheth held the manor, and members of the Culcheth family continued to reside in Culcheth at Culcheth Hall until 1747. In 1601, John Culcheth paid his overlord, who at the time was Thomas Ireland of Bewsey and Baron of Warrington, 100 marks for all the rights, suits, services, etc., that Thomas Ireland had in Culcheth, thus freeing the Culcheth family from their age-long subservience to the Barons of Warrington. With the end of the male line of the Culcheth family in 1747, the estate was ultimately possessed in 1824 by Peter Withington and during the 19th century three successive squires of Culcheth were all named Thomas Ellames Withington. The second of these gentlemen was the last resident owner of Culcheth Hall, a church-warden of Newchurch for 56 years and one who indulged in planting his estate extensively with trees.

Ecclesiastically the separation of Culcheth from Winwick occurred much later than the separation of its civil subservience to the Barons of Warrington. A separate parish for Culcheth and Kenyon was created in 1845 under the Winwick Rectory Act and the incumbent of the Church was styled Rector of Newchurch since the name Newchurch had been attached to the chapel of ease dedicated to the Holy Trinity and erected in 1528. This church, reconstructed on two occassions, was finally destroyed by fire in 1903 and the present church was built in the following year.

following year.

The name of Culcheth in recent years has been carried far from Lancashire by two different kinds of temporary residents. Between 1946 and 1950 an emergency training college for teachers was established in hutments near to Newchurch Rectory, and known officially as Risley Training College, Culcheth, and to those who served there as "Little London". These buildings still exist and now form part of later development in the area by the U.K.

Atomic Energy Authority. Many employees of this organisation, however, have settled in the area with the result that Culcheth, like Appleton, has acquired in recent years a distinctly urban and modern appearance – complete with a pleasing county branch library, shopping precinct and a distinct aura of prosperity and well-being.


## BEWSEY

. Within two centuries of the Norman Conquest of England, Warrington was developing into a prosperous market town and the need for a castle in a strategic position to guard the ford across the Mersey was no longer necessary. The seventh lord of the manor of Warrington, William le Boteler, therefore, decided to build himself a new home nearer to the pleasures of the forest and at a convenient distance from the centre of the growing town.

The site selected was at Bewsey in Burtonwood and the land was purchased from Robert de Ferrers about the year 1264. A part of William's new estate had previously belonged to the Abbey of Tiltey in Essex and during the time of the monks' ownership they had established a grange within an enclose of the wood or park which they had called "beau site". Bewsey means "beautiful site" and it is quite evident that successive members of the Boteler family found it beautiful for they continued to reside at Bewsey Hall until the Boteler estates passed to Robert Dudley, Earl of Leycester in 1586.

A survey of 1586 says "The Manner howse of Bewsey . . . invyroned with a Fayre moat, over which is a strong drawe bridge. The house is large but the one halfe of it beinge of very old buyldinge is gone to decaye . . . The other halfe is of new buyldinge and not decayed . . ."

Bewsey Hall is easily the most romantic house still standing in the neighbourhood of Warrington. James I spent a night there in August, 1617, when he knighted Thomas Ireland who had purchased the estate from the Earl of Warwick.

In the days of the Boteler family the Hall was the scene of a number of exciting events that have been celebrated in prose and ballad so that almost all books about Lancashire contain some versions of a number of legends associated with Bewsey Hall.

During the 19th century the northern wing of the old Elizabethan Hall was taken down and a new wing of Georgian design erected in its stead. The Hall was then for a time the home of the Rector of Warrington, the Rt Rev Horace Powys, later Bishop of Sodor and Man. Later in the century this Georgian wing was removed and all that remains today is the old Elizabethan southern wing, still surrounded by the depression that formerly was a moat.

After World War I, Bewsey was selected as the site of one large post-war housing development by the Warrington Corporation, so that the growing town of Warrington was only separated from the ancient Manor House by the width of the Sankey Canal. To cater for the needs of this new estate, Bewsey School was opened in 1934. Only a few years later, the development of land in Burtonwood for military purposes meant that Bewsey Hall became the centre of a thickly populated area and well-known to thousands of American Servicemen: indeed, for a short period in recent years, the Hall had an American family as its tenants.


## ANTROBUS

Antrobus is a hamlet within the lordship of Over Whitley and lies between Stretton and Great Budworth. Although the main road from Stretton to Budworth passes through part of this widespread hamlet the traveller must take a secondary road in order to pass through the centre of the village where the church and school are situated.

All those who are named Antrobus take their names from this Cheshire hamlet, which appeared in the Domesday Survey as Entrebus. The Concise Oxford Dictionary of English Place Names dismisses Antrobus without attempting a definition on the grounds that the name is "Hardly English", but other etymologers have shown that the two components of the name "Entre-bus" are derived from the Latin "inter" and Old French "bus" or "busc" from which comes "bois" meaning "a wood". The name, therefore, means "Amid the woods" and in the Domesday Survey it says "there is a wood there one league long and half a league broad".

In spite of Domesday recognition, the village of Antrobus is of modern origin. The Church, the National School and a Wesleyan Methodist Chapel were all built in the first half of the 19th Century and the road through the village is flanked with houses belonging to the 20th Century. The history of this village is hidden in farms and houses scattered amongst the 2,000 acres comprising the township. The ancient hall was taken down about the year 1830 but before that two ancient families had lived in the locality for several hundred years. In 1850, one of the principal landowners in the township was Sir Edward Antrobus, a descendant of the family who, having first settled in the township and assumed the name of Antrobus had continued to reside there until Henry Antrobus sold his estates to Thomas Venables in the reign of Henry VI. After an interval of about 400 years, during which time the Venables family and their descendants were the principal landowners, the estate was re-purchased by Sir Edward Antrobus a descendant in the male line of Henry Antrobus.

The name of Venables has earned for Antrobus a special place in the history of England for it was Robert Venables of Antrobus who achieved considerable distinction during the Civil War as one of Oliver Cromwell's generals and also as the author of a book on angling. Robert Venables's career as a soldier was long and illustrious having served from the outset first under Sir William Brereton and then, as a Lieutenant-Colonel, he was wounded in the siege of Chester. In 1649, he was made Commander-in-Chief of Cromwell's forces in Ulster and in 1655 he was sent as a general with an undisciplined and ill-equipped army to the West Indies. His army succeeded in taking Jamaica, which has ever since remained a British possession. After his return to England he was made governor of Chester by General Monck and in 1662 he published "The Experienced Angler, or Angling Improved" to which book was prefixed a letter by Izaak Walton addressed "to his ingenious friend the author".

## GRAPPENHALL

The first glance along the cobbled street towards Grappenhall Church usually causes the visitor to pause and catch his breath. The scene is full of beauty and surprise; the surprise of finding everything that tradition demands of an English village beautifully standing so close — and yet so remote — from the considerable urban landscape to the north.

An ancient church, stocks, cobbled street, inviting pubs, a hall, a school — all pleasantly set among trees, while around the corner is a cricket ground in a setting that would be acceptable anywhere in England.

Nothing could be more romantic and even the name of Grappenhall is pleasant to the ear, and creates mental images that, alas, are far removed from the true meaning of the name!

The meaning of Grappenhall, indeed, simply serves to remind all who enjoy the romantic prospect of such a village that the essential elements of life connected with food and shelter must come before beauty and romance. Consisting of three elements — as it did in the Domesday Survey when it was recorded as "Gropenhale" — the first and third elements "grop" and "halh" are Old English and mean respectively "a ditch or a drain" and "a piece of flat alluvial land by the side of a river". Remembering, therefore, that the Parish of Grappenhall once extended as far as the south bank of the Mersey the name means: "a ditch or drain through the alluvial land by the side of the river". It is possible, of course, that the name may refer, either to Lumb Brook or Morris Brook, both of which pass through Grappenhall and in former years, entered the Mersey.

People had settled in Grappenhall over 2,000 years before the Domesday Survey was written, and the evidence of the Middle Bronze Age settlement in Grappenhall is now preserved in the Warrington Museum.

A medieval survey of land in Grappenhall belonging to the Legh family, part of a manuscript written by Peter Legh in 1465, mentions many roads, fields and streams, such as "Catriche Lane", "Lumme Brooke", Middilhurste", "Marfenne Medo" and "Stanylandys" that are still recognisable today. It also mentions features that have disappeared such as "Grappenhall Cross" and the "Fountain of St. Leonard the Abbot". The Survey makes it clear, however, that hard at work at either end of this extensive parish were two mills – "The Herr (higher) Milne" and "The Lagher (lower) Milne". It is clear these were two water mills powered by the two brooks running through the Parish.

An 18th century account book of the surveyors of the highway for the Township of Grappenhall shows how the men of the parish made good the roads each year and not only includes items for stones, cinders and slag, but also includes payments for liquor for workmen. Both of these manuscripts are preserved in Warrington Library.

Perhaps it is most interesting, however, to observe from the earlier manuscript that many families living in Grappenhall in the 15th century bore the same names as many families living there today namely: Antrobus, Bowden, Caldwell, Cartwright, Domville, Handkinson, Kerfoot, Naylor, Reddish, Stockton, Singleton, Tomlinson, Warburton and Wilkinson.


## WINWICK

Winwick stands about the same height above sea-level as the Cheshire parish of Grappenhall and like Grappenhall it was inhabited by settlers of the Middle Bronze Age more than 2,000 years before the Domesday Survey was compiled. The various Bronze Age remains found at Winwick are fully recorded and are also described in the "Victoria County History of Lancashire".

St. Oswald's Church is mentioned in the Domesday Survey but the name of Winwick itself does not appear in this unique record. The name, however, consists of an Anglian personal name, Wineca, and an Old English element "wic" meaning "dwelling place" so that Winwick means "the dwelling place of 'wineca'!" When the name of Winwick first occurred in a written record in the year 1170 it was spelt "Winequic" and in another record 22 years later it appeared as "Wynewhik".

The Church was founded some time after the death of Oswald, the Christian king of Northumbria who was slain in battle with Penda of Mercia in the year 642. Local legend places the site of this battle at Winwick but most historians consider that the site of the battle was at Oswestry.

Fragments of an ancient pre-Norman sculptured cross are preserved in Winwick Church and it is thought that the subject of the sculpture could be the dismemberment of Oswald, although it is equally possible that the subject could be martydom of Isaiah.

Winwick Church

Orford Hall (demolished 1935)

At the beginning of the 19th century the Parish of Winwick embraced 26,502 acres and the benefice was considered to be the richest in the kingdom. Its value in 1835 was said to be £7,000 a year, of which £3,000 was from tithes. It was, however, due to the munificence and efforts of the Rev J.J. Hornby, Rector of Winwick from 1812 to 1855, that two Acts of Parliament were passed in 1841 and 1845 resulting in a division of this great Parish into eight separate parishes and chapelries.

Red Bank, Winwick was the scene of the greatest battle of the Civil War in Lancashire when in August, 1648, Oliver Cromwell pursued and fought an invading force of about 24,000 Scots under the command of the Duke of Hamilton. This battle started in Preston and continued for 30 miles until the Scots made their last stand at Winwick. Over 1,000 men were killed at Winwick and 18 years later a young mercer of Ashton-in-Makerfield, Roger Lowe, recorded in his diary "there was the head of some Christian lay bare to publicke view above ground . . . I went to bury it . . . It was supposed to have beene a Scott, and theie slaine when Duke Hamilton invaded England."

About the same time a traveller named Kuerden described Winwick Rectory as "a princely building, equal to the revenue". This old rectory was situated in a park in which the County Mental Hospital, opened in 1902, was built. Before this various absentee parsons had leased the rectory and one of the lessees, Gowther Legh, founded a grammar school in Winwick in the reign of Henry VIII. The endowment was not very substantial but the school sent boys to the universities in the 17th century. By 1865 it was a small boarding school and it ended in 1890 when the endowment was combined with the Dean School in Newton.

## BRADLEY

Several places named Bradley are to be found in Lancashire and in Cheshire, and since the name means quite simply "Broad lea", this is scarcely surprising.

There are two places named Bradley within four miles radius of Market Gate, one in Lancashire to the north west of Winwick Church and one in Cheshire to the south east of Grappenhall Church. Both are ancient manors and evidence of the antiquity of both places may be gleaned from the two halls that were respectively the residences of the possessors of each manor for many centuries.

The Lancashire Manor of Bradley lies within the township of Burtonwood, and after this manor had passed from its first possessor, the Haydock family, through marriage, to the Legh family, Sir Peter Legh in the year 1465 recorded a detailed description of his home there as "a fair new hall with three new chambers and a fair dining-room with a new kitchen, bakehouse and brewhouse with a new tower of stone with turrets and a fair gateway . . . and one ancient chamber called the Knyghts Chamber, all . . . surrounded with a moat having a drawbridge."

A farmhouse now stands where this ancient hall formerly stood. In 1900 however, a photograph shows the old gateway still standing, although in September, 1666, Roger Lowe of Ashton had recorded in his diary that: "I went to my brother's into Burton Wood, and on Lord's day morneinge we came for Ashton and cald to se Braidley Hall, which I admird to se so goodly a fabrick lying wast."

The manor house of Bradley within the township of Appleton, Cheshire still stands surrounded by a moat and is now known as Bradley Hall Farm. The house, though beautifully modernised by the present owners still contains much evidence of its antiquity. In 1465, Sir Peter Legh of Bradley, Lancashire, also recorded that a croft of one of his Grappenhall tenants extended on the west "as far as the land leading to the hall or Manor of Bradleigh". This Manor of Bradley was originally held by the Baguley family and afterwards by the Donyels or Daniers, from whom it passed in the reign of Edward III to the Savages. It then passed to the Greggs and then to the Egertons until in the 19th century it was sold to William Fox of Statham.

An ancient landmark of Bradley was Bradley Cross, which once stood on the highway between Warrington and Knutsford. This cross was mentioned when evidence was being given at the Warrington Friary in September 1386 in the Scrope versus Grosvenor dispute concerning a shield of arms. A witness named John de Massey swore he had seen the challenged arms upon the cross at Bradley in Appleton and that they were painted there by the Grosvenors more than 50 years before. Unlike Appleton Cross, no trace of Bradley Cross now remains to be seen.

Bradley Brook, however, still flows from the 200 feet contour of this Manor in a north easterly direction to Lymm.


## BRUCHE

Bruche is the name of an ancient manor within the parish of Warrington as well as the name of a family who belonged to that manor for more than 300 years until the reign of Queen Elizabeth the First.

The boundaries of this manor were described in the 15th century as being: "situate on the south of a certain heath called le Bruche hethe, and extending from thence towards a certain land leading from the town of Weryngton as far as the town of Wulstone, and so from the said lane as far as the water of Mersee, which said Manor and all its members . . . lie in breadth between . . . le Bruche brook on the west and . . . le Wulstone brook on the east."

In the 13th century the name first appeared as "del Bruch". It was usually spelt "Bruche" but occasionally as "Briche" and on Saxton's map of Lancashire in 1577 it appeared as "Bryche". Ekwall, in his "Place names of Lancashire" considers that the name is derived from the Old English "bryce" meaning "breaking" in the sense "broken up ground, new-cultivated land".

Bruche Hall was the seat of the Bruche family until the manor was sold to Peter Legh of Bradley early in the 17th century. At the beginning of the 19th century the estate and hall had become the property of a soap manufacturer named Jonathan Jackson, who became bankrupt as a result of action by excise officers, and in 1824 the Bruche estate was purchased by Thomas Parr for £19,200.

The occupant of the hall in 1908 was Colonel J.D. Buckton and by 1927 the hall (which has subsequently become a convent) together with 11 acres of ground, had been purchased by the Roman Catholic community for educational purposes. The plot included the site chosen for the erection of St. Oswald's Church, the foundation stone of which was laid on May 29, 1927 by Dr Keating, Archbiship of Liverpool. Nearly 40 years later a new and bigger St. Oswald's Church was opened when in June, 1965, Dr G.A. Beck, Archbishop of Liverpool, blessed the new church.

Not very far from Bruche Hall a collection of buildings was erected in 1940 to 1941 to provide hostel accommodation for workers engaged on wartime munition production at Risley, but before being occupied for this purpose the buildings were acquired by the U.S. Army Authorities as a drafting pool and transit camp for American servicemen.

Soon after the end of World War II the buildings were put to a different use when, in 1946, they became a Police Training Centre. With new and improved accommodation at Bruche, "No. 1 District Police Training Centre" now provides accommodation for 480 students, sufficient to cater for the needs of all police forces in the district, which covers a wide area in the North of England.

Bruche has also been an area of considerable housing development in the post-war years and in 1961, land sufficient for the erection of 200 houses off Bruche Avenue North belonging to the Bennett family of Bruche Farm was auctioned in Warrington, so that the only green oasis now remaining in Bruche is the park situated around Bruche Hall and known as Bruche Park.


## WILDERSPOOL

The combination of a brewery and a football stadium together with the notoriety of an unwelcome level crossing have almost made the name of Wilderspool as widely known as Warrington in which county borough it is now entirely situated.

Formerly Wilderspool was a hamlet within the County of Cheshire, and it is often thought that the name is fairly modern. This was disproved many years ago, however, with the discovery of the name of Wilderspool in a charter of the reign of Henry II at the beginning of the thirteenth century, where the name is spelt "Wildrespul". The first part of the name is the Old English "Wild deor" meaning "a wild beast, a deer" and the second part means "a pool, pond, a pool in a river, a creek or a stream". The name, therefore, means "the pool of the wild beast".

After the establishment of the Legionary fortress at Chester by Agricola, a Roman station was established at Wilderspool. Some antiquaries believe that the name of this settlement was "Veratinum" but as this has not yet been established beyond all doubt, the station is always located on maps of Roman Britain as at Wilderspool.

It is evident that a highway from Warrington along the bank of the Mersey to Stockton Heath and Stretton must have been made soon after the first bridge was built in Warrington about 1305, and as this highway was subject to constant flooding from the Mersey a causeway, or a road raised on stone arches, was constructed in the first half of the 17th century.

Wilderspool Causeway thus came into being and extended from Warrington Bridge for a distance of 910 yards, and the stone arches erected over two centuries ago still remain beneath the modern macadam road surface. The course of the river was altered with the advent of the Manchester Ship Canal and the old river bed behind Wilderspool Causeway is now filled in.

This ancient highway has always been a busy thoroughfare. In the Civil War it was the scene of a battle when the Earl of Derby sent his men along it in 1643 to engage the Parliamentary troops at Stockton Heath. Its pavements have subsequently echoed to the footsteps of workers at the Wilderspool Brewery and the Wilderspool Ironworks as well as at other industrial enterprises either side of the Causeway.

Thousands of men and women have wound their way from the Bridge to the Football Stadium and thousands more have travelled its length by tramcar, bus and motor car. Almost as many thousands have experienced delays as a result of the creation of a railway level crossing which came into being when a railway bridge across the Mersey was erected in 1854 and Wilderspool railway station on the Wilderspool Altrincham line was closed. This irritating and costly impediment to the free movement of road traffic was only removed by the construction in the years 1955-57 of the new Wilderspool Bridge over the railway.

Probably few districts of Warrington have experienced quite so many changes as have taken place within the length of the Causeway and at the same time have succeeded in retaining such a dignified atmosphere.

# THELWALL

Although Thelwall is not the oldest name within the neighbouring district of Warrington, it is the only name to appear in a written record before the Domesday Survey.

The fact that the name of Thelwall was recorded in the Anglo-Saxon Chronicle has perhaps had an unfortunate effect on modern Thelwall so that the visitor to this Cheshire village becomes aware of a pseudo atmosphere springing from Victorian Gothic and twentieth century Anglo-Saxon.

This is a great pity because Thelwall contains some charming half-timbered cottages; it once possessed a fine Georgian hall and certainly there is enough genuine antiquity in Thelwall to excite interest if only Edward the Elder could be placed into proper perspective.

While successive generations of Thelwallians have been busily engaged in ensuring that an entry in the Anglo-Saxon Chronicle should not escape notice, a fine Georgian hall has been allowed to fall into decay and disappear while the family connection with Thelwall of Dr Thomas Percival, who achieved immortality for his book on Medical Ethics and his part in the founding of the Manchester Literary and Philosophical Society, have been largely ignored by those who have written about Thelwall. Dr Percival's grandfather, Peter Percival, was born at Thelwall and is mentioned in an old deed at present hanging on a wall in the Cottage Hotel.

Thelwall is not mentioned in the Domesday Survey but the name consists of two old English elements meaning "a pool by a plank bridge". There was an ancient ferry across the Mersey until the Manchester Ship Canal was constructed and then a ferry service across the Canal was maintained.

This ancient township, having been under ecclesiastical control after the Norman Conquest, eventually became possessed by the Clayton family and then by the Brookes, Moores and Pickerings. The Pickering family did not enter upon the Thelwall scene until 1662 and it was a member of the family who built Thelwall Hall, an impressive Georgian structure that was allowed to deteriorate and finally disappear after it had suffered from military occupation during World War II.

A war memorial in the form of an imitation Anglo-Saxon cross was erected in the village and unveiled by General Sir Richard Butler in 1924. A translation of an entry in the Anglo-Saxon Chronicle is carved on the pedestal of this cross and the same entry also appears on an outside beam of the Pickering Arms as well as being attached to a photograph of one page of a manuscript copy of the Anglo-Saxon Chronicle in Thelwall Church, which was constructed in early English style in 1843.

The churchyard contains the grave of Sir Peter and Lady Rylands, while a stained glass window in the church in memory of this local industrialist was unveiled and dedicated in 1950. The bottom panel of this window depicts a wire-drawer at his bench.

The name of Thelwall has become known to all motorway users in recent years as a result of the construction of the Thelwall Viaduct on the M6 and it is fitting that this modern structure should have utilised pre-stressed concrete which depends upon stress-relieved wire produced by the organisation with whom Sir Peter was so intimately connected.


## DARESBURY

As the birthplace of Lewis Carroll, the village of Daresbury attracts hundreds of visitors each year principally to see the stained glass windows in All Saints' Church depicting characters from "Alice in Wonderland".

In recent years, however, no village near to Warrington has attracted more distinguished visitors than Daresbury and for reasons totally unconnected with its literary associations. These visitors have included Princess Marina, the Prime Minister, Lord and Lady Leverhulme as well as many of the country's leading scientists and research physicists, and they have visited Daresbury either because of the Nuclear Physics Laboratory or because of the residential centre of adult spastics at Daresbury Hall.

The old village of Daresbury, however, has been left largely untouched by modern developments and retains its old world charm as it looks upon the surrounding countryside from an elevated position giving views of the Mersey and the Lancashire hills. It is thought that Daresbury is unique among the local villages in possessing a name apparently unconnected with any physical or geographical feature, and takes its name instead from some ancient family who once lived there.

The name indeed is thought to be derived from the words "Deors burg", but the earliest written record containing the name is a Chester Court Record of about 1250 where it appears as "Derisbury".

As an ancient Manor, Daresbury was held after the Norman Conquest by a family named Daresbury until it passed to the Daniels about 1344. A Randoll de Deresbury was Mayor of Chester 1277-79. John Daniel sold the manor to George Heron in 1756 and the new owner rebuilt Daresbury Hall which after various other owners had lived there was sold to the National Spastics Society in 1965 for £6,500 and subsequently adapted at a cost of £25,000 as a training centre for adult spastics.

On June 16, 1967, the Prime Minister, Mr Harold Wilson, officially opened the £4m Daresbury Nuclear Research Laboratory where research physicists from a number of universities including Liverpool, Manchester and Glasgow, are conducting experiments. The Research Centre is not visible from the village itself where the Church attracts a steady stream of visitors because of its associations with Lewis Carroll, whose real name was Charles Lutwidge

Dodgson and whose father was the Vicar of Daresbury from 1827 to 1843. A church existed in Daresbury from 1159 and the Church registers date from 1617. In 1773 the church was rebuilt by the lord of the manor and again in 1870-72 it was almost completely restored. In 1933, an appeal was made for funds for the provision of a memorial window which depicts Lewis Carroll as well as characters from "Alice". A more recent tribute to "Alice" takes the form of a weather vane, made in 1953 by the local blacksmith Mr Colin Dale and erected on the chimney of the Smithy and later given to the school.

The school was originally founded in the year 1600 by Richard Rider of Preston Brook.

Perhaps the greatest tribute paid to Lewis Carroll, however, by those who have lived in his birthplace is the numbers who have called their daughters "Alice"!


## LATCHFORD

Latchford, once a large township in the County of Cheshire, now forms a substantial part of the County Borough of Warrington and indeed, a part of Latchford together with a comparatively small portion of Thelwall, became a part of Warrington when Warrington became a Municipal Borough in 1847.

The ancient ford, whereby the crossing of the Mersey was made before the first bridge was built certainly was the origin of the name of Latchford which means quite simply: "A ford over the Laecc or stream". The present writer has suggested that the part of Thelwall, formerly next to this ford and which became part of Warrington with Latchford in 1847 may have been the scene of Edward the Elder's fortification described in the Anglo-Saxon Chronicle in the year A.D. 923.

Extending from Warrington Bridge to south of the Manchester Ship Canal, the township of Latchford once enjoyed its own annual fairs granted by charter to Sir John Daniell in 1367.

St. James's Church formerly stood not far from Warrington Bridge on Knutsford Road. This church was opened in 1777 and its first minister, the Rev James Glazebrook inaugurated what was probably the first Sunday School in England there on April 4, 1779. Being in need of extensive repair the church was taken down in 1829 and a new church was built on Wilderspool Causeway within the year following.

Not far from the old Church on Knutsford Road there stood the cotton factory of Peel Ainsworth which became the first cotton factory in the North of England to be powered by steam when a Boulton and Watt steam engine was installed there in 1787.

This ancient township was first intersected by a canal in 1801 when the Old Quay Canal was opened, enabling boats to proceed from Howley to

Runcorn without having to wait for a tide on the River Mersey. Nearly a century later another Canal intersection occurred with the construction of the Manchester Ship Canal and the erection in Latchford of the locks as well as two high level bridges and one swing bridge.

Christ Church, Latchford in Wash Lane, was erected in 1861 and the parish was formed from the Parish of Grappenhall in 1866. The Church stands on the fringe of the estate of what was formerly the residence of the Broadbent family, but this estate and house have now made way for road widening purposes as well as for the addition of a small portion of land to the area surrounding the new Boteler Grammar School. This school was an ancient Warrington foundation and was moved from its original home in Warrington to Latchford in 1940. Older schools in Latchford were replaced in 1908 by Bolton Council School and the large post war housing estate at Latchford soon necessitated the erection of new schools, first the Richard Fairclough School in 1934 followed by the provision by the Roman Catholic community of schools associated with St. Augustine's Church.

Much of the urban development of Latchford followed the provision of adequate public transport which began in the 19th century with a railway station on the L. and N.W. Railway and later with the addition of a number of horse-drawn buses which were displaced by the opening of the first electric tramcar route to Latchford on April 21, 1902. Incidentally the last electric tram ran along the same route on August 29, 1935.

Today, not far from the old tram terminus in Latchford, exists one of the busiest shopping districts of Warrington and the adjacent Latchford housing estate is now bisected by a busy main trunk road which provides Warrington's second road crossing on the River Mersey at Kingsway Bridge which was opened in 1935.


## HOWLEY

Howley, like Dallam and Wilderspool, is an ancient part of the County Borough of Warrington and all three have been considerably scarred within the past two centuries by industrial development.

It was necessity that prompted men to settle and live in Howley in the first instance and necessity rather than deliberate choice explains why the majority of residents of this locality have dwelt there ever since.

A bend of the River Mersey forms the southern boundary of Howley and the name is a compound of two Old English words "holh" and "leah" meaning "hollow meadow". As a low-lying area bounded by a river it has been subjected to floods and mists throughout many centuries and would never have been chosen deliberately as a place of residence but for the fact that a small mound which formerly stood near to the present Parish Church afforded a strategic position from which to control the passage of the river via the ancient ford at Latchford.

The Romans used the ford when they constructed a road from Wilderspool through Wigan to the north and this road passed through what is now the rectory garden, but there is no evidence to show that anyone had settled on the north bank of the river at Warrington until after the Romans had departed from this country. Certainly the Romans had created their settlement on the south bank of the river at Wilderspool and it is only from the Domesday Survey that we are able to deduce that a subsequent settlement was made in Howley on the north bank which ultimately had at its centre a Norman castle clearly intended to control the river crossing. The town of Warrington, therefore, first began to grow in Howley around this castle and the neighbouring Parish Church, and it was only after the lords of the manor deserted their castle in Warrington for Bewsey, when they had built a bridge across the river that Warrington began to develop around this bridge leaving the Parish Church as one traveller said about 1540 "at the Tayle of al the Tounne".

The earliest maps of Warrington made in 1772 and 1826 show Howley as an area consisting almost entirely of open fields still bounded on the south by the river and on the north by Church Street. Both maps show a lane which on the 1772 map is described as "Road to Mersey Mills Howley &c." and on the 1826 map as "Howley Lane". Howley Quay, however, appears on the 1826 map and one of the main reasons for the considerable industrial development to take place in Howley during the nineteenth century was the construction of the Old Quay Canal at the end of the eighteenth century thus enabling boats to proceed from Howley to Runcorn without having to wait for a tide on the river.

Church Street is probably the oldest thoroughfare in Warrington apart from the Roman road. It was used in medieval times as a route from the neighbouring berewicks of Sankey and Penketh to the home of the lords of Warrington. The dead from these places were brought for burial in the church yard and it is evident that the best hostelries were to be found in this street as late as the seventeenth century since both Cromwell and the Earl of Derby favoured inns in Church Street when they stayed in Warrington. Industrialisation in the North West soon placed Church street on the main thoroughfare from Liverpool to Manchester and in the few decades preceeding the construction of the East Lancashire road, steam wagons carrying bales of cotton were a considerable hazard as they rattled and belched along this venerable highway.

Howley and Church Street house the first school to be established in Warrington that provided elementary education for all comers, and near to this National School there also stood Warrington's first workhouse. Although scarred by the nineteenth century, Howley is now slowly being tidied and

33

renovated but some of its scars still need drastic surgery.

## WOOLSTON

Woolston-with-Martinscroft is a joint township on the high road from Warrington to Manchester: this high road is one of the oldest in Lancashire. Only four roads were shown in Lancashire in 1675 in Ogilby's "Britannia" and the Warrington to Manchester road was one of the four. This became a turnpike road in the 18th century when slag from the Warrington Copper Works was used in its construction. Unfortunately the course of this road appears to have been little changed since then in spite of heavy traffic, considerably increased in recent years by placing on it an access point to the M6 at the Woolston end of the Thelwall Viaduct. Clearly it would have been in the best interest of all concerned if this old road had been straightened and widened at Woolston before the recent rapid urban development there had been permitted to take place.

For centuries after the Norman Conquest, Woolston was a tiny backwater, remote even from neighbouring Warrington to which it was connected by an early and primitive road. Communication also existed between Woolston and Thelwall by means of a ferry across the River Mersey until suddenly in the 18th century Woolston found itself connected to Warrington and Manchester not only by a turnpike road, but also by a short canal constructed as part of an early river navigation scheme designed to eliminate the long bends in the river in its course from Warrington eastwards.

The first Woolston Cut was made about 1720 and less than a century later this was replaced by the Woolston New Cut. Even the New Cut now ends abruptly in Woolston, and has not been used for more than 30 years. Recently proposals have been made to fill it in order to eliminate a danger to life and to create extra land for development.

The name of Woolston, which first appears in a charter dated about 1180 consists of two Old English elements the first of which is a personal name, either "Wulfes" or "Wulfsiges", followed by "tun". Martinscroft similarly means a small place, or croft, belonging to someone named "Martin".

In 1292 Robert de Woolston was a witness to a charter granted to the people of Warrington by William le Boteler and a family named Woolston resided there until the manor passed in the early 15th century by marriage to the family of Hawarden of Flintshire and then again by marriage from the Hawarden family in 1575 to the Standish family.

These families resided at Woolston Hall which stood in the vicinity of what is now Hall Lane. The Hall possessed a domestic chapel and here, Benedictine priests ministered to the spiritual needs of Warrington and Woolston Catholics from the latter part of the 17th century until Father Shuttleworth, O.S.B., came to Warrington from Woolston in 1771. A Catholic Church dedicated to St. Peter was opened in Woolston in 1835 and a Catholic school was built in 1840 to accommodate 120 children. In 1895 there were 64 children in attendance at this school. A Wesleyan Chapel erected in Martinscroft in 1827 still exists, but the rapidly-growing community now needs a new Anglican Church. The Vicar of Padgate (Rev J.O. Colling) has recently successfully managed to achieve a start on the building of this in Woolston at the junction of Hillock Lane, Dam Lane and Warren Lane.

Many Warringtonians were grateful during a hot summer in 1934 when the first open air swimming pool which could be heated artificially was opened in Woolston on May 19, 1934. Known as "The Lido" it proved a great attraction but a succession of wet summers cooled early enthusiasm and the swimming pool fell into disuse.

Near to the Lido site a shopping precinct has been developed in more recent years and in this precinct a fine branch of the Lancashire County Library is now nearing completion. Woolston now has an air of growing prosperity that would be considerably enhanced if much needed improvements to the A57 trunk road were to be given urgent attention.


## STOCKTON HEATH

Stockton Heath is now a compact and fully developed suburban parish of small area and high population bounded on the north by the Manchester Ship Canal, on the south by the Bridgewater Canal and extending from Walton in the West to Grappenhall in the East.

It provides a busy shopping centre for a much wider area and remains pleasantly attractive in spite of its rapid and somewhat haphazard method of growth. It does not appear in Arthur Mee's book on Cheshire in "The King's England Series", nor was it named on any map printed before 1739 when it featured modestly as "Stoken" on Moll's map of Cheshire. "Stoken" it remained on Bowen's map of 1777 only to disappear completely from Cary's map of 1824, from which it may safely be assumed that it was a hamlet of little consequence and no development until after the first quarter of the 19th century.

Nevertheless the name of Stockton is of some considerable antiquity and a family named Stockton dwelt in the hamlet of Stockton from the end of the 13th century until at least the end of the 15th century. In 1288, one Geppe de Stockton was fined at Chester in company with Godfrey de Lacheford and Ralph the reeve of Lachisford; and hereditary land in "the hamelete of Stokton" belonging to Robert Stokton is mentioned in the Legh Survey of 1465.

The name is a compound of two Old English elements: "Stoc" and "tun", or possibly "Stocc" and "tun". "Stoc-tun" means the tun belonging to a cattle or dairy farm, and "Stocc-tun" means a homestead built of logs. It is thought that the first alternative (i.e. that the name is derived from "Stoc-tun") is the most probable explanation of the name.

Originally Stockton Heath was merely a part of the township of Appleton from which it was created a separate civil parish by a Local Government Order dated October, 1897, hence "Victoria Square". The ecclesiastical parish is slightly older and was formed from the parishes of Great Budworth and Runcorn in 1838. On October 12, 1838, the first parish of St. Thomas was built and consecrated, but the rapid growth of Stockton Heath after this date was such that this first church was taken down and the present church, erected in its stead, was consecrated on July 31, 1868. The celebration of the centenary of this event taking place this year.

A group of Independent Methodists however, had established a place of worship in a barn in Stockton Heath in 1806 and a more permanent home, "Providence Chapel", was built by this group and opened in 1828. "Rules and regulations of the Sick Club for the children of Providence Chapel, Stockton Heath" were printed in 1833.

Unfortunate soldiers killed in battle between Parliamentary and Royalist forces were taken in April 1643 to Great Budworth for burial and the parish registers there record this battle as having taken place at "Stockton Heath".

A century later a plan of the rivers Irwell and Mersey also shows "Stockton Heath" as a place near Warrington. Shortly afterwards this hitherto little-known hamlet began to become widely known to travellers using the Bridgewater Canal as a means of transport since a coach, known as a "boat coach", met canal boats at London Bridge, Stockton Quay for the conveyance of passengers to Liverpool, Chester and elsewhere.

A Scottish novelist, James Grant, wrote his book "Lucy Arden" while residing at Stockton Lodge, a house which subsequently became a private school and which now has disappeared to make way for modern housing development.

The rapid development of modern Stockton Heath however, followed the provision of electric tramcars in 1902 and 1905. This was the first tramway route to be closed when it was decided to replace trams with buses in 1931.

In 1908 Stockton Heath was described as a garden city and fortunately the roadside tree planting which formed part of this project still makes this busy urban parish a pleasant place for residents and an attractive feature to visitors.


## MOORE

As a personal name, Moore occurs as frequently as Clarke and there are 48 entries for Moore and 50 for Clarke in the current issue of "Who's Who".

There are also 63 individuals named "Moore" in the "Dictionary of National Biography" including painters, politicians, writers, soldiers, sailors, physicians, surgeons, ministers, a gardener and a librarian. Yet none of the individuals named Moore, past or present and listed in these national works of reference, appears to have had any connection with Moore, Cheshire. This is a curious circumstance as there are only two places named "Moore" in Bartholomew's "Gazetteer of the British Isles" and only "Moore, Cheshire" is listed in "The Concise Oxford Dictionary of English Place Names".

Many families named Moore, therefore, must have taken their name from Moore in Cheshire and a family so called belonged to Moore as early as 1172 since a charter of Richard of Moore, quitclaiming to John, the Constable of Chester and the Abbey of Stanlaw the land which John had given to him, is reproduced in "Facsimiles of early Cheshire Charter", edited by Geoffrey Barraclough.

Professor Barraclough dates this charter between 1172 and 1178 and says: "Richard himself is a fairly well-known figure who was a tenant of the Constable of Chester on both sides of the Mersey in Runcorn and in Widnes. At a later date he received lands in Lancashire and at Runcorn, on condition that he and his heirs maintained a boat for the ferry across the Mersey at Runcorn." Among the large number of Cheshire men who opposed King Henry IV at the Battle of Shrewsbury on July 21, 1403, and who incurred forfeiture of their land in consequence were Randel del Moore, William de Crue and Sir Piers Dutton.

Moore originally formed part of the barony of Halton and was given by Roger Lacy, the Constable of Cheshire, to his brother Richard who later died of leprosy and was buried in the Chapter House of the Cannons of Norton. A large estate in Moore was purchased by Richard Rutter who was buried at Daresbury in 1623. The descendants of Richard Rutter continued to live at Moore until Rebecca Rutter married Peter Kyffin Heron of Daresbury Hall in the 18th century. The possessor of Moore Hall in the year 1850 was the Rev George Heron and another principal landowner at this time was Dennis Milner of Moore House.

A later occupant of Moore House, Miss Mary Milner, presented to the village "The Milner Church Institute" in 1907. Miss Milner laid the foundation stone of this centre of social and recreational activity on July 20, 1907, in memory of her father and mother, Nathaniel and Anne Milner of Moore. Anglican church services are held in this Institute once each month as there is no Anglican Church in Moore. A Methodist Chapel, however, was built in 1812 and rebuilt in 1870. A village school was also built in 1877 for 50 children but modern housing development on the west side of Moore has been accompanied by the recent erection of the "Moore County Primary School".

Much of Moore fits the meaning of the name which is Old English Mor meaning "moor" or "fen", because the cutting of the township into strips by canals and railways has meant that parts are isolated and undeveloped and in consequence most development until very recently in Moore has clung to the sides of the road from Warrington to Runcorn. This roadside village contains some pleasant old houses and farms.

Near to the former L.M.S. railway line in Moore, an A.A. battery was placed to help the defence of Merseyside in World War II. Slightly farther north, the Moore Lane Swing Bridge across the Manchester Ship Canal (at present closed for repair) will perhaps be used more extensively for road traffic in the near future since an 18-acre site nearby has been chosen for the development of a large warehouse for the Du Pont Co. (U.K.) Ltd. This warehouse will be 650 feet by 200 feet and there will also be an extensive office block with parking facilities for cars and lorries.


## FIDDLERS FERRY

Although Fiddler's Ferry is simply an ancient ferry across the Mersey and situated in Penketh it has gradually assumed the role of a separate locality to the extent that when it was decided to build a 2,000 megawatt coal-fired power station near to this ferry the proposed station was known from the outset as the Fiddler's Ferry Power Station.

Considerable argument has always surrounded the origin of the name of this ferry. There are those who believe that the name originated with the name of a former licensee of the Ferry Inn named Fidler: others are persuaded that a fiddler used to accompany the ferryman on his journeys across the river. Both of these explanations, however, have a touch of improbability. A more plausible explanation, in view of the great antiquity of this ferry, is offered in the "Victoria County History of Lancashire" where it says that the name is derived: "Perhaps from (Adam le) Vieleur, the (supposed) original grantee of the manor (of Penketh)." Vieleur of course, can easily be construed as violer, a player of the viol or fiddle.

"Go to Fiddler's Ferry" used to be a polite way of consigning someone to Hades but it is difficult to imagine why this expression should have gained currency locally since the view of the Mersey at this point possesses great beauty and Fiddler's Ferry has had much to offer local sportsmen over a long period of time.

The Ferry was the starting point for certain events in the Warrington Regatta which took place annually more than a century ago, while only in April 1968 the Fiddler's Ferry Sailing Club opened a new clubhouse at Penketh Locks.

In 1919 a concrete barge was launched at Fiddler's Ferry. This was the Elmarine, stated at the time to be the lightest seagoing concrete barge in the world and the construction of which, at the Concrete Seacraft Co., Ltd., Fiddler's Ferry, had created a record in the building of concrete ships. The Elmarine weighed 250 tons designed for the local wheat-carrying trade, was 95ft. in length, 21ft. 4in. beam and 8ft. draught.

When the first modern industrial canal was opened in 1757 it connected the Mersey at Sankey Bridges to the Parr Colliery near St. Helens. This canal, the Sankey-St. Helens Canal, was subsequently extended by Acts of Parliament on two occasions; the first of these occurred in 1762 resulting in an extension to Fiddler's Ferry and the second in 1830 so that the canal ultimately terminated at Widnes.

After having sprung into modern prominence as the terminal of a canal in the 18th century, the Ferry next acquired a railway station situated on the old Whitecross to Runcorn Gap line, subsequently acquired by the L.N.W. Railway Company.

Many Warringtonians became familiar with Fiddler's Ferry however, because of the Golf Club which was originally known as the Mersey Golf Club, and which seems to have commenced about 1895 continuing until soon after a fire destroyed the club-house a few years ago. Many notable personalities of Warrington once enjoyed membership of this club and its closure has been regretted.

The old Ferry Inn, however, has recently been modernised and has become a popular rendezvous, while the Fiddler's Ferry Power Station, which is considered to be vital to the needs of the North West, now provides a landmark that makes this ancient locality the most readily discernible spot in the environs of Warrington and its surrounding area.

## BANK QUAY

A survey of the possessions of the lord of the Manor of Warrington taken on April 19, 1587 shows that a widow named Elizabeth Fakener and another lady named Jane Parpen both held separate tenements and two plots of land each called the "Bank Fyelds". It also shows that the Bank Fyelds lay between a lane, now called Liverpool Road, and the River Mersey.

In Lancashire place-names, "bank" mostly means "hill", but it also means "sea-shore" or "bank of a river", and in Warrington, "Bank Fyelds" the site of Bank Quay, obviously take their name from their situation on the bank of the Mersey as do Bank Hall and Bank House.

Bank Quay has been an industrial area for nearly three centuries, and it was the first great industrialist of the area, Thomas Patten, who said, in a letter written in 1697, that he had made the Mersey navigable from Liverpool to Warrington. Patten did this in order to ship copper ore to his works at Bank Quay, which is shown on a map of the Mersey in 1712 as "Bank Key".

Fearnhead, James Cropper's Agricultural School

Halton Castle

Belmont House, Great Budworth

Stretton Hall, Stretton

An Act of Parliament in 1721 for making the Mersey and Irwell navigable to Manchester also states that: "the said River Mercy hath been heretofore and now is navigable from Liverpool to Bank Key."

It was Patten's son, also called Thomas, who built Bank Hall, now the Warrington Town Hall, in 1750. The great grandson of this Thomas Patten was John Wilson Patten, later Lord Winmarleigh, and he sold Bank Hall and Bank Park to the Warrington Corporation in 1872. Colonel Wilson Patten and George Crosfield contributed £12,500 of the total cost (£22,000) and Warrington's first public park, Bank Park, was opened to the public on June 20, 1873.

Adjoining Bank Park, is Bank House now the Borough Treasurer's Office, and this was once the home of the second Mayor of Warrington, William Allcard, who was also one of the three engineers to work with George Stephenson on the construction of the Liverpool-Manchester Railway.

The Patten family had other interests than copper at Bank Quay in the 18th century since a glassworks had also been built there in 1750 by Robert Patten and others which passed into the ownership of Perrin, Geddes and Co. The last firm to manufacture glass at Bank Quay, however, was Robinson, Son and Co., and this firm transferred the business to Birmingham in 1933.

Although George Crosfield became a grocer in Warrington in 1777 and later moved to Lancaster, his fourth son Joseph returned to Warrington in 1814 after his father had viewed "some premises near Bankey suitable for a Soapery". Thus began the manufacture of soap in Warrington by Joseph Crosfield at the age of 22.

The River Mersey and the 18th century canals encouraged other manufacturers to establish their premises at Bank Quay and these included the mill originally rented, and later purchased and used as a flour mill, by James Fairclough. These mills were remodelled and enlarged in 1915. The Bank Quay Foundry Co. in the mid-19th century cast a huge press which was used in the construction of the Britannia Bridge across the Menai Straits. The press was exhibited in the "Great Exhibition" at the "Crystal Palace" and since it was of enormous size and weighed more than 60 tons, it was conveyed to its destination on a special train consisting of 11 trucks and two "break" vans.

It was in 1837 that a railway line from Birmingham to Liverpool and Manchester passed through Bank Quay and the first Bank Quay Station (on the north side of Liverpool Road), was opened. The present Bank Quay Station was originally erected in 1868 with high and low level platforms. Recently this station has been the subject of a considerable face lift as a result of the modernisation plans for Joseph Crosfield and Sons Ltd., including improvements to the rail links with the works.

Perhaps the most interesting commentary on the changing nature of Bank Quay, however, is the fact that after Joseph Crosfield established his soapery

42

at Bank Quay, he elected to live on the north side of Liverpool Road, opposite the works, in a house called Mersey Bank which is shown on a map of Warrington in 1826. At that time this house was surrounded by open fields!

## OUGHTRINGTON

Arthur Mee describes Oughtrington, in his book on Cheshire in "The King's England Series", as "A little neighbour for Lymm". Now, since the Lymm Grammar School is now situated in Oughtrington, it is perhaps not surprising that there are so many people who regard this "little neighbour" as an integral part of Lymm. In spite of its close proximity to Lymm, however, Oughtrington was a distinct entity long before it was constituted a parish out of the second mediety of the old Parish of Lymm in 1874 and formed into an ecclesiastical parish in 1881.

A family taking their name from the place resided at Oughtrington Hall as early as the 12th century: this family became extinct when Margery, the daughter and heir of John de Hughtrington married Richard Leigh of West Hall, High Legh.

The estates ultimately descended to Trafford Trafford who rebuilt Oughtrington Hall about 1817 and special comment about this is made in Ormerod's "Cheshire" where it says: "The principal gates, and entrance lodge, are from an elegant design by Harrison."

Trafford Trafford died in 1859 and the Oughtrington estate consisting of about 1100 acres was conveyed to G.C. Dewhurst of Manchester in 1862. This transaction brought to Oughtrington a man who became a great benefactor to the locality since he not only built Oughtrington Church in 1872 and became its patron but his benefactions also included the gift of land and money for the building of a new Grammar School in Lymm in 1882.

When the Oughtrington Estates were again sold in 1911 the gift of the living was transferred to the Bishop of Chester. The name Oughtrington means the "tun" or farm of the people of Uhtred, and there are more than a score of Cheshire places similarly ending in "-ington" so that such places as Carrington, Cuddington, Partington means the tuns or farms of the people of Cara, Cuda and Pearta.

Near to Oughtrington Hall stands Oughtrington House, once the residence of Joseph Watts, maltster, who offered it for sale about the year 1862 when it was stated that the view from the house was "not to be surpassed in any situation in England". This house was subsequently the residence of members of Dewhurst, Miller and **Mandelberg** families until it was purchased soon after the second world war as a home for crippled women.

This institution has an interesting history since it began with the evacuation during the blitz of a number of crippled women from Liverpool to Cotebrook near Tarporley where they found shelter in the village hall under

43

the care of members of the Society of Friends. With the end of the war the villagers wanted to use their hall for other purposes and the evacuees were moved to Penketh. Very soon afterwards Oughtrington House was purchased as a permanent home for them and re-named "Cotebrook". The hostel is now organised as a non-profit making society having a Quaker Chairman and known as Cotebrook Ltd: accommodation for about 30 crippled women is thereby provided.

The end of the war also resulted in the purchase of Oughtrington Hall by the governors of Lymm Grammar School. By December 1945 the Hall was in use by the school and by 1957 with the addition of new buildings around the Hall, the school was situated entirely in Oughtrington.


## RISLEY

When the Risley estates were auctioned in 1872 they comprised a few scattered farm houses including Risley Old Hall and Risley New Hall. Risley Old Hall was then described as "A Farm House, with two barns, stable, shippon, piggeries etc. Fold yard, moat and orchard." Risley Moss was also shown on the estate plan and as late as 1924, Kelly's Lancashire Directory described Risley simply as "A small scattered village in the township of Culcheth."

Since then, of course, Risley has been the site of a Royal Ordnance Factory, a Royal Naval Station, a Home Office Remand Home and as the Headquarters of three groups of the United Kingdom Atomic Energy Authority as well as being designated as part of the New Town of Warrington.

The name of Risley is derived from two Old English words "hris" and "leah" meaning "twigs, brushwood" and "tract of open ground" respectively, so that Risley means an area of open ground covered with twigs or brushwood.

Originally Risley belonged to Culcheth, and when Gilbert de Culcheth was killed in 1246 his estates passed to his four daughters (Margery, Elizabeth, Ellen and Joan) who married four sons of Hugh de Hindley. The part of the Culcheth estates known as Risley passed at this time to his daughter Ellen, whose husband Robert elected to be called "Risley". Thus a Risley family came into being and this family resided in Risley until the beginning of the 18th century when the manor was acquired by the Blackburne family.

Perhaps the best-known member of the Risley family was Thomas Risley who was born in 1630 and educated at Warrington Grammar School. He went to Pembroke College, Oxford, in 1649 and was elected a Fellow in 1654. Being unwilling to comply with the terms of the Uniformity Act, he surrendered his Fellowship on August 24, 1662 and settled on his estate at Risley where he formed a Nonconformist congregation and built, at his own

The Old Farm, Moore

Victoria Square, Stockton Heath, 1908

Church Street, Warrington, 1907

expense, a small chapel in Fifty Croft, Cross Lane which was vested in trustees on March 25th, 1707. This chapel still exists and was the burial place of Thomas Risley, its builder and founder, who died in 1716.

A special railway station was constructed on the Cheshire Lines Railway in World War II for those employed at the considerable Royal Ordnance Factory built there. When this Factory was closing down the same site was chosen by the United Kingdom Atomic Energy Authority and in February, 1946, the nucleus of the Production Division consisting of 12 men and women, moved into their new Headquarters at Risley. Today, Risley is the headquarters of the Engineering Group, the Production Group and the Reactor Group which employ at Risley about 3,500 men and women.

Near to the Royal Ordnance Factory in World War II was sited HMS Ariel, which stood derelict after the war until it was decided in 1958 to build a Remand Centre, which houses now about 600 prisoners.

A large part of Risley is now included in the area designated as the New Town of Warrington and most probably, therefore, will become the location of still further development on a considerable scale, with many new homes and people being settled in this rapidly-changing area.


## STRETTON

Concerning Cheshire, Arthur Mee says: "many of the great homes of county families are now farmhouses, but many of them keep the beauty which prosperous owners gave to them. Few of England's counties can show such a wealth of black and white timbered houses as Cheshire."

Many of these black and white timbered farm houses are to be seen within a few miles of the centre of Warrington and one of them is known as Stretton Hall. Originally this was the manor house of the Starkey family who possessed Stretton from the reign of Henry II until the beginning of the 18th century. Stretton Hall is an Elizabethan structure with a beautiful front and when it was auctioned in 1884 it was described as "an excellent country residence for a gentleman however good his position". Clearly this statement was no exaggeration for the property was then sold for £8,660 to Mr Henry Neild of Whitley.

The Roman road from the South to Wilderspool passed through Stretton and the name of Stretton is derived from this fact, and means the tun on the "stret" or road.

For centuries Stretton has been, and still remains, the home of an agricultural community. This fact is reflected in various entries to be found in the Stretton Town Book 1791-1834, now preserved in Warrington Municipal Library. In this book were recorded annually the payments made by the Constable for sparrow heads. Sparrows were a great nuisance to farmers and the Constable paid sums of public money for their heads and eggs. In 1827, for example, he paid £3 8s. 2d. for "818 sparrow heads at 1d. per head"; 15s. 2½d. for "365 young sparrow heads at ½d. per head", and 7s. 5d. for "356 sparrow eggs at ¼d. per egg". The Constable's accounts also show that when he held a prisoner in custody, expenses for food and drink were paid to the proprietor of the Cat and Lion, an example being a payment of 7s. 10d. to: "the Cat and Lion when James Davies was in custody for stealing Wm. Darbyshire's potatoes."

A road in Stretton known as "Pewter Spear Lane" was once a private road to Appleton Hall and as several Cheshire Squires fought in the Battle of Poitiers it is thought that the name of this road might have been corrupted from "Poiters Pierre", otherwise a person named Pierre brought to Stretton at the time of Poitiers.

Like the neighbouring Parish of Appleton, Stretton once possessed a thorn tree and also possessed village stocks which stood under the thorn tree. The stocks, however, were demolished in the 19th century, the last stump being used on a weighing machine to steady the vehicles brought to be weighed on the machine.

Stretton Church, dedicated to St. Matthew was originally erected in 1827 on the site of an ancient chapel of ease but was restored in 1870 under the direction of Sir G. Gilbert Scott and possesses a very pleasing appearance. Next to the Church stands a village school, erected in 1838 as a "National School" for 140 children. Although the Church, the school and the Cat and Lion are pleasantly grouped together in the centre of the ancient township it is unfortunate that they also stand today at the junction of extremely busy main roads so that to photograph these pleasing buildings is apt to be somewhat hazardous!


## PADDINGTON

Situated between the ancient Manor of Bruche and the Township of Woolston, Paddington is an almost fully developed locality carved from the Manor of Bruche.

The name of Paddington is the invention of a 19th century manufacturer, Robert Hatton, who erected a soap works there in 1820. It would seem that at first the name only applied to the works but quickly extended to the surrounding locality, so that when the soapery was auctioned in 1844, it was described as being "situate at Paddington, near Warrington". Paddington as a locality is now shown on Ordnance Survey maps.

As the invention of one man, it is not easy to state with accuracy precisely what prompted his choice of name. An obvious guess would be that the name is a combination of Padgate and Warrington since the manufacturer in

47

question had been sued for creating obnoxious smells in Warrington with an earlier soap works and had been compelled to move to the district next to Padgate. Another suggestion with some local currency is that the same manufacturer had associations with Paddington, London and that this prompted his choice of name, but this does not seem to have been clearly established.

The Paddington soap works featured in an exciting case of conspiracy to defraud the Government of duty within a few years of its establishment. Other soap manufacturers in Warrington noticed that the Paddington soap was being sold at a price lower than soap of the same quality made elsewhere and as a result Excise Officers kept a careful watch on the Paddington works. Nothing untoward was discovered for some time until a new officer making a surprise visit noticed a trap door in the office floor being lowered. He found that this trap door led to a large vaulted chamber were contraband soap was made and the manufacturers were required to pay £6,340 in double duty. This alarmed the creditors of the soap manufacturers to such an extent that the manufacturers were forced into bankruptcy.

The Paddington works later became the site of a glue works and the smell from this works at one time can have been little less obnoxious than that which caused the earlier soap manufacturer to move from Warrington.

In spite of these industrial settlements in the area the countryside in Paddington remained open and attractive until recent years. The river bank from Paddington Lock on the Woolston New Cut, and a path through the fields from Manchester Road to Green Lane, Padgate, both attracted Warringtonians on weekend strolls until urban development spread over these open spaces.

Paddington House was once the home of a former Mayor of Warrington, Alderman Arthur Bennett, whose passionate regard for Warrington's past led him to collect many curious remains in the grounds of his house. Some of these remains, including stones from Victoria Bridge, Warrington, and the Warrington Training College, are still to be seen at the house which is now an attractive residential hotel.

A Warrington Directory for 1908 shows that Paddington extended at least to the Dog and Partridge Inn, which is listed under Paddington, and under the same heading also appears: "Edward Scholtze, glue extractor; Edward Gorton and Co. Ltd., chemical manufacturers; and Arthur Bennett, J.P., chartered accountant, Paddington House."


FEARNHEAD


Fearnhead is the northern part of the ancient township of Poulton with Fearnhead which extended from the River Mersey to the boundary of

Winwick. Although this township is situated in a flat, low lying area which only stands at 45 feet above sea-level the name is derived from two Old English elements "Fearn" and "heafod", meaning fern and hill respectively. The name of Fearnhead, therefore, means "a fernclad height".

Originally it was an area of wood and moss which has been brought under cultivation over many centuries and remains primarily agricultural today. A family named Fearnhead held lands there from the end of the 13th century when Richard de Fernyheued was living at the same time as his neighbour Henry de Bruche, until the 17th century when the will of Thomas Fearnhead, a yeoman, was proved.

In the 19th century, Fearnhead was selected by a Liverpool shipowner named James Cropper as the site of an experimental agricultural school. Cropper was a Quaker and had inherited an estate from his father at Fearnhead. He had been interested for many years in establishing a school in which boys would be engaged in agricultural labour and ultimately built his school house next to Fearnhead House. He proposed that the labourers should share the profits of cultivation and also ensured that his pupils received school education as well as acquiring manual skills. Cropper described his school in a pamphlet entitled "Some account of an agricultural school for orphans at Fearnhead, near Warrington", and this pamphlet was printed at Warrington in 1839.

Fearnhead was also selected as the site for playing fields, used for many years by the pupils of Warrington Secondary School. Bounded by Powell's nurseries and the Fearnhead Golf Course, the playing fields provided football and cricket grounds together with tennis courts and Wednesday afternoons were devoted to the weekly exodus of the school from Warrington to Fearnhead. Part of the old Golf Course has since been used as a site for Padgate Training College, but the remainder still provides the cheapest game of golf in the vicinity of Warrington.

After water works had been established at **Winwick** and Houghton Green a number of inhabitants of Fearnhead who had private water wells were exempted from paying water charges under agreements drawn up when it was considered that their private supplies would be affected by the establishment of the large pumping stations nearby.

Fearnhead Cross is now a road junction in the centre of this ancient township and a roadside cross once stood at this point.

An exceptionally full set of town books containing the accounts of the Surveyors of Highways, the Constables and the Poor Books of the townships of Poulton and Fearnhead are preserved in Warrington Municipal Library and in one of these books is recorded a bequest in 1722 of £100 by "Peers Legh Esquire, Late of Bruche" to the poor of "Poolton and ffearnhead" and the entry describes how this sum is to be used for the distribution of woollen and linen cloth to the "poor of ye above said Townshipps".

Bruche Hall (demolished 1971)

Risley Chapel Built in 1707

# HALTON

Standing on a rocky height giving commanding views over a great distance, Halton Castle was once the residence of the Constables of Chester, who were also the Barons of Halton possessing extensive privileges granted by the Earl of Chester.

Halton stands in the centre of a group of townships named after their approximate location to this formerly important centre namely Norton, Sutton, Weston and Aston. The honour of Halton, however, at one time possessed jurisdiction over 37 townships in Cheshire including Thelwall, Stretton, Appleton and Walton, and a wide variety of offences committed in these places were tried and punished at Halton.

In 1474, for example, two Welshmen from Mold who had committed a burglary at Keckwick were committed to Halton Castle, only to break out complete with fetters and chains. When they were recaptured they were tried by the seneschal and were hanged at Halton.

William Beamont suggested that the name of Halton itself meant "high town". The name, however, consists of two old English elements "halh" and "tun" and the meaning of "halh" varies from "a piece of flat alluvial land by a river" to "the spur of a hill" including a third possibility, namely "a corner, angle or secret place".

Halton means therefore, the "tun" in or by a "halh" whichever meaning of "halh" is most appropriate to Halton, Cheshire.

The romantic remains of Halton Castle attract many visitors as does the Castle Hotel which was built within the grounds of the castle, and formerly housed the ancient court in which hundreds of offences were tried.

It was the commanding position of the rock on which Halton stands that prompted the Norman barons to erect a castle guarding the Mersey at this point. Hugh Lupus, Earl of Chester, gave Halton to his cousin Nigel, making him at the same time his Marshal and the Constable of Chester. This first baron of Halton built the Castle but little of its original Norman state remains as the Castle, having been first garrisoned by the Royalists in the Civil War and then by Parliamentarian troops, was later dismantled and reduced to a ruin.

Next to the Castle there now stands St. Mary's Parish Church, a stone building with a spirelet designed by Sir George Gilbert Scott. The vicar of Halton is also the custodian of Sir John Chesshyre's Library, a simple stone building standing next to the Vicarage. This Library was founded in 1733 and contains an interesting catalogue written on vellum which also states the rules. It was provided partly to create a private study for the vicar and at the same time was to be open every Tuesday and Thursday for clergymen and other persons of letters. The Latin inscription containing the name of the founder is still to be seen over the doorway, but the door does not appear to have been opened very recently.

In Main Street stands the Trinity Methodist Church, also a stone Gothic building with a spire, erected in 1875 at the expense of Thomas Hazlehurst. Brooke's almhouses were founded in 1769 and endowed with £54 12s. 0d. a year for six poor and decayed honest servants; whilst a Grammar School, founded by an unknown benefactor, was endowed with about £44 a year.

This romantic and ancient township is now to become the scene of modern development that will result in the influx of about 10,000 new residents. Plans for the development of the north and east of Halton from Summer Lane and Halton Brow round the northern slopes of the village to the eastern side near Norton Lane were announced at the end of 1966. This development is due for completion in 1971.


## GREAT BUDWORTH

Great Budworth was formerly the second largest parish in Cheshire and extended from Stockton Heath to Northwich, 51 miles in length and 10 miles in width. The Tudor charms of the village surrounding the ancient church fortunately has been preserved largely because the main road from Warrington to Northwich passes to the west of the heart of the village which stands on a hill.

This village cannot fail to charm any visitor with its array of half-timbered houses with their twisted chimneys. Its beauty as well as its history has been well and truly preserved for all time in a book, published in 1951, and written by Mr A.W. Boyd entitled "A Country Parish". This book contains 34 magnificent colour photographs and 48 black and white photographs by C.W. Bradley that demonstrate quite clearly the truth of Arthur Mee's statement that "Great Budworth ... is as lovely as any Cheshire village, a rare bit of Tudor England".

Dedicated to God and All Saints, the 14th century church is an impressive building containing monuments of the Warburton and Poole families as well as the remains of the great Cheshire historian, Sir Peter Leycester.

It was Leycester who said that the name of Budworth was from two words "Bode" and "Worth", meaning a dwelling by the water. This regrettably is not a correct interpretation as the second element "worp" means "homestead" while the first element "Budda", is a personal name.

A cobbled street next to the Church called School Lane contains the village school, while nearby in the Churchyard is a school founded about the year 1600, by John Dean. This school was endowed with the interest of £200 given by Mr Pickering of Thelwall and Mrs Glover. The remains of the village stocks stand outside the lychgate of the Churchyard.

At the time of the Domesday Survey, Budworth was held by William fitz

Nigel, Baron of Halton, but in the reign of Henry III was possessed by Geoffrey, son of Adam de Dutton who resided in Budworth and was also known as Geoffrey de Budworth. His grandson, Peter, removed to Warburton and assumed that name.

The "Cock Inn" on the main road is an ancient foundation and in the 17th century was visited by Drunken Barnaby who composed verses in Latin and in English about each of his stopping places.

Near to the Cock Inn is Belmont House, now a private school, but originally built as a residence by J.H. Smith Barry who desposited in it a valuable collection of pictures and statues that was later removed to Marbury.

About 1950 when workmen were making alterations to an old country house in Budworth, the owner noticed a peculiarity in the soil being thrown out of a hole. A chemical test on this soil proved it to contain pure alluvial gold but only in tracer quantities. This deposit was found in several places in the vicinity but fortunately not in sufficient quantity to promote a gold rush that might have destroyed the charm of this village forever.

## SOUTHWORTH WITH CROFT

Situated exactly half-way on the road from Winwick to Culcheth, the village of Croft is comparatively free from modern development and is a place of charm and surprise. Southworth consists only of Southworth Hall which was formerly the home of an ancient family but which was occupied and used as a farmhouse in the 19th century.

The two places nevertheless are united as a joint township known as Southworth-with Croft. As early as 1212 Croft was held by Gilbert de Croft who possessed this manor on condition of the service of falconer to the Lord of Makerfield. Gilbert also held Southworth but before 1219 he had granted Southworth to Gilbert, son of Hugh de Croft, who assumed the name of Southworth and thus became the founder of the Southworth family which continued to hold the manor of Southworth and Croft until the beginning of the 17th century.

It was as the result of the marriage of a Gilbert de Southworth in 1325 that this family came to posses a part of the Manor of Samlesbury and at the beginning of the 17th century it was from Thomas Southworth of Samlesbury that Sir Thomas Ireland of Bewsey acquired the manors of Southworth and Croft, the reason for the collapse of the Southworth family resources being a succession of fines, forfeits and imprisonments consequent upon the adherence of the family to the Roman Catholic faith during the reign of Elizabeth.

A century later, however, the manor was once more held by a Roman Catholic family, the Gerards of Ince, and was bequeathed in 1743 to Thomas

Fairfield Hall, Manchester Road

Warrington Road, Preston On The Hill c.1907

Gerard, a Jesuit priest. When Charles II lodged for a night in August 1651 at the house of Sir William Gerard, a letter written about the occasion described Sir William as "a subtle jesuited Papist".

Both Southworth and Croft are ancient names consisting of Old English elements. Southworth consists of OE "sup" meaning South, and "worp" meaning "homestead" or "enclosure". Croft is OE meaning "a small piece of arable land, a field".

Since the Southworths and Gerards were Roman Catholics it is scarcely surprising to find that Croft possesses a large Roman Catholic Church which is dedicated to St. Lewis. The dedication followed from the fact that the priest in charge was a French refugee named Louis Richebeque and this Church was opened in 1827. Nearby now stands a new Roman Catholic School. Croft became a separate parish following the Winwick Church Act of 1841 but the Church of England Church in Lady Lane, Christ Church, Croft, was built in 1832. A Unitarian Chapel was also opened at Croft in 1839.

The village school, enlarged in 1893, now stands at a road junction and is known as Croft County School. Nearby is a pleasant Village Memorial Hall opened in 1965, the foundation stone having been set by Joseph E. Birchall on April 26, 1965.

Early in the 19th century two Friendly Societies of Croft held their meeting in the Joiners Arms while a third Society, the Croft Junior Female Friendly Society, met at the Admiral Rodney.

Although some modern housing development is now taking place in New Lane, Croft remains largely undisturbed, pleasant and somewhat remote in spite of a war time invasion that left behind hutments subsequently used to house refugees from Egypt at the time of the Suez crisis.


## RIXTON-WITH-GLAZEBROOK

The Glazebrook and the Sankey Brook were formerly the eastern and western boundaries respectively of the ancient Parish of Warrington. Rixton-with-Glazebrook, containing the ancient chapelry of Hollinfare, was the eastern extremity, therefore, of the Parish of Warrington. Today, however, the name of Hollinfare has taken precedence and Hollinfare is now a civil parish consisting of the township of Rixton-with-Glazebrook and the village of Hollins Green.

The Glazebrook flowed from the north into the River Mersey, but as the Mersey and Manchester Ship Canal are now coincident across the southern extremity of this parish, the Glazebrook now flows into the Canal.

Glazebrook takes its name from the brook and the first part of this name "Glas" is an old river name although two other meanings of "Glas" are "bright" and "green or blue". Rixton consists of a personal name "Ric" and

55

"Tun". Both Rixton and Glazebrook are mentioned in 13th century records. "Le Fery del Holyns" is mentioned in a murder case recorded in the Assize Rolls of 1352 and the ferry across the Mersey at this place was used by the Duke of Cumberland in December 1745 in his pursuit of the Young Pretender. The first element of the name of Hollinfare is Old English "holegn" meaning "holly", whilst "fare" means "ferry" or "ford".

The parish is very much an agricultural area largely untouched by urban development, although one concession to modernity is a country club at Glazebrook.

Ancient halls at Rixton and a fair sprinkling of chapels and churches, however, betoken an area rich in romantic family and personal history exceeding most other places within the neighbourhood of Warrington.

The name of Alan de Rixton occurs in records repeatedly between 1200 and 1332 so that successive lords of the manor bore the same name and in 1292 one of these gentlemen was fined "because he stood in the hall for pleas of the Crown without warrant and being solemnly called would not come".

In 1384, William, son of Matthew de Rixton sold all his lands in Rixton and Glazebrook to Richard de Mascy. A grandson of this Richard de Mascy named Thomas who died in 1464 was a Rector of Warrington in 1435, and before the end of the 15th century another member of the family, Hamlet de Mascy, endowed a chantry in the chapel of Hollinfare. The family adhered to the Roman Catholic faith after the Reformation. The Mascy family lived at Rixton Hall and although reduced in circumstances through penalties inflicted because of their recusancy, survived until the 18th century. The ancient chapel at Hollinfare was rebuilt in 1735 and constituted the Parish Church of Hollinfare in 1874. This church, which is now dedicated to St. Helen, was restored in 1882.

The Roman Catholic Church of St. Michael in Moss Side Lane was built in 1831, and there are three Methodist churches in the Parish.

The main road through the Parish is the road from Warrington to Manchester and a bar erected on this road to increase toll in 1831 was pulled down by the people of the parish.


### FAIRFIELD

Although Fairfield has simply been the name of an electoral division of Warrington since 1890, the name of Fairfield is of a somewhat greater antiquity and was the name of a house, subsequently known as Fairfield Hall, erected in the mid 18th century for Miss Anna Blackburne with a special view to housing her collection of ornithology.

Miss Blackburne was the only daughter of John Blackburne of Orford Hall and both father and daughter achieved considerable reputations for their interest in natural history.

Anna Blackburne corresponded with Linnaeus who named after her one of the American Warblers (Sylvia Blackburniae) and another naturalist, John Reinhold Forster, named a genus of New Holland plants after her (Blackburnia). She died at Fairfield on December 30, 1793, and among her benefactions was a legacy of £100 to the Warrington Blue Coat School.

At first Fairfield Hall was called Fairfield House and a century after its erection it is shown standing completely surrounded by open fields on the 1851 Ordnance Survey Map of Warrington. On this map, the house stands on a site which is now the junction of Manchester Road and Fairfield Street and it is named on the map as "Fairfield House". Clearly this house gave a name to the locality because nearby a "Fairfield Cottage" is also shown. A map published in 1890, however, shows that "Fairfield House" had become "Fairfield Hall" and "Fairfield Cottage" had become "Fairfield House" whilst a "Fairfield Tannery" owned by William Mortimer and Co., had also appeared between the two houses. Both Fairfield House and the Tannery had disappeared by the time the 1928 map was compiled but Fairfield Hall remained.

After the death of Miss Blackburne, the Rev Edward Lloyd opened a private academy for the education of youths of a higher class at Fairfield Hall after surrendering his post as Second Master of the Boteler Grammar School, but by 1844 the Hall had become the residence of John Fitchett Marsh who became the first Town Clerk of Warrington.

Later in the century the Hall was rented by the Warrington Training College as a residence for the lady Superintendent of the College as well as for students.

The Warrington Training College stood almost opposite to Fairfield Hall on a site adjoining St. Elphin's Park, and the fine array of buildings which comprised this College were regrettably destroyed by fire on December 28, 1923.

Before the Second World War, the site of Fairfield Hall was used for air raid shelters and subsequently the site was used for the erection of buildings housing the local offices of the Ministry of Social Security.

Fairfield Street is now known by all who have to take a driving test in Warrington but the Street also contains Fairfield School, a Church of England foundation originating with the old Mount School, although the buildings in Fairfield Street were not opened until 1894 when Mrs L.M. Stansfield was headmistress.

Improvements to Fairfield School were given final Ministry approval earlier this year.

The Town of Warrington in 1772

# HIGH LEGH

Intersected by the highway from Warrington to Knutsford, the extensive township and scattered village of High Legh is situated midway between Grappenhall and Mere and embraces about 4,500 acres.

Until recently there were two principal halls at High Legh, the East Hall (later known as High Legh Hall) and the West Hall, both situated so close together that the grounds of both are only separated by a high brick wall. Both halls have been demolished within the past seven years. In the 13th century the manor was held in moieties by two branches of the Legh Family. In 1888, J.P. Earwaker said "these two families of the Leghs do not appear to be descended from any common ancestor . . . they have lived side by side for the past 600 years and the only difference now is that the members of one family spell their name LEGH and those of the other LEIGH." The private chapels of both families still remain: the chapel of High Legh Hall now stands unused in the centre of a group of new houses and bungalows and is one of the oldest buildings in High Legh, having been erected in 1581. The chapel of the West Hall, known as the Church of St. John was erected in 1893 to replace an earlier chapel destroyed by fire in 1891.

These circumstances led to the composition of the following lines by the Rev A.J. Richardson in 1879:

'Tis an odd state of things that a stranger would see,
If he came on a visit perchance to High Leigh;
To his mind it would cause great confusion and bother,
To find things so mix'd up the one with the other:
Two establishments separate, two Halls, and two Squires,
Two parsons, two chapels, two bells, and two choirs!
Whilst the magnates themselves couldn't fairly agree
As to the spelling correctly the name of "High Leigh".

The name of course is now spelt "High Legh" and most of High Legh is held by the Cornwall Legh family now living at High Legh House.

Two more Halls still stand within the township: Swineyard Hall, formerly the seat of a younger branch of the Leghs of East Hall, and Northwood Hall, also once the property of the Leghs of East Hall. Both properties were offered for sale in 1919 by direction of Lt. Colonel Hubert Cornwall Legh. In the sale catalogue Swineyard Hall was described as: "This charming old-world residence, in the black and white checkered design, is partially surrounded by a moat, and affords a comfortable and commodious domicile . . . the interior fittings of rare old oak are delightful, the massive oak beams are introduced in the fabric in an unique manner, and the ceiling in the principal room is in harmony with the general genuine antique and substantial fabric."

When the main highway was diverted in 1854, the Red Lion Inn and the old smithy were demolished and as a result High Legh found soon afterwards that there was no public house within convenient distance, a state of affairs that lasted until 1948 when the Bear's Paw, which appeared on the Estate Plan of 1919 as "Bear's Paw Farm", was granted a license at the Altrincham Licensing Sessions and became an inn again as it was in the earlier part of the nineteenth century.

In Northwood Lane is an ancient Independent Methodist Church once used by Robert Moffat who came to work at High Legh as a gardener's boy and who was inspired to become a missionary in Africa. He became the father-in-law of Dr Livingstone and a plaque still exists in the old gardens of East Hall to the effect that "Robert Moffat lived and worked here 1813-1814."

An ancient cross was accidentally damaged during recent building developments in the grounds of the West Hall and although its future is still uncertain it is hoped that it will be restored and re-erected.


## PRESTON ON THE HILL

Preston On The Hill is a township, containing the village of Preston Brook and situated between Daresbury and Sutton.

The road from Warrington to Frodsham as it passed through Preston Brook used to be viewed with trepidation by an earlier generation of road users, for the steep descent through a cutting, ending in a sharp bend over the Bridgewater Canal, could easily lead to disaster.

At Preston Brook, roads, canals and railways come together, and it was because of canals that Preston Brook became widely known as a busy centre for the transhipment of goods from the narrow boats of the Trent and Mersey Canal to the wide barges of the Bridgewater Canal.

The two canals were joined at Preston Brook, after the Duke of Bridgewater had undertaken to extend his canal to join the Trent and Mersey Canal and then to construct at his own expense the final section from Preston Brook to the Mersey. When this junction had been effected the Duke was able to charge an extra levy on goods passing from the Trent and Mersey Canal over the final section.

Large warehouses were constructed at Preston Brook in consequence and now that the use of these warehouses has declined one of them has been converted into a canal-side club. Not far from this club is the Preston Brook tunnel through which the canal passes for a distance of three quarters of a mile.

Preston means the tun, or home of the priest. It is perhaps coincidental that next to Preston-on-the-Hill there formerly stood Norton Priory which had moved from Runcorn to Norton in the mid-12th century and when a list of the possessions of the abbey were made four centuries later, a tenement at

60

Preston was included.

As the road to Preston Brook leaves Daresbury it passes a large house known as The Oaklands which is now standing empty. This house is actually situated in the neighbouring township of Newton by Daresbury although it is generally thought to belong to Preston Brook. From 1922 until 1948 the house was the home of an ancient Warrington Charity – The Warrington Blue Coat School. The school moved to The Oaklands on April 26, 1922 from Winwick Road, Warrington, and like similar establishments ceased to provide a home for boys and girls after the passing of the Children's Act of 1948.

## BOLD

A romantic legend is associated with the name of Bold, which is a township lying between St. Helens and Warrington within the Parish of Prescot.

This legend which is based on an ignorant interpretation of the name of Bold, is associated with the Bold family who had an unbroken connection with the township from the 12th to the 18th century. The origin of the family is lost in antiquity and according to the legend the founder of the family obtained his name by slaying a griffin or dragon that lived upon Bold Heath. For this bold deed the dragon slayer was given as much land as the beast's hide would encompass and the name of "The Bold".

"Bold" however, is Old English and means "dwelling, house, palace".

All three meanings are appropriate to Bold in which township the family erected not only dwellings and houses in which to live, but also one building that could be fairly described as a palace.

In 1616 Richard Bold built Bold Old Hall, surrounded it with a moat and left his initials together with those of his wife Anne (a daughter of Sir Peter Legh of Lyme) carved on the door. This Old Hall managed to survive a new and palatial Hall completed in 1732 under the direction of the eminent Italian architect Leoni.

Bold New Hall was sold by Henry Bold-Houghton in 1858 and was purchased by an eccentric Wigan cotton-spinner named William Whiteacre Tipping for £120,000. He was unmarried and is said to have lived in about four rooms indulging in such pleasures as cock-fighting and visits to the Tipping Arms often with £1,000 or so in his pocket. He also hoarded gold coins in buckets, finally dying intestate in 1889. About 10 years afterwards the estate was purchased by a syndicate, registered as the Bold Hall Estate Limited, and the Hall was then taken down and a colliery opened.

The New Hall, therefore, disappeared leaving the Old Hall to become a farmhouse.

In 1946 the Bold Estate was sold once more. The sale excluded the Old

Bold Hall and consisted of 12 farms and 13 cottages, and the estate was purchased for £69,600 by Councillor Roger Fleetwood Hesketh, of Meols Hall, Southport on behalf of himself and his brother, Mr P. Fleetwood Hesketh. It was stated after the sale by Councillor Fleetwood-Hesketh that the estate had been purchased partly for sentimental reasons because they were descended from the Bold family.

Farnworth Church at Widnes contains the Bold chapel and in this chapel are the marble figures of Richard Bold, 1635 and his wife and also a white marble monument to Mary Bold, who married Prince Sapieha of Poland and died in 1824 without issue.


## WHITECROSS

Whitecross is now an electoral division of the County Borough of Warrington and its boundaries embrace a heavier concentration of 19th century industrial and housing development than any other part of Warrington.

It is scarcely surprising, therefore, that in connection with recent plans for the expansion of Warrington, Whitecross should have been selected for a considerable experiment in urban renewal and it is, from the ashes of this great industrial scar that the new Warrington will first appear. Already a new dual carriageway is being carved through this highly-developed area and old buildings are rapidly disappearing to make way for a brand new Whitecross.

When modern municipal government first came to Warrington in 1847 the town at first was divided into five wards known simply as North East, North West, South East, South West and Latchford wards, and thus Whitecross at first was part of the North West area of the town and it was only in October 1890 that Whitecross first became a separate ward of that name.

The name of Whitecross now belonging to this district as well as to many organisations, both civil and industrial within the area, springs from the fact that a white cross stood for many centuries in the middle of the road leading from Warrington to Sankey.

In a Survey made in 1465 the district was described as the "suburbs" of Warrington when a dwelling house belonging to a man named Henry Bullynge was located as being "near to the White Cross, which stands in the way leading from the aforesaid town as far as the bridge of Sankey."

The precise location of this cross is shown on an early map of Warrington compiled in 1772 as being at the junction of what is now Liverpool Road and Green Street, while nearby stood an ancient bowling green that has been a recent casualty in the path of the new dual carriageway.

The white cross could have been a wayside preaching cross used by friars from the Warrington Friary as a spot to preach to local inhabitants, or more possibly it was a roadside cross used as a convenient place for a funeral procession to rest in times when burial grounds were not so numerous as they are today.

The existence of this cross has not only determined the name of the district but has also given a name to institutions that have carried the name to all parts of the world.

In the middle of the 19th century when a railway line was constructed from Warrington to Runcorn Gap the Warrington terminal for the first year was at Whitecross Station. Ten years later, in 1864, the Whitecross Wire Company Ltd., was founded and the products of this firm, bearing not only the name of Whitecross, but also an emblem in the form of a white cross, have been sold throughout the world.

Standing in Whitecross Ward and surrounded by a heavy concentration of industry is the Warrington General Hospital and the buildings of the former Whitecross Institution which was originally known as the Workhouse. Three new hostels, the first of which is known as Orford Hall in Capesthorne Road and opened in October 1967, have now replaced the Whitecross Homes as accommodation for old people. The old buildings of Whitecross and Aikin Street Hospitals have been merged with the General Hospital which is, like the area in which it is situated, gradually achieving a more modern appearance.

## NORTON

Once the location of an ancient abbey and later the seat of a large landowner, Norton is principally known today for a considerable landmark erected by Liverpool Corporation towards the end of the 19th century. This landmark is a water tower 113 feet in height and 80 feet in diameter and it was constructed in red sandstone as part of the scheme for the supply of water to the City of Liverpool from Lake Vyrnwy in Montgomeryshire. The tank in the tower holds 672,000 gallons of water and this is carried from the tower under the Mersey by means of a tunnel 900 feet long and 10 feet wide.

The small village of Norton is close to this tower and is one of four Cheshire townships whose names are associated with their geographical location in relation to Halton at their centre, namely: Norton, Sutton, Weston and Aston. The name of Norton, therefore, means "North farm" or "homestead".

Norton Priory was originally established at Runcorn by William Fitz Nigel, second baron of Halton, in 1115 and dedicated to St. Bertelin a little-known saint whose feast occurs on September 9. The Priory was transferred to Norton in 1134 where it became one of the largest houses of Augustinian Canons in the country. It became an Abbey about 1422 and was finally dissolved in 1536-7.

At about the time when Norton Priory was as its peak, and possibly just

The Warrington Academy 1762

Original Home of The Warrington Library
Barbauld Street

before it became an Abbey, a large statue of St. Christopher was erected at the Priory appropriately looking across the Mersey.

This statue, which still exists, is 11 feet high, and although it has suffered some damage in recent years it still remains as a fine example of medieval sculpture belonging to the end of the 14th century. A few years ago the statue was inspected at Norton with a view to determining its future home. Various suggestions were made and possible homes suggested were: Chester Cathedral, Liverpool Cathedral and the Walker Art Gallery. The statue was eventually removed to Liverpool for repair work at the Walker Art Gallery.

After the dissolution of Norton Priory it was sold by the King to Sir Richard Brooke for £1,512 1s. 9d. in 1545 and remained in the possession of the Brooke family until recent years. The Priory was converted to a residence by the Brooke family and the old house was finally demolished in 1928.

Part of the old abbey, including an ancient doorway, still remained after the demolition of the house, however, and the statue of St. Christopher was still standing against a wall at Norton in 1962.

At the time of the construction of the Bridgewater Canal, it was necessary for the final part of the canal from Moore to Runcorn to pass through land owned by Sir Richard Brooke and the negotiations concerning this land delayed the completion of the canal for several years with the result that the quay at Stockton Heath became an important terminal for passengers and goods traffic until the canal finally reached Runcorn.


## HILL CLIFFE

A perforated stone hammer of the Neolithic period found at Hill Cliffe by the late Colonel Brereton Fairclough and now exhibited in the Warrington Museum is one of the oldest objects found in the Warrington area and together with a polished hand axe or celt, found at Orford, indicates that Neolithic men inhabited North Cheshire and South Lancashire.

Hill Cliffe itself is the most beautiful part of Appleton and appeared on Saxton's Map of Cheshire in 1577 as "High clyff hill". Certainly the sudden rise from Walton to the lych-gate of the Hill Cliffe burial ground provides one of the most attractive features of the landscape in the Warrington area . . . and a view of the Mersey Valley from Liverpool to Manchester that is unsurpassable.

The burial ground is attached to the ancient Baptist Chapel in Red Lane, dates from the year 1661 and contains stones inscribed as early as 1664.

Some stones in the graveyard bearing much earlier dates than this were dates cut in the 19th century according to William Beamont.

Beamont also considers that the Chapel was first built after the year 1688, although it appears to be evident that a congregation existed at Hill Cliffe before that date. He also gives adequate reasons for not accepting the widely accepted tradition that Cromwell worshipped at Hill Cliffe during his three-day sojourn in Warrington in 1648.

The chapel was enlarged and a building for the Sunday School erected about 1800 and the chapel was rebuilt in 1841 while the Rev A. Kenworthy was the pastor. Between 1860 and 1870 the burial ground was enclosed with the substantial stone wall that is still standing.

Just above the burial ground contractors have been busily engaged since May 1967 in the construction of a new underground reservoir designed to hold 10 million gallons of water. When complete the reservoir will be covered with a mound of earth and will gradually fit the surrounding landscape. This reservoir is situated quite close to existing reservoirs located on the golf course, the highest part of Hill Cliffe, where the ground reaches an elevation of 345 feet. The oldest of these two reservoirs has a capacity of 1¼ million gallons and was completed in 1903 in connection with Houghton Green Pumping Station so that water was pumped from Winwick to Hill Cliffe, whilst the second reservoir erected in 1949-51 has a capacity of six million gallons.

Surmounting the oldest reservoir is a stone obelisk with four lions at its base. This did not exist before the year 1850 but it is shown on an Ordnance Survey map, surveyed in 1873-7, standing at the highest point of Hille Cliffe on land belonging to Colonel Lyon's Appleton Hall Estate.

The purpose of the obelisk is somewhat obscure and it is possible that it was erected to mark the highest point of Hill Cliffe. It is clear, however, that it was re-erected as a result of the construction of the first reservoir in 1902-3. It also stood near to where some masonry, described in a Directory of 1850 as being "surmounted by a square flag staff" and "used as a beacon in the time of the French war", was also standing.

In 1968 the lych gate of the Hill Cliffe Baptist Chapel burial ground, was damaged by a contractor's vehicle and an appeal has been made for donations to restore this attractive gate which is a favourite viewpoint for visitors to Red Lane.


## WARRINGTON

The modern town of Warrington is divided into two halves by the River Mersey and only two bridges for road traffic connect the two parts of the town.

The Mersey has always divided those who have dwelt on its banks in this locality and in the past the division has occasionally amounted to enmity. But it is because it has always been possible to cross the river at Warrington that a town came into being and in modern times the river has played no small part in the industrial development of the town.

Communities were settled on either side of the river in the Bronze Age and Warrington was a point of entry for Bronze Age metal workers who manufactured their goods in Ireland and traded them in South Lancashire and North Cheshire. The Romans created an industrial settlement on the South bank of the Mersey at Wilderspool and crossed the river by way of the ford at Latchford. The Anglo-Saxons settled on the North bank of the Mersey near to the Parish Church and later the Normans built a castle close to the church to guard the ford and river crossing.

In Anglo-Saxon times the Mersey was a boundary between the two ancient kingdoms of Mercia and Northumbria and thereafter the north bank of the Mersey at Warrington has always belonged to a different administrative or ecclesiastical area from the south bank.

Warrington itself grew up on the north bank in the County of Lancashire and after the first bridge had been built at the beginning of the 14th century, deep divisions occurred between the lords of the manors dwelling on the opposite sides of the river concerning the tolls and charges collected from those who wished to cross the river by the various means available – namely by ford and ferry, or by bridge. The ford and ferry tolls belonged by right to the lords of Grappenhall in Cheshire and the bridge tolls were collected by the lords of Warrington in Lancashire.

This division clearly amounted to enmity in the 14th century, for when John le Botiller was engaged in the task of rebuilding Warrington Bridge in the year 1364 he had to seek royal protection from his enemies.

It is scarcely surprising, therefore, that the name of Warrington should have created a division of opinion among etymologists who are unable to state definitely the meaning of the name.

There seems no doubt, however, that the name is Old English and the difference of opinion lies in the interpretation of the first element, "*Waer*". On the one hand it is thought that this could be a personal name so that Warrington would mean "The tun of Waer's people" or, "The tun of the followers of Waer". On the other hand, this first element can be identified with OE "Waer" or "waering" meaning weir, dam. Both interpretations are given by Ekwall in "The Concise Oxford Dictionary of Place Names" while in the English Place-Name Society's book on "English Place-Name Elements" it states simply: "Wering, Waering OE, 'river-dam', is possible in (A) Warrington La (tun)."

There seems, however, to be a third possibility advanced by those etymologists who have studied the Roman name of Warrington. The Roman name of Veratinum has been considered by many to belong to Warrington and although this has been stated to be "illusory" in a post-war publication of the late Professor I.A. Richmond it has not been finally disproved. Those who consider that the name of Veratinum belongs to Warrington believe that an ancient British word variously spelt as: "Gweryt", "weryt" or "werid", and meaning "ford", is involved.

Remembering first the dictum laid down by Samuel Johnson who wrote: "The name is exhausted by what we see. We have no occasion to go a distance for what we can pick up under our feet . . . it turns to be a mere physiological name"; and second, that the one physiological feature of Warrington responsible for its very existence was the river crossing which for more than 2,000 years was a ford, it is difficult to be persuaded that the ford was not connected with the name of Warrington.


## The Street where you live – ACADEMY STREET

Although so named because the Warrington Academy was situated between Mersey Street and Buttermarket Street, the street, which ultimately cut through the Academy buildings, was not made until after the Academy was dissolved.

The Warrington Academy was founded in 1757 and opened in the building known as the "Old Academy" in Bridge Street on October 20, 1757. It remained there until 1762 when new premises were erected between a part of Buttermarket Street – originally known as Bow Street – and Mersey Street. These premises formed three sides of a square and the open side was on the north. Here the Academy remained until 1786 when it was finally dissolved and the buildings were sold.

Half the proceeds of the sale and the Library were given to a newly-established Academy in Manchester and which is now situated at Manchester College, Oxford, where a Warrington window commemorates the association with Warrington.

Donbavand's Map of Warrington in 1772 shows the Academy buildings standing before the street was made but with a passage known as Academy Place leading from Buttermarket Street into the Academy buildings.

Later Academy Place became Academy Street and continued through to Mersey Street as shown for the first time on the 1884 map. The street was constructed between 1850 and 1867 and therefore passes through the Academy buildings, some of which remain on either side of the street.

On one of these buildings two plaques commemorate the association of Joseph Priestley and William Enfield with the Academy. The association of a third tutor of the Academy, John Holt, is denoted by the street name plate fixed to the part of the Academy building still standing at the junction of Academy Street and Holt Street.

After the Academy was dissolved, the Warrington Mechanics Institution was established in the same buildings and this is shown on a map of 1850.

This society existed for the educational improvement of the artisans of

James Brindley

Warrington and amonst many other activities organised what was possibly the first travelling library in England, drawn through the streets by a horse!

Academy Street provided a home for the Warrington Conservative Association from 1872 until 1884 when the Association moved to Sankey Street. Among other inhabitants the street was the home of John Jackson, a Quaker philanthropist who gave a large collection of early printed books to the Warrington Municipal Library and also of Colonel Brereton Fairclough who became a member of the Warrington Library and Museum Committee and is remembered for archaeological work on Roman Warrington.

It is interesting also that one inhabitant of the street in 1867 was Stephen Moss, and a firm of blacksmiths of the same name still have premises at 57, Academy Street.


## ACKERS LANE

Early post-war development as well as paper and other urban debris floating upon what was once a beautiful stretch of water, are slowly transforming the area known as Ackers Common, or "The Ackers", from a scene of rural beauty into a scene that would no longer attract the attention of such an artist as Oswald Garside who once portrayed a cottage in Ackers Lane.

Today Ackers Lane connects Fairfield Road and Ackers Road, but an Ordnance Survey map of 1873 shows that before the Manchester Ship Canal was cut, Ackers Lane began at Wash Lane and contained the Baptist Chapel at the junction with Loushers Lane. It then proceeded to Chester Road and also to Hunt's Lane by means of a Y-shaped junction. Ackers Road, therefore, was once part of Ackers Lane and has only been known as Ackers Road since 1914.

The same map also shows the area known as "The Ackers", together with "Ackers Pits" while nearby was a mill pond and flour mill fed by Lumb Brook.

As early as 1465, a field called "Le Akkirs" is mentioned in a survey of land belonging to Peter Legh where it says: "William Mury holds of the said Peter . . . one parcel of land containing an acre and more . . . enclosed with hedges and ditches called le akkirs which parcel lies in breadth between the arable land of the said Peter on the east and part of Lacheforthe Heath on the west and extends in length from a certain lane leading from Lacheforthe towards the township of Knottisforthe on the south as far as another part of . . . Lacheforthe Heath on the north."

The route along Ackers Lane from the ford at Latchford and across Ackers Common was used by the Earl of Derby's soldiers on April 3, 1643 when the Earl inflicted a defeat upon Parliamentary soldiers under the command of Sir

William Brereton in Stockton Heath. It is also evident that the same route had been used for centuries before this, since a bronze palstave belonging to the late Bronze Age was found on Ackers Common and is now exhibited in the Warrington Museum.

Ackers Lane lies on one side of Ackers Pits which were shown on Bryant's Map of Cheshire in 1829 and which have been used by local anglers at least since 1904 when the "Year Book of the Warrington Angler's Association" stated that the stocking of Acker's Pit was "to be proceeded with at once".

In spite of urban debris floating on the surface, the "Pit" still is the home of swans and other birds and, clearly, if modern planning is exercised with imagination, some of the attractiveness of this locality could be preserved for many years to come.

The name "Ackers" appears to be derived from an Old English word "Aecer" meaning a plot of arable or cultivated land, although the original sense was "wild undeveloped land" and later "a piece of land cleared for use". Obviously the area must have been cultivated in medieval times since the water mill driven by Lumb Brook (faint traces of which still remain) is also mentioned in the 1465 Survey.

Registers and rate book show the occupant of the "House, mill and land" at 'The Ackers' to have been Joseph Blinston from 1842 until 1871.

Ackers is also the name of a local family since a James Ackers married An Williamson at the Warrington Parish Church on November 4, 1640. There are five individuals named Ackers in the March 1968 issue of the Warrington and District Telephone Directory.


## ALLCARD STREET

Appropriately situated near to the Dallam railway sheds and the main railway line from Warrington to the north, Allcard Street is a cul-de-sac in the centre of the southern side of Folly Lane.

It is almost a century since the street was built: it was first listed in the local burgess lists in 1881 and shown on a map of the Borough in 1884. Railway workers and their families have been residents of this street from the outset and among the occupants in 1908 were listed a railwayman, a fitter, a signalman and an engine-driver.

William Allcard, after whom the street was named, drove one of the railway engines on the occasion of the opening of the Liverpool to Manchester Railway on September 15, 1830. He was a railway engineer of distinction and was actively associated with the municipal, industrial and social life of Warrington in the mid-19th century.

Allcard was born in Derbyshire in 1808 and was named as an apprentice in a list of persons to be employed by George and Robert Stephenson on the

71

Liverpool and Birmingham Rail Road in 1823. And after George Stephenson had been appointed as Chief Engineer on the Liverpool and Manchester Railway project in 1826 three engineers were appointed to serve under him, namely Joseph Locke, John Dixon and William Allcard.

After the Liverpool and Manchester Railway was opened in 1830 a single track junction was constructed from Newton to Warrington and in 1837 this junction railway became part of the Grand Junction Railway. Allcard took a post as locomotive engineer on this railway and became associated with William Buddicom who was Locomotive Superintendent at the Liverpool works.

Allcard's name appears frequently in the minutes of the Directors of the Grand Junction Railway for 1837 and 1838 and in March 1839 he purchased a Grant Junction locomotive called the "Doctor Dalton" for £600.

In the same year he became the tenant of Bank House in Sankey Street, Warrington, now the offices of the Borough Treasurer of Warrington.

Soon afterwards Allcard went to France with Buddicom where they opened a locomotive works near Rouen and built the famous Buddicom engines which became standard on the Paris and Rouen Railway. One of these locomotives was exhibited at the Festival of Britain's South Bank Exhibition in 1951.

The Crewe railway works supplanted the Liverpool (Edge Hill) works in 1843 by which time Allcard had returned from France to Warrington, for he purchased a plot of land adjoining Bank House in 1843 and rented a further plot in 1847 indicating an expanding business interest in Warrington where he was also the joint lessee of a billiards hall in Spring Gardens (later Bold Street).

In 1847 Allcard stood unsuccessfully as Liberal candidate for Warrington in a Parliamentary election but became Warrington's second Mayor in 1848-9. He was again Mayor of Warrington in 1851-2 and left the town for his native Derbyshire in 1854. He died at the early age of 52 on August 5, 1861 at Burton Close, Bakewell.

It is not known who decided to perpetuate his name in Warrington by giving it to the street made some 20 years after his death and situated so close to the scene of his pioneering efforts on the earliest railways ever constructed.


## ARPLEY STREET

Although there are frequent references to Arpley, Arpley Meadows and Arpley Common fields in local records from the beginning of the 15th century, Arpley Street was not so named until 1879.

Before this date the street was known, first as Slytchers Lane and later as Slutchers Lane. Slytchers Lane is mentioned in a Survey of 1465 and is shown as Slutchers Lane on the 1851 Ordnance Survey Map. The northern part of Slutchers Lane was paved and re-named Arpley Street in 1879. Originally Slutchers Lane had connected Sankey Street with Broad Arpley Lane running across Arpley Meadows and the lane passed over the Warrington and Garston Railway line by means of a level crossing. Arpley Street now simply connects Sankey Street and Wilson Patten Street. Slutchers Lane still exists to the south of the railway line.

The name of Arpley consists of two Old English elements – "eorp" and "leah" meaning dark meadow.

Built in the days before the advent of public transport, the new houses of Arpley Street became the homes of Warrington shopkeepers and works managers, and also became the home of two important Warrington Institutions.

Because of the building of Warrington Central Station on the Cheshire Lines Railway, a new home had to be found for a school known as People's College. This school was originally situated in Newton Street but the school site was purchased by the Cheshire Lines Railway Committee. A new school was erected in 1871 in Slutchers Lane to which extensions were added in 1882 and 1889 after this part of Slutchers Lane had become known as Arpley Street.

People's College provided an elementary education for many Warringtonians and had originated as a combination, in 1858, of evening classes with a school provided by the Warrington Education Society, the object of which was to provide education for the working classes "without regard to religious distinctions".

At first, objections were made about the name of People's College on the grounds that the inhabitants were led to believe that the school was something more than an elementary school. The objections were of no avail, however and from 1858 the school continued to be called People's College. The schools organised by the Warrington Education Society operated until 1902 when they were handed over to the Warrington Education Committee.

At the other end of Arpley Street, new Central Police Offices were opened by the Mayor (Alderman Henry Roberts) on October 11, 1901. The new Police Station, which cost £30,000, was described in a directory of 1908 as "palatial" and it contained a handsome court room which became known in the town as "The Palace of Justice".

These buildings replaced the Old Bridewell in Irlam Street which had been in use throughout the 19th century and which had been condemned year after year by Her Majesty's Inspectors of Constabularies.

The architect of the new Arpley Street premises was Mr R. Burns Dick, of the firm of Cackett and Burns Dick of Newcastle-on-Tyne.

# AIKIN STREET

Although it is possible that Aikin Street was named after a distinguished family, it was most probably named after two members of the family only, both of whom were named John and both of whom were tutors at the Warrington Academy.

That the street was not named after all the members of this family is evident since another street, Barbauld Street, is named after a daughter of the elder John Aikin, Anna Laetitia, who married Charles Rochemont Barbauld. Seven members of the family were sufficiently distinguished to appear in "The Dictionary of National Biography" and of these it was the elder John Aikin who first had any association with Warrington.

He was born in 1713 in London where his father, a Scotsman, had a business. Although placed in his youth as a clerk in a mercantile house, Aikin quickly showed his love of study and after entering Kibworth Academy, proceeded to Aberdeen University which subsequently awarded him the degree of Doctor of Divinity. He is usually distinguished from his son John by this degree since his son's degree was Doctor of Medicine and thus the two John Aikins are often known as John Aikin D.D., and John Aikin M.D.

John Aikin, D.D., became one of the three original tutors at the Warrington Academy when it opened in October 1757 and his son, John, was one of the first pupils.

According to a modern American, Professor Aikin "brought to Warrington the embodiment of a liberal spirit and a richly stored mind", while Professor George Saintsbury states that Aikin was "the first systematic lecturer in English literature". By this he meant in any educational establishment anywhere in the world, for at the time of the establishment of the Warrington Academy the education curriculum was extremely cramped and limited to the well trodden paths of theology, philosophy and Latin grammar.

The importance of the Warrington Academy, indeed, lay in the fact that the tutors were permitted to experiment by introducing entirely new subjects into the curriculum and the first to do so was John Aikin. Unfortunately the elder Aikin, unlike other tutors at the Academy, published no books although the influence he exerted upon his pupils has been well attested, particularly by William Turner who wrote a lengthy description of his life and methods in an "Historical account of the Warrington Academy" published 1813-15.

Apart from Aikin Street, the only memorial to Aikin in Warrington is a plaque in Cairo Street Chapel which states in Latin that he was for 23 years a Professor at the Warrington Academy, first in Languages and Literature and then in Divinity.

His son John became a tutor at the Academy in Chemistry, Anatomy and Physiology from 1770 to 1779 and became distinguished as the author of many books which included a General Biography in 10 volumes, a Medical

Biography, as well as some notable "Essays on song writing". He also assisted other men, including John Howard, with their literary work which was printed in Warrington.

Aikin Street was built about 1869 and first appears in the Warrington Burgess Roll for 1870, incorrectly spelt "Aiken Street".

The men from whom the street is named are certainly more illustrious than this street ever was, but which once lent its name to a hospital – the Aikin Street Hospital – in which beds were provided for the treatment of the elderly sick and longstay orthopaedic cases as well as paediatric infectious diseases. Originally this hospital was built as an Isolation Hospital in 1879, but since April 1967 the Aikin Street Hospital has been absorbed into the General Hospital.


## BEAMONT STREET

Almost exactly a century ago (in December 1869) a resolution of the Warrington Town Council stated that the new street leading from Heath Lane should be called Beamont Street. Heath Lane was subsequently re-named Kendrick Street. In 1870 Beamont Street simply contained dwelling houses on both sides that were occupied by skilled tradesmen – joiners, a cabinet maker, a saddler, a file cutter, a whitesmith, a glass engraver, a hamper maker and a machine painter.

The Warrington Infirmary was not built until 1876 (it was officially opened on January 24, 1877) and the dwelling houses of Beamont Street were not disturbed until extension to the Infirmary were erected 30 years later.

The street was named after William Beamont, the first Mayor of Warrington in 1847-8 who records in his diary on January 5, 1877: "In the afternoon I attended a meeting of the Dispensary to arrange for the opening of the new hospitals on the 24th inst." The Dispensary had been situated in Buttermarket Street from 1819 and as Beamont was prominently concerned with work of this Institution, a fitting memorial to his efforts was ultimately established in the new Infirmary with the naming of a "Beamont Ward".

Probably no one ever worked so long or so selflessly for the good of Warrington as William Beamont.

He was born on September 19th, 1797 and baptised at the Warrington Parish Church. Throughout his professional life as a solicitor he worked in an office in the Warrington Market Place and after his death on June 6, 1889 his widow continued to lavish support on local charities that had benefited from the efforts of this noble Warringtonian.

It was Beamont who advocated municipal government in Warrington to replace the old body of Police Commissioners, resulting in the Royal Charter whereby Warrington became a Municipal Borough in 1847. As the first Mayor of the new borough he spent hundreds of pounds of his own money to complete and connect sewers. He was prominently concerned with the establishment of the Warrington Museum and Library in 1848 and also contributed largely to the erection of the School of Art. He built and endowed St. Ann's Church and provided an endowment for Orford where he had lived and taught as a Sunday School teacher.

His most lasting memorial, however, was his work as a local historian. Many of his books were published at his own expense and the major works were published by learned societies and notably by the Chetham Society.

These books are still widely used by all those interested in the local history of Warrington and its neighbourhood and create great respect for the name of William Beamont in academic as well as local circles.

But for Beamont's painstaking efforts as a local historian there can be no doubt that a large part of the detailed knowledge of the past history of Warrington would have been lost for ever, for he gained access to many private collections of documents of local interest and was instrumental in acquiring many of these invaluable sources of information for permanent preservation in the Warrington Municipal Library.

Regrettably no one has yet written a biography of this most distinguished Warringtonian, although his name was further perpetuated by the existence in Beamont Street of a printer and publisher who, in recent years, published under the imprint of "The Beamont Press", the work of later historians of Warrington.


## BLUECOAT STREET

The Warrington Co-operative Society have occupied premises on the site of the Warrington Bluecoat School in Winwick Road since 1923. Bluecoat Street is on the northern side of these premises and, perhaps significantly named is "Oliver Street" on the southern side.

A charity school situated in Georgian premises occupied this same site from 1782 until 1922, but this charity, known as the Bluecoat School, did not begin here, nor did it cease to exist in 1922. Indeed, the charity had its beginning in 1665 when a Mr Allen of Westminster willed to the Church-wardens of Warrington a legacy "... to put out 5 several poor boys at 14 to apprenticeships to some handicrafte trade ..."

Many Warringtonians subsequently bequeathed and donated money to this charity and especially did they do this after the charity became purely educational in the year 1711. It was then determined to make the boys fit for apprenticeships by putting them to the Charity School, "there to learn the knowledge and practice of the Christian religion as profest in the Church of

England, to learn to read, write" &c.

Twenty-four boys were put to school, all with blue caps and bands and the "blew boys" attended a school belonging to Trinity Chapel in buildings behind the Church.

About 50 years later girls were admitted to the school and in 1782 new premises, capable of accommodating boarders, were opened on the Winwick Street site. In 1820, besides 24 boarders there were also 120 boys and 30 girls attending as day scholars under a monitorial system of instruction.

A Government Inspector investigated the Charity in 1858 and considered the school "to be one of the best" but nearly 10 years later a protracted discussion took place in the correspondence columns of the local press as the result of charges levelled at the Trustees of the School by Dr James Kendrick. He had been honorary medical examiner of the children in the school and resigned this post in 1866 following his discovery that his dietary table was ignored and that the scholars were living in "revolting conditions of dirt and disease".

Dr Kenrick's charges were ultimately published in a pamphlet entitled: "The Warrington Blue-Coat School Exposure" and although his charges were indignantly denied and ridiculed by the Trustees, the abuses complained of by Dr Kendrick were nevertheless corrected by the Trustees so that the Institution continued to earn the respect of the people of Warrington and to produce a number of distinguished men and women.

The school was moved from Winwick Street and Bluecoat Street in 1922 to The Oaklands, Preston Brook and although this Institution ceased to function as a school in 1949, the funds of the Charity are still administered by the Warrington Church of England Educational Trust.

Bluecoat Street itself has only ever had dwelling houses on the side opposite the school, and first appears in a Burgess List in 1878 although the street is shown un-named, on the 1851 and 1875 maps of Warrington.

The empty school premises were acquired by the Warrington Co-operative Society in 1923. A bakery was opened on the site in April 1933 and a new group of buildings on the site now houses the Co-operative Halls as well as the office block, a youth club, garages and other departments of the Society.


## BRIDGE STREET

Many distinguished Warringtonians have been actively associated with Bridge Street during the seven centuries since the street was first made. The name of Bridge Street, however, is not as old as the street itself, for immediately after it was made, following the construction of the first road bridge across the Mersey in Warrington at the end of the 13th century, it was known as the "New Street".

Sankey Street and Church Street, both leading to the old centre of Warrington near the Parish Church, are the oldest streets in Warrington and the original purpose of the "New Street" was simply to provide a thoroughfare across the new bridge.

The earliest reocrd of the development of this street occurs in the year 1323 when William le Boteler granted to Robert, son of Adam Dun of Warrington, a piece of land in the New Street. After this the centre of Warrington quickly moved from Church Street to the New Street and Market Gate, and thenceforth the New Street became a street of shops, hostelries and houses.

to Bridge Street soon after a substantial stone bridge (the third on the same spot) was opened in 1495.

In an Easter Roll of moneys due to the Rector of Warrington dated 1580, is listed about 40 residents of "The Bridge Streete", and this is the earliest record of the name of Bridge Street. The record is preserved appropriately in the British Museum.

During the following century the name of Bridge Street occurs frequently in the Parish Church Registers until eventually the street was shown on the 1772 map of Warrington together with the names of three hostelries including one, The Lion, which still exists.

On the opposite side of the street about this time stood another public house, The White Bear, the landlord of which was Peter Stubs who began to manufacture files at the White Bear in addition to his other occupations as innkeeper and brewer.

At the turn of the century there were 20 public houses in Bridge Street and these were listed in the 1826 Directory. Six of these public houses (Lion, Feathers, Higher Seven Stars, Roebuck, Royal Oak and Packet House) remained after the street had been almost entirely rebuilt and widened between 1883 and 1908.

In the process of widening Bridge Street, new buildings were erected before the old ones were demolished and the last of the old buildings to disappear stood in front of Hodgkinson's new store. A shop belonging to W. Hodgkinson is listed in a Directory of 1887 and an advertisement in a Directory of 1891 describes W. Hodgkinson as "Costumier and Silk Mercer" stating that "a large staff of experienced dressmakers (were) kept on the premises.". Before this store closed in 1962 it had probably become the most sophisticated store in Warrington selling an extensive range of goods from perfumes to furniture.

The 1891 Directory is the earliest Directory to list a Bank in Bridge Street, the National Provincial at No 31, and it also shows that the premises at No 78, now occupied by Martins Bank, were then the showrooms of a well known cabinet maker, S.E. and R. Johnson.

78

Now that the needs of Bridge Street traders have had to bow before the needs of modern traffic, emphasising the original purpose of the street which was to provide a road approach to an important crossing of the River Mersey, it might be some small comfort for those affected most by modern traffic regulations to realise that the problem was just as acute before the advent of the motor car.

As long ago as 1813, the Warrington Improvement Act provided that wagons, carts, carriages and stage coaches should only be permitted to stand in the streets for the purpose of unloading or loading and to remain longer incurred a penalty of five pounds with the possibility of removal to a Pound and further penalties.

Obviously the rapid growth of traffic now requires far more than regulations and an additional bridge has become a most urgent need both for the flow of traffic and the convenience of trade.

## BARBAULD STREET

Friar's Gate and St. Austin's Lane both lead into Barbauld Street from Bridge Street and Bold Street respectively, and these two street names are almost the only reminder of the fact that Barbauld Street itself passes over the remains of an ancient Friary and was formerly known as Friar's Green.

Friar's Green was the oldest part of Barbauld Street and is shown as such on the 1884 map of Warrington leading from Friar's Gate to Bridge Foot. An earlier map of 1772, however, shows that the part of the street leading from Friar's Gate as far as Stanley Street was then called Chancel Street and the street then continued as a narrow lane, called Friar's Lane, as far as Bridge Foot.

After the widening of Bridge Street between 1883 and 1908, an extension of Friar's Green was made in the direction of Rylands Street and by 1901 the whole street had evidently become known as Barbauld Street because it is so named in the Register of Electors for 1901. Very strangely, however, it was not until October 1907 that the Warrington Town Council formally resolved "That the new street behind Bridge Street be named Barbauld Street."

It is possible that the reason for this delay was occasioned by the fact that the street was in the process of being re-made, the older Friar's Green having contained, in 1851, a saw mill, a tannery, a cotton manufactury and the original home of the Warrington Library and Museum.

Mrs Barbauld, after whom the street is named, was the daughter of John Aikin, a tutor at the Warrington Academy. While living in Warrington before her marriage as Anna Laetitia Aikin, she formed a romantic attachment with two young men associated with the Academy circle. One was John Howard, the prison reformer, and the other, an 18-year-old pupil at the Academy, was Rochemont Barbauld, the grandson of a French Huguenot, who had fled to England hidden in a cask.

Before her marriage Anna Laetitia was aware of the hereditary insanity affecting Rochemont Barbauld yet she nevertheless decided to marry him in the year 1774. At this time she was 31 years of age, and had just published her first very successful volume of poetry.

The newly-married couple removed to Palgrave in Suffolk and established a school for boys. This school though successful did not prove remunerative and in 1785 the Barbaulds removed to Hampstead and finally to Stoke Newington. Because the marriage proved to be childless the Barbaulds adopted a young nephew, Charles Rochemont Aikin, and Mrs Barbauld proceeded to write a number of books especially for this little boy.

The first of these books "Lessons for Children" and a later book, "Hymns in Prose", were both widely used and were the first books written specifically for children. "Hymns in Prose" was translated into five languages and many English editions were produced.

Mrs Barbauld established herself as an author and was friendly with Coleridge, Southey and Lamb. Unfortunately her husband's mental illness became worse and after attempting to murder her he died insane in the year 1808. Mrs Barbauld continued her literary work after her husband's death and died at Stoke Newington in 1825.

In addition to the honour of a long entry in the "Dictionary of National Biography", Mrs Barbauld was the subject of a book published in 1958 entitled "Georgian Chronicle, Mrs Barbauld and her family" by Betsey Rodgers. It was also in 1958 that Barbauld Street became part of the circulatory traffic system whereby one-way traffic proceeds from Warrington Bridge into Bridge Street.


## WATERWAY STREETS

A group of avenues on the Latchford Housing Estate, all first named between 1930-34, are associated by name with the network of waterways (river, canals and brooks) that create so many transport problems in Warrington.

The avenues concerned are situated near to Kingsway Bridge and all are connected to Bridgewater Avenue which is one of the longest avenues on the Estate. They are: Brindley Avenue, Worsley Avenue, Morris Avenue, Brook Avenue and Mersey Walk.

It seems most probable that the naming of these avenues was determined by the fact that Morris Brook, which runs through Grappenhall and which was intersected by both the Bridgewater and Manchester Ship Canals, joins the River Mersey close to Kingsway Bridge.

At the time of its construction and for many years afterwards, the Bridgewater Canal attracted considerable attention as an engineering feat, for it was the first arterial canal to be constructed. It was thus distinct from previous lateral canals, like the Sankey Canal which had been constructed alongside the banks of a river, and it crossed valleys with the aid of aqueducts, tunnels, cuttings and embankments.

The object of the Canal initially was to facilitate the transport of coal from the Duke of Bridgewater's estates around Worsley to Manchester, and at Worsley the Canal entered the coal mines directly so that barges were loaded in a series of underground waterways.

At Barton, near Eccles, the Canal originally crossed the River Irwell by means of an aqueduct which became an engineering wonder of the world after it was opened on July 17, 1761. Parliamentary powers to enable the Canal to be extended through Cheshire to link Manchester and Liverpool were obtained in 1672, but the progress of the Cheshire extension was considerably delayed as a result of negotiations with landowners, notably Sir Richard Brooke of Norton, and the whole Canal was not finally opened until 1776.

Before traffic along the Canal was able to reach Runcorn, however, both goods and passengers were travelling as far as Stockton Quay. Passenger services had begun in 1769 and by 1781 a daily service was in operation (on weekdays) from Manchester to Stockton Quay, Preston Brook and Runcorn as well as from Manchester to Worsley and Runcorn to Worsley.

The receipts from fares in 1781 amounted to £1,326 and the journey from Runcorn to Manchester took eight hours at a cost of 2s. 3d. in the general quarters or 3d. 6d. for special accommodation. By 1800 passenger receipts had risen to £4,787.

The engineer responsible for the most ingenious features of the Canal was James Brindley, a largely self-taught millwright. After serving a seven-year apprenticeship as a millwright with Abraham Bennett of Sutton near Macclesfield from 1733 to 1740 Brindley worked as a millwright until he was engaged in 1758 by Earl Gower of Trentham to survey a waterway intended to link the River Trent and the River Mersey. His activities on this project, which did not commence until 1766, brought him to the notice of the Duke of Bridgewater who first employed him in connection with the Bridgewater Canal in 1759.

Having achieved considerable fame as a result of the construction of the Bridgewater Canal, Brindley next surveyed the Coventry, Oxford, Birmingham, Staffordshire and Worcestershire, Chesterfield, Droitwich, Chester, Bradford, and Huddersfield Broad Canals. Generally he laid out the basic pattern of England's inland waterways and his canals linked the Mersey, Trent, Severn and Thames.

The Bridgewater Canal also gave a name to another street in Warrington in 1877 when Bridgewater Street, a cul-de-sac off Howley Lane, first appears in the Register of Electors.

# BUTTERMARKET STREET

Once the busiest and most important street in Warrington, containing more public buildings than any other street, Buttermarket Street has gradually been supplanted in importance by other streets, but nevertheless still contains some fine buildings.

Although one of the oldest streets in the town, it remained nameless for several centuries and simply appears in a 15th century survey as "the street leading to the church".

The name of "The Buttermarket" is first recorded in the Parish Church Registers in February 1648 and the 1772 map of Warrington shows that "The Buttermarket" extended only from Market Gate to Scotland Road. The street from Scotland Road to Mersey Street, was then called "Bow Street". By 1826, however, Buttermarket Street extended from Market Gate to Mersey Street.

While nothing is known of a butter market it is reasonably certain that such a special locality for this market must have existed in order for the name to have been applied to the street.

This does not mean, however, that the whole street was given to the sale of butter for at least one ancient building in the street, near to Market Gate, was only demolished just before the first World War having stood as a famous inn (The Old Fox) from the late 16th century. When it was decided to demolish the "Old Fox" as part of the widening of Buttermarket Street the Town Council resolved on April 4, 1911: "That on completion of the purchase of the 'Old Fox Inn', the building be carefully taken down for re-erection in some other part of the town." Accordingly the timbers were numbered and then removed to Victoria Park where a concrete foundation was laid for the re-erection of this ancient hostelry. Unfortunately the First World War prevented the completion of this project and as late as 1933 the rotting timbers of the "Old Fox" were still lying in the park.

At the other end of Buttermarket Street the first permanent home of the Warrington Dispensary was erected in 1819 and this building (now part of St. Mary's School) also housed an interesting medical library. After the Dispensary had moved to new premises in Kendrick Street in 1877, the library was put into store and was ultimately bought by Sit William Osler for the Johns Hopkins Medical School in America.

On the opposite side of the street from the Dispensary, the Warrington and District Trustee Savings Bank acquired a site for a new building in 1829 and after a tender had been accepted for this building for a sum of £970 the bank was moved to these new premises in 1831.

Next to the Dispensary stood Allen's Cotton Factory and the destruction of this factory by fire enabled the site to be purchased for the erection of St. Mary's Church, which was opened in 1877. The architect of this attractive

82

church, E.W. Pugin, was the son of the famous Victorian reviver of Gothic architecture in England.

Opposite Scotland Road, in a quiet secluded setting, stands the Friend's Meeting House and this place of worship is shown on the 1772 map.

Many living Warringtonians, however, will associate Buttermarket Street with Warrington's first super-cinema, The Empire which was locally owned, and which opened in 1921 with a comedy "Why girls leave home". Always a popular rendezvous, The Empire showed silent films to the accompaniment of a 10-piece orchestra until the "talkies" came along.

The first talking picture to be shown was "The Broadway Melody" on September 9, 1929 and the orchestra soon ceased to be. When this cinema closed in October 1961 the last film shown was "All hands on deck" and soon the building was demolished to make way for a supermarket and cafe.

## BOLD STREET

Created in the mid-19th century Bold Street was developed fairly quickly and has remained ever since as a collection of harmonious and pleasing buildings.

In 1839 a lane known as Ashton's lane wended its way through neatly laid out gardens. It was in this year, however, that a new street was created in place of the lane and the Minutes of the Police Commissioners refer in December 1840 to "the new street called Bold Street".

The connection of the Bold family with Warrington and in particular with the Patten family of Bank Hall, was recognised in naming this street which very quickly assumed an air of dignity that has never been lost.

Pleasing dignity was certainly achieved when the first public building was erected in the street in 1849-50. This was the Bold Street, Wesleyan Methodist Church and the site for this church was secured in Bold Street, Spring Gardens after consideration had first been given to the feasibility and desirability of extending an existing chapel in Bank Street.

Once the decision had been taken to build a new church on a new site, a chapel in Burnley was selected as a model and an architect, Mr James Simpson of Leeds, was appointed. The stonework was constructed with stone from Hill Cliffe and the total cost of the church, £4,723 15s. 7d. was raised by subscriptions, donations and bequests.

The foundation stone was laid on July 9, 1849 and the church was opened on April 12, 1850.

Within six years of the opening of this noble building Bold Street was selected as the appropriate location for the new home of the Warrington Museum and Library. The cost of this was restricted to £2,000 and much of this was raised by means of a bazaar. This building took much longer to complete than the Church. After the foundation stone had been laid by William Beamont on September 20, 1855, it was not until June 1857 that the old premises in Barbauld Street were closed for three weeks to enable the books and specimens to be moved to their new home, in which it had been decided to incorporate a new home for the School of Art as well as a house for the Curator and Librarian.

An artist's sketch of Bold Street in 1855 shows that the two houses on either side of the street, and now occupied by Robert Davies and Co., Solicitors and Edwin Over, Dental Surgeon, were already erected; 21 years later "The Warrington Club", had been established and was occupying premises on the opposite side of the street from the Bold Street Methodist Church. The first Committee of this Club consisted of: J. Charlton Parr, Peter Stubs, T.G. Rylands, James Marson, Charles Broadbent, John Crosfield, John White, William Sharp, E.J. Nicholson, Thomas Draper, John Dun and J. Paul Rylands.

A second church appeared in Bold Street in 1883. The reason for the appearance of this Church was that a section of the congregation of St. James's Church had united to form a branch of the Reformed Church of England. At first services were held in the Public Hall but in 1882 a site was acquired in Bold Street and the Church known as Emmanuel Church was dedicated on March 1, 1883.

A service of induction for the present rector, the Rev W.B. Makin was conducted in this Church by the Diocesan Bishop, the Right Rev J.D. Burrell, on January 17 this year.

Queen's Gardens, which add so much beauty to Bold Street, were dedicated on April 3, 1897, the 50th anniversary of the Incorporation of the Borough of Warrington, while recent development at the north end of Bold Street has resulted in the opening of a modern public house complete with a "Dallam" lounge.


## CAIRO STREET

The two early maps of Warrington, compiled in 1772 and 1826 respectively, do not show Cairo Street although they both show a lane leading from Sankey Street to the chapel now known as Cairo Street Chapel. This chapel is the oldest dissenting chapel in Warrington and the land upon which it is built was secured by a deed dated 1703 between the Minister, Dr Charles Owen, and the Earl of Warrington. This deed refers to "all that later erected building or meeting house". The present Chapel was built in 1745 and was altered and repaired in 1863.

Various ministers of this Chapel have had considerable influence in shaping other Warrington institutions. The Warrington Academy was founded in

Warrington very largely as a result of the enthusiasm of John Seddon who became Minister of Cairo Street Chapel in 1746. A century later, Dr Philip Carpenter, whose ministry extended from 1846-1861 worked vigorously in connection with matters of social importance including sanitation, an industrial school and the publication of a "Town Council Reporter". Perhaps the most lasting project with which Dr Carpenter was indirectly concerned, however, was the Warrington Co-operative Society and the close proximity of the principal store and office of the Warrington Co-op to Cairo Street Chapel is more than accidental.

The first secretary of the Warrington Co-operative Society, and the first man to sign the Co-op's Register of members was Frederick Monks, who subsequently founded the Whitecross Wire Co., and later Monks Hall and Co. Frederick Monks was a member of Cairo Street Chapel and was one of a number of young men who took residence at the home of the minister, Dr Carpenter, near to the Chapel in Cairo Street.

It was here that he inbibed new social doctrines with the result that he went to Rochdale in August 1860 to obtain practical information on the working of the Rochdale Pioneer Society.

The resolve to establish a Co-operative Society in Warrington was recorded in August 1860 and on August 31, 1860 Frederick Monks undertook the duties of Secretary to the Committee. In October the Society's first shop on the corner of Cairo Street and Sankey Street was rented for £21 per annum, and from this first shop with 108 members in 1860, the Society had grown by 1960 to an organisation with 45,610 members, 61 stores, 41 bread rounds, 51 milk rounds and 1,047 employees.

Cairo Street itself, which now connects Sankey Street and St. Austins Lane with junctions at Egypt Street and Suez Street, was first created and named in 1846 and the three streets associated with the French in Egypt appear in the Warrington Burgess Roll of 1847. The South Lancashire Regiment behaved gallantly at Aboukir and Alexandria in 1801 so that the Regiment was rewarded with the Badge of the Sphinx and the word "Egypt" inscribed on its colours and crest. In 1829 naval lieutenant Thomas Waghorn established the overland route Alexandria – Cairo – Suez which by 1845 had reduced the passage from London to Bombay to 30 days. These momentous events were duly remembered in Warrington when the new streets were named in 1846.

Before Cairo Street received its name, another church had been established in St Austin's Lane known as Friars Green Church. This Church is shown on the 1826 map as "Methodist Chapel", a reminder that the Quaker – Methodists who built it as their first home originated in Warrington. It was rebuilt in 1859 and is now known as Friars Green Independent Methodist Church and has its main entrance in Cairo Street.

# CHURCH STREET

Church Street is so old that there was a time when it was merely a thoroughfare leading to the Church. At first there were so few inhabitants that it was not even necessary to give it a name, and for this reason very early records of the name of the street do not exist.

A history of Warrington could be written based on the history of this street, for the town of Warrington first developed around the Parish Church after the Anglo Saxons had settled in Lancashire. After the Norman Conquest, the Church, together with the Castle of the early Norman lords of the Manor of Warrington situated on the Mote Hill next to the Church, continued to be the centre of Warrington until the growing prosperity of the community resulted in the introduction of markets, fairs and a bridge across the River Mersey in the last quarter of the 13th century. The centre of Warrington then changed and new streets became sufficiently numerous to require names, so that Church Street was also named and appears in a Medieval survey as "Le Kyrke Street".

Today the graceful spire of the Church rises to 281 feet above street level and all who walk along this street towards the Church can have no doubt that the street came into being in order to lead to this historic edifice. The spire is little more than a century old however, and was added in 1860 when the present tower was built as part of a reconstruction that commenced in 1859.

This reconstruction, according to a former Rector, amounted to the building of the fifth church on the same site.

The centuries from medieval to modern times are fused together in the buildings standing in this street as they blend agreeably together to remind the passer-by of the variety and wealth of activity – religious, civil and industrial – that has stretched across a period of more than 1,000 years.

Ancient half-timbered cottages have been restored by the Lancashire Steel Corporation and a plaque on these cottages explains that a nearby hostelry was used by Oliver Cromwell in 1648. On the opposite side of the street stands Warrington's first elementary school, erected in 1833 and opened in February 1834 when 328 boys and 204 girls presented themselves. This school was built because of the enthusiasm of the Rector, the Rev H. Powys, who managed to secure a tiny portion (£415) from a Parliamentary grant of £20,000 in aid of schools supported by the National and British and foreign School Societies. Local donations and subscriptions were added and a tender for the building of £645 was accepted.

The rules provided that: "Each scholar must pay 1d. to the master or mistress every morning, and no child will be suffered on any account to remain in arrear."

Not far from this school stood Warrington's Workhouse, which opened in 1729 and continued in Church Street until 1851. A description of the building in 1765 indicates that in the hall could be seen an iron bridle and a pair of handcuffs and that the dining-room for inmates had six long tables and 11 long forms without any back rests.

Almost immediately opposite stand the new premises of the Warrington Trades Hall and Labour Club, the erection of which began in 1960 and which replaced the early club where the meetings of the local executive of the Labour Party led to an expression which indicated that "Church Street" had merely become a synonym for the local Labour Party. Labour and Capital are both represented in this street, however, for on the same side is the Head Office and factory of one of Warrington's largest industrial undertakings, Rylands Brothers Ltd., whose product has also served as another synonym for the local Rugby League Football Club — "The Wirepullers". Between these two organisations stood "The Star Kinema" which closed in 1956 after 40 years of film entertainment. In 1914 prices at this cinema ranged from 2d. to 1/-.

Today Church Street is a bus route, but before buses, electric tramcars in the first quarter of the 20th century had run along the street side by side with steam wagons which spluttered and rattled as they carried cotton from Liverpool to Manchester. Every variety of road transport has passed along this ancient highway for 10 centuries and throughout this long period of time inhabitants of the extensive Parish of Warrington have also wended their way on foot to the Church that is the raison d'etre of the street.


## CHESTER ROAD

It is reasonable to suppose that any principal thoroughfare leading from one ancient town to another historic city and named after the latter would itself be ancient in origin. In the case of Chester Road, Warrington, however, such an assumption would be false for the road was created in connection with the construction of the Manchester Ship Canal and in 1908 there were only 14 houses situated in Chester Road. As recently as 1929 the undeveloped land between Chester Road and Wilderspool Causeway was known as the Chester Road Flying Ground and was used for aerial displays by Sir Alan Cobham's Flying Circus.

A plan published as a supplement to the Warrington Guardian on December 8, 1883, shows proposed alterations in the course of the River Mersey and intended roads and railways. This plan shows the diversion of the River Mersey from Walton Bridges to Warrington Bridge together with an intended new road from Lower Walton to a junction with Wilderspool Causeway. It also shows that it was intended to use the old course of the River Mersey behind Wilderspool Causeway as a large dock and that entrance to this dock was to be effected by a junction of the Ship Canal and river at

Oldest House in Warrington in Cockhedge Lane

Dallam Lane Brewery in 1896

Walton. The river diversion shown, as well as the creation of the new road, duly materialised before the Manchester Ship Canal was opened in 1894 but the creation of a dock behind Wilderspool Causeway was not effected so that a Directory of Warrington published in 1908 stated that: "Warrington is greatly disappointed that the Manchester Ship Canal Co., have been unable to fulfil their undertaking to construct docks here. The Corporation have now relieved them of this obligation . . . the Canal Company have, however, provided a wharf for local traders at the point where the Mersey joins the Canal."

A bridge constructed over the old course of the Mersey to carry the new Chester Road across both the River and the Old Quay Canal has recently been examined by the Ship Canal Co., and found to be in need of major repair work. This bridge offers a good view of the disused part of the Old Quay Canal which formerly connected the River Mersey at Howley with the river at Runcorn in order that ships need not wait for a tide on the River. Since the Ship Canal was constructed, however, the useable portion of the Old Quay Canal ran simply from Manor Lock to the Swing Bridge at Stockton Heath.

Houses erected on one side of Chester Road formerly had an open view across Arpley Meadows but in 1937 production commenced in a new factory erected by Thames Board Mills Ltd., and which has subsequently been extended so that the factory extends along the length of the diverted river bank. Owing to the boggy nature of Arpley Meadows the foundations of the factory required 4,000 piles in which 10,400 tons of concrete together with 220 miles of reinforcing steel were used.

A much-needed additional road bridge, planned to cross Chester Road, the river and Arpley Cricket Ground was submitted for approval in 1963 but this scheme has failed to materialise and the most recent development along Chester Road has consisted in the erection of a new public house and restaurant known as the Riverside Inn which is built on stilts to provide car parking accommodation under cover on the ground. This new inn was opened in September, 1965. Near to the road bridge across the old River course a new road has also been constructed in recent years to connect Chester Road and Wilderspool Causeway. The Causeway, of course, used to be the old thoroughfare used by those who wished to travel by road from Warrington to Chester.

## CROSFIELD STREET

Developed on land lying between Bank Park and the main railway line from Bank Quay to the north, Crosfield Street first appears on a map of Warrington in 1884, exactly a century after George Crosfield married Elizabeth Key in Warrington. George and Elizabeth Crosfield were the parents of the founder of the firm of soap makers, Joseph Crosfield, the fourth son of the marriage who was born in Warrington on October 5, 1792.

The railway from Bank Quay, as far north as Newton-le-Willows, had been in existence from 1835 and was originally constructed as part of the Warrington to Newton Railway which had its original station in Dallam Lane and a short branch line (used mainly for goods traffic) from Jockey Lane to Bank Quay.

After the Grand Junction Railway from Birmingham to Liverpool and Manchester via Crewe, Warrington and Newton Junction was opened in 1837, Dallam Lane Station continued to be used for local passenger trains until 1839, but after this, Dallam was used only for goods traffic and Bank Quay Station was used for passengers. The original Bank Quay Station was situated next to Bank Quay Bridge and was only moved to its present location in 1868.

Like the railway, Bank Park existed before Crosfield Street was made. The Park was originally the grounds surrounding Bank Hall which had been erected in 1750 as a private residence. In 1872 (one year before another railway, the Cheshire Lines loop to Central Station, threatened to create additional noise and smoke at the rear of Bank Hall) the Hall and Gardens were offered to the Warrington Corporation by Colonel Wilson-Patten for £22,000 and the sale was completed in 1873 after George Crosfield (the eldest son of Joseph) had given £9,500 towards the purchase and Colonel Wilson-Patten himself had donated £3,000. George Crosfield had deplored Warrington's lack of parks and open spaces and hoped his gift would benefit public health and recreation.

The first resident of Crosfield Street, Thomas Williams of the firm of Williams and Clay, marble masons, appears in a Burgess List of 1878, so that Crosfield Street was created and named within five years of the opening of Bank Park to the public partly as a result of the generosity of George Crosfield. The street was therefore named after a member of the Crosfield family and it clearly serves as a reminder of the prosperity created in Warrington by all the members of this family.

The first member of the Crosfield family to reside in Warrington was also named George: he came from Kendal in 1777 to take a situation in a Warrington grocer's shop in Sankey Street belonging to the Quaker, Samuel Fothergill. George Crosfield soon acqquired the ownership of the business and at first lived over the shop with his family.

Premises at Bank Quay suitable for a soapery were purchased by Joseph Crosfield in 1814 and thereafter members of the Crosfield family took an active interest in the affairs of Warrington. George and John (the eldest and youngest sons of Joseph Crosfield) were members of the Warrington Town Council. John became Mayor of Warrington in 1882 and was made a Freeman of the Borough in 1891.

The Crosfield family were Quakers and it would have been appropriate if a Friend's Meeting House had been erected in Crosfield Street. Instead, the street was chosen as a suitable location for the only Welsh Calvinistic Methodist Church in Warrington in 1891. Members of this denomination had previously worshipped in Warrington from 1884 at premises in Bewsey Road, the Market Place and Bold Street, until the chapel in Crosfield Street was opened in April 1892.

## COCKHEDGE LANE

A public right of way along part of the narrow lane from Scotland Road to Fennel Street and now known as Cockhedge was established in the 15th century. This fact is recorded in the Legh Survey of 1465 where it states that the 12 jurors had made a way on the western side of the acre of land known as "Cocage".

The name of this street and the field of the same name is associated with the ancient sport of cockfighting. Before this sport was made illegal early in the reign of Queen Victoria, a number of places in the Warrington area were habitually used for cockfighting and local records show that in 1515 the 16th lord of the Manor of Warrington arranged with the Bishop of Ely (a former Rector of Winwick) to have a cock-fight at Winwick every Saturday.

Cockfighting was forbidden during the Commonwealth and permitted once more under licence after the Restoration. Although made illegal in the mid-19th century, cockfights have continued in various parts of the county in secret to the present day.

The oldest building in Warrington, except the church, formerly stood in the angle formed by Fennel Street and Cockhedge Lane. This was an ancient house which survived until the early part of the 20th century. It was occupied at the end of the 19th century, by Mr Samuel Welsby, a local seedsman. William Beamont stated that this house had survived from the 15th century, the oldest portion of the house being built of sticks and clay laid skilfully across great oak beams.

Not many years ago Cockhedge was almost synonymous with the cotton factory which dominated ône side of Cockhedge Lane and which has survived to concentrate on spinning yarns for the tufted carpet trade as well as weaving dress materials from man-made fibres. The Cockhedge Factory was first occupied in 1831 by the firm of Hadfield and Frost who were cotton spinners and weavers.

At this time there were a number of cotton manufacturers in Warrington, but the Cockhedge mill was destined to become the sole survivor. It was taken over in 1854 by Armitage and Ward and in 1871 was occupied by Armitage and Rigby, the name still attached to the modern Cockhedge

Factory where cotton spinning has been replaced by other processes.

On the opposite side of Cockhedge Lane from the factory stands the Ashton Hall, a centre of Roman Catholic welfare and social work. This Hall was built by a former Rector of St. Mary's, Father V. Wilson, in 1915 and named after Mr John Ashton, whose generosity had practically provided the shell of St. Mary's Church. When Mr Ashton died in 1875, fellow solicitors erected a window and a tablet to his memory in the Church.

Cockhedge once teemed with life but clearance of old dwelling houses has left large car parking areas where people were once herded together, and only two groups of houses and a public house now remain on either side of this ancient lane.

## DALLAM LANE

An Ordnance Survey of Warrington made in 1849 shows that Dallam Lane from Tanners Lane to Jockey Lane was almost entirely bordered by open fields.

On the western side, of course, there was the single track of the Warrington and Newton Railway with the Dallam Railway Works situated at the junction of Jockey Lane and Dallam Lane. A little nearer to the town centre, almost opposite to Stamford Street and standing side by side, were the Dallam Iron Works and the Dallam Lane Pottery. The only other industrial building in Dallam Lane at this time was the Hope Cotton Mill at the junction of Hope Street and Dallam Lane. All these buildings were comparatively new in the year 1849 and until the beginning of the 19th century, Dallam Lane had been a thoroughfare, little more than a country lane, leading from Warrington to the ancient hamlet of Dallam.

A family taking its name from this hamlet was evidently of some substance during the 16th and 17th centuries since one member of this family at least was entitled to bear arms (Ermine, two flanches, each charged with a doe passant) and four members of the family were accorded entries in the Dictionary of National Biography because of their skill as organ builders.

The Dallam Iron Works, which became the Dallam Forge Co. Ltd., in 1865, made bar iron plates and railway axles and this led to the establishment of another company on nearby land, the Warrington Wire Iron Co., primarily to supply the needs of the wire trade. These two companies were amalgamated in 1874 with the collieries of Pearson and Knowles of Wigan, as the Pearson and Knowles Coal and Iron Co. Ltd., and later this undertaking became part of the Lancashire Steel Corporation stretching along a large area on the western side of Dallam Lane.

Soon after the mid-19th Century the firm of Peter Walker and Son acquired the mill site on the east of Dallam Lane after their smaller brewery in King Street (established in 1846) had proved successful and Walker's Warrington Ales began production at the Dallam Lane Brewery with a weekly output of 500 barrels which increased to 10,000 by 1897. This brewery is now known as the Tetley Walker Brewery which in 1967 was extended at a cost of £3m. for a weekly production of 20,000 barrels and is one of the largest breweries in Europe designed and built for automated control.

Other industries established in Dallam Lane include Whyman's Foundry Co. Ltd., promoted by Thomas Whyman in 1901, and the Longford Wire Co. Ltd., established in 1874 at the northern end of the Lane.

Perhaps the most interesting feature of Dallam Lane, however, is still to be found at the "town end" where there is still standing a railway shed which was part of the original terminal of the Warrington and Newton Railway which must be counted as one of the most historic railways in Great Britain.

## DELVES AVENUE

From the junction of Lodge Lane and Folly Lane, Boteler Avenue leads to Delves Avenue and Haryngton Avenue, which form two sides of the Bewsey housing estate recreation ground. The other two sides of the recreation ground are bounded by Troutbeck Avenue and Bagot Avenue. The names of all these avenues belong to men and women who were residents of Warrington and Bewsey in the 15th and 16th centuries.

Richard Delves was the Rector of Warrington from 1486 to 1527 and his sister Margaret Delves was the wife of Sir Thomas Boteler, the founder of the Boteler Grammar School.

The centre of the complicated series of family relationships which resulted in the names of Haryngton, Gerrard, Saville, Troutbeck, Delves and others being assigned to the avenues of the Bewsey housing estate, however, was undoubtedly Sir John fitz John le Boteler (1429-1463), the 13th Lord of the Manor of Warrington, whose tomb and effigy is situated in the former Boteler Chapel of Warrington Parish Church and it was almost certainly the romantic and mysterious aspects of this man's life and family that appealed to the imagination of Alderman Arthur Bennett who was Mayor of Warrington when the lay-out of the Bewsey estate was adopted in 1926, thus prompting the selection of ancient family names for the avenues of the estate.

Sir John's father, who had married Isabella Haryngton, died mysteriously at the age of 28 in the year 1430. His widow was forcibly abducted from Bewsey Hall at 5.0 a.m. on July 22, 1437, by William Pulle of Liverpool and carried away to Bidston where a marriage took place following threats and force. After being carried from Bidston into Wales she was ultimately rescued by Sir Thomas Stanley. Sir John succeeded to his father's estates at the age of one and was first married at the age of 15 to Margaret Gerrard, the daughter of Peter Gerrard of Kingsley and Brynn in Cheshire, who had purchased the young boy's wardship. Of the six children of Sir John Boteler and Margaret Gerrard, the eldest son married Ann Saville and died without issue in his father's lifetime, and three were married to members of the Troutbeck family. (Another member of the Troutbeck family was destined to become Sir John's third wife).

Sir John next married Elizabeth Dacre in 1454 but this marriage was set aside and declared void in 1458. Two years later Sir John married his third wife, Margaret Stanley, whose first husband Sir William Troutbeck of Dunham had been killed at the Battle of Blore in 1459. The only child of this marriage was Thomas Boteler who became the 15th Lord of the Manor of Warrington in 1471 and who was the founder of Boteler Grammar School.

The Boteler family are perhaps best commemorated in Warrington because of this ancient foundation, and the relationship between the Rector of Warrington and the founder of the Grammar School perhaps caused Richard Delves, the Rector, to bequeath to the schoolmaster "a bord cloth of diaper and his mass-book of parchment in print". Richard Delves died in 1527 and was buried in the chancel of the Parish Church while the bodies of his sister Margaret and his brother-in-law Sir Thomas were buried in the Boteler Chapel so that when the antiquary Dodsworth visited the Parish Church on March 31, 1625, he states that he then saw the arms of Boteler and Delves paled, with an inscription beginning: "Pray for the souls of Sir Thomas Boteler knyght and dame Margarete his wife . . ."

It is, therefore fitting that on the Bewsey estate, which adjoins the ancient home of the Boteler family, the names of Boteler and Delves should be joined by two avenues so named.

## ELMWOOD AVENUE

Between the end of the 19th century and the beginning of the First World War, the east of Warrington was developed fairly rapidly from Fairfield Street to Padgate Lane. In the 1908 Directory of Warrington for example, only one half of Fothergill Street appears and most of now familiar avenues leading from Padgate Lane had not been built.

Perhaps it was because there were streets leading from Padgate Lane called Oakland Street and Brookland Street as well as a much older thoroughfare known as Gorsey Lane, that prompted the Street Improvement and Lighting Committee on May 5, 1910 to resolve that certain new streets be named Oakwood Avenue, Elmwood Avenue as well as Pinewood, Ashwood and Briarwood Avenues. This certainly appeared to be a break with the tradition of naming streets after people or events and much more recently a similar idea has been used in naming avenues at Orford after places in the English Lake District.

Elmwood Avenue first appears in the Burgess List for 1910 when the residents of numbers 2, 6 and 8 were listed as Thomas Hackett, Percy R. Walker and James Barnes. Two years before Elmwood Avenue was so named, however, a site had been secured by the Wycliffe Congregational Church for a second Congregational Church to replace a mission which had existed since 1872 in premises belonging to the Cockhedge Mills.

The Elmwood Avenue Congregational School and Chapel was opened on September 11, 1913 and this church remained in these premises until 1934 when, during the pastorate of the Rev E.P. Willcocks, a new church was erected on the site at the junction of Elmwood Avenue and Oakwood Avenue.

The new Congregational Church was opened on October 10, 1934 and in the following year Wycliffe Church granted full independence to their former mission.

This fact was duly recorded in an illuminated address presented to Wycliffe by Elmwood Avenue a year later when Mr J. Phoenix, secretary of the Elmwood Avenue Church, expressed appreciation for the help rendered by the Wycliffe Church.

The new church was thus erected on the opposite side of Oakwood Avenue from a school that had been its neighbour for 20 years. The foundation stone of Oakwood Avenue School had been laid in November 1914 by Sir Peter Peacock but the first part of the new school was not opened until April 1917, and then only as a temporary junior mixed school with Mrs C.E. Cooke as head teacher.

Only in August 1919 were the school buildings completed, providing separate accommodation for boys, girls and infants. One interesting feature of this school was that it was provided with hot baths for washing and many of the pupils at Oakwood in the early post-war years enjoyed this innovation.

The first Headmaster of the Boys' School was Mr F.H. Longshaw and the Head teacher of the Infants' Department was Miss E. Gandy.

At the time Oakwood Avenue School was built it was claimed that no other elementary school in the town was so pleasantly situated and today the Oakwood Avenue Recreation Ground, together with the tree lined avenues bearing sylvan names in the locality, still help to maintain the pleasing environment considered to be so important when this school was first erected.

## EVELYN STREET

A former headmaster of Evelyn Street School, the late Mr Stanley C. Jones, affirmed that Evelyn Street was named after the famous English diarist John Evelyn and that Samuel Street was similarly named after the diarist

Joseph Priestley: Tutor At
Warrington Academy

Orford Branch Library Poplars Avenue

Samuel Pepys. Mr Jones also believed that in the case of Samuel Street the Christian name was chosen because the use of the surname would have created too many problems of pronunciation.

While Mr Jones was the headmaster a school magazine was produced entitled "Evelyn's Diary" and this was used to record events that had taken place in the life of the school. Fortunately those who write diaries do not always confine themselves to a mere record of events. It was Somerset Maugham who once said: "Keep a diary and one day it will keep you" and those who have profited from this advice have generally included in their diaries personal feelings, outspoken comment as well as the record of events with which they have been associated.

The two most beloved English-diaries, however, were those written by John Evelyn and Samuel Pepys who were not only contemporaries but friends, and the two streets in Warrington bearing the names of these two seventeenth century celebrities are appropriately adjacent to each other, Samuel Street leading from Wellfield Street into Evelyn Street. Both streets appear in the 1897 Burgess List and both lie very close to the Borough boundary. John Evelyn wrote his diary with a reader in mind and often quoted from other sources in order to give useful information and yet he remains most readable where his own observations, phraseology and experience are used.

Pepys, on the other hand never intended his Diary to be read by others and to prevent this he used a shorthand system and a cipher of his own invention which was patiently deciphered a century after the diarists's death by a Cambridge graduate named John Smith.

The Evelyn Street Council School was opened in 1912 by Councillor Henry Roberts and was planned with well-equipped, light and properly ventilated class-rooms, large halls, handwork and science rooms and spray baths in the midst of an area of industry and tight-packed industrial housing.

It is to the everlasting credit of the first teachers at this school and particularly, the first headmaster, Mr A.N.B. Appleton, that the school, instead of being adversely affected by its environment, exercised a beneficial effect upon the neighbourhood from the outset.

This creditable Evelyn Street tradition was pursued and continued by successive teachers and notably by Mr Stanley C. Jones who succeeded Mr Appleton as headmaster.

It was the first headmaster who once said that Evelyn Street was unknown to most of the town until the school was opened there and one could write of various teachers at this school, as John Evelyn wrote of Samuel Pepys, that they were "particular friends . . . very worthy, industrious and curious . . . universally beloved, hospitable, generous, learned in many things . . ."

John Reinhold Forster: Tutor At Warrington Academy

# FORSTER STREET

Extending from Winwick Road on the west to Orford Lane on the east, Forster Street is a quarter of a mile in length and now forms part of the boundary between the Orford and Howley Wards. The street first appears in the 1882 Burgess List and by 1908 there were more than 150 houses in terraces on the two sides of this long street. The only relief to the terraced houses is provided by the Gospel Hall which was erected in 1898 on the north side of the street between numbers 98 and 108, and which is listed in the 1968-9 Free Church Directory as one of four halls in the Warrington area belonging to the Christian Brethren.

The man after whom this street was named, Johann Reinhold Forster, lived in Warrington for two years only almost exactly two centuries ago and his accomplishments as a scientist and scholar still attract the attention of modern scholars throughout the world. In recent years an American professor crossed the Atlantic especially to study the life of this man and in so doing he visited Warrington in order to inspect original correspondence written by Forster while he was a tutor at Warrington Academy.

Johann Reinhold Forster was born on October 22, 1729, at Dirschaw (now Tczew) in Polish Prussia where his father was burgomaster, and in his youth he quickly acquired a remarkable knowledge of foreign languages including oriental tongues. His first occupation as a minister of religion did not prove sufficiently lucrative to provide for his family and he accepted a post in Russia to superintend new colonies at Saratov. Forster, however, was not possessed to the most docile kind of personality, as a letter written in Warrington shows, and he quickly left Russia because he had offended his Russian patron.

He next came to England in 1766 and after supporting his family by translating Kalm's "Travels into North America" (an edition of which was printed in Warrington in 1770) Forster accepted a post in 1768 as teacher of French, German and Natural History in Warrington Academy where he remained until 1770. While in Warrington his eldest son, Johann Georg Adam Forster, was a pupil at the Academy and Forster also became friendly with a local naturalist, Miss Anne Blackburne of Orford, after whom he named a genus of New Holland plants that he discovered when he accompanied Captain Cook on his second voyage around the World between 1772 and 1775.

Forster's son also accompanied Captain Cook on this voyage of discovery and when the voyage was over Reinhold was about to write a book about it only to discover that Captain Cook himself was engaged upon the same task and the admiralty ordered him not to write about it at all. He complied with this order and persuaded his son to write instead so that the story of "A voyage round the world in His Britannic Majesty's Sloop, Resolution, commanded by Captain James Cook, during the years 1772, 3, 4 and 5," and written by George Forster was published in 1777 exactly three weeks before Captain Cook's narrative appeared.

As a result of the publication of their book the Forsters were compelled to leave England. George Forster died in Paris at the age of 39 while his father died at the age of 69 in Hallé.

Forster's extensive museum containing thousands of botanical specimens collected in the South Sea Islands was purchased after his death by William Roscoe of Liverpool who transferred it from Germany to the Liverpool Botanic Garden. Many of these specimens are still preserved in the Herbarium of the Liverpool City Museums.

## FROGHALL LANE

Widespread clearance of large areas in the Whitecross area is rapidly causing complete streets to disappear so that before many more years have passed the fact that these streets once existed will be known only from old maps and old records. This is a situation that has happened before, for the creation of railways in the 19th century was the cause of the disappearance of some streets and a number of interesting buildings in Warrington.

A map of Warrington compiled in 1772, for example, shows a street running parallel to Bewsey Road from Froghall Lane at the southern end to Lovely Lane at the Northern end. This street was known as Bellmans Lane and it appeared on subsequent maps of Warrington from 1826 to 1851. It was not shown on the 1884 Survey because by that time the Cheshire Lines Railway had been constructed and the loop of this railway from Bewsey to the Central Station caused the whole of Belman's Lane to become extinct.

The purchase of property for the construction of this part of the Cheshire Lines Railway also resulted in the demolition of a building that gave its rather intriguing name to Frog Hall Lane. This building is shown, unnamed, on the 1772 map but on the 1851 Ordnance Survey Map the same building is named as "Frog Hall".

"Frog Hall" evidently existed long before the 1772 map was compiled, however, for an Indenture dated June 5, 1733 between George, Earl of Warrington and Mathew Lyon shows that among other properties sold by the Earl to Mathew Lyon was a "Messuage or Tenement commonly called Froghall together with the Close or field thereto adjoining and belonging, situate and being on Warrington Heath within Warrington aforesaid late in the possession of Mathew Jenkinson, Husbandman as Tenant to the said Mathew Lyon".

This indenture gives us, therefore, the name and description of one tenant of Frog Hall, but unfortunately all attempts to discover subsequent occupiers until the Hall was demolished in order to make way for the railway have so far failed.

The plan showing the property acquired by the Railway Company in 1865 shows that Frog Hall was one of the dwellings purchased but nothing seems to be known of this building immediately prior to its demolition.

Froghall Lane now runs from Frog Hall Railway Bridge, to the junction with Bewsey Road. Two earlier maps of Warrington (1826 and 1851), however, show that originally Froghall Lane proceeded as far as Little Sankey Green Lane. Today, of course, the street running from Froghall Bridge to Green Street is known as Priestley Street.

A number of the houses in Froghall Lane are large and spacious and were originally substantial town dwellings.

Two of these houses were used in 1908 to accommodate private schools, one belonging to Miss Marion Campbell and the other to Miss Lloyd-Williams. A well-beloved teacher of music, Mr W.H. Payton, also lived in the street and at a later stage, a doctor who endeared himself to hundreds of Warringtonians, Dr George Sinclair, displayed the Sinclair tartan at his home and practice in Froghall Lane until he returned to his native Edinburgh upon his retirement.


## FRIARS GATE

Modern Warringtonians will know Friars Gate principally as that part of a one-way traffic system from Barbauld Street to Bridge Street containing the Palace Theatre. Memories of this theatre will probably stretch back to the time when it was a variety theatre known as the Hippodrome — when it was built in 1907 it was called the Palace and Hippodrome. In 1931 it was converted to a cinema, was closed in 1957 and re-opened in 1961 only to become a bingo hall in 1964.

Friars Gate, however, is much older: it may be older than Bridge Street.

Although the earliest record of the name of Friars Gate appears to be an entry in the Warrington Parish Church Registers recording the burial on April 28, 1639 of Alice Harrison "of the ffriers gate", this street or passage leading to the Friars Church is as old as the Church itself and the earliest parts of this church, according to one realiable authority, could be dated around 1280.

The Austin Friars, who built the Church, were active in England from 1256 onwards and the presence of the Friars in Warrington is recorded in an action tried at Lancaster in 1292.

The Church was large and had a square tower which is depicted in a drawing of the centre of Warrington made about the year 1580. By this time the Friary had been dissolved by Henry VIII and the various buildings belonging to the Friars, including the Church, were granted by the King in

1540 to Thomas Holcroft who sold them three years later to John Cawdwell for £126.

The deed conveying the property to John Cawdwell refers to the "late house of Austen Friers of Weryngton ... nowe dissolved, with all his messuages, housses, buyldings, barns, stabuls, duff housses, orchards, gardens, lands and grounds (etc)". But John Cawdwell convenanted "Not to lette or interrupte the inhavitauntes of the towne of Weryngton aforsayde for the usage of the churche of the late Freirs" which was then known as Jesus Church.

Efforts were made by interested people to ensure that the Church continued to remain as a place of worship after the sale of the Friars property and it probably continued to be used until about 1640, but by 1700 only a single arch of this ancient church remained.

Subsequent building completely covered the site so that in the early 19th century no part of the old Friary remained above ground and it was only by excavations made in 1886 and 1931 that the plan of the church was revealed. The names of St. Austin's Lane, Friars Gate, Friars Lane and Chancel Street on early maps of Warrington, however, had remained to indicate the site of this ancient foundation before the site was excavated.

In the early 19th century Friars Gate was the earliest home of the Warrington Branch of the District Bank which opened in Friars Gate in July 1831 and remained there until 1857.

The 1908 Directory of Warrington also shows that a Christadelphian Meeting Room was situated in Toft's Assembly Rooms in Friars Gate and that William Coates and Son, shirt, jacket and overall manufacturer of Friars Gate also had a telephone number. (Telephones in Warrington were first organised by the National Telephone Company at 60, Horsemarket Street from 1890 to 1892 and at 8, Scotland Road from 1892 to 1912.)


## GREENALL'S AVENUE

For nearly 2,000 years, Greenalls's Avenue was part of a thoroughfare from Wilderspool to Chester but its name is only **three-quarters-of-a-century** old and dates from the time when it became a cul-de-sac following the construction of the Manchester Ship Canal.

Soon after the Romans had established themselves in Chester about the year A.D. 70, the conquest of Northern England was commenced under the leadership of Agricola who proceeded with such speed that his son-in-law, Tacitus, was able to record in his life of the general that: "In the course of the third year (of Agricola's administration) the progress of the Roman arms discovered new nations, whose territories were laid waste as far as the estuary, called the Firth of Tay" and "The country, as far as the Romans advanced,

*The school-church that William Beamont knew. This is now the Infants' School.*

Orford School, Long Lane

Statue of Lt. Col. W. MacCarthy O'Leary, Queen's Gardens

was secured by forts and garrisons."

The first tiny Roman settlement at Wilderspool, therefore, dates from this early period and the Roman road from Chester to Wilderspool would also have been quickly constructed.

Various excavations of the Wilderspool site have shown that during its occupation, which lasted for about 300 years, it was used primarily as an industrial settlement for the manufacture of articles of pottery, glass and various metals. Indeed as a result of a re-examination of the site in 1966 opinion seems to favour the idea that Wilderspool developed into a workshop to supply the needs of the Romans in Chester.

Knowledge of this local Roman settlement, however, had lain buried for centuries until in 1787 Edward Greenall, during the building of Wilderspool House, discovered a number of Roman remains on the site, and this discovery was followed by the discovery of further remains during the cutting of the Old Quay Canal between 1801-3. Other discoveries followed and the site has subsequently been explored systematically by competent archaeologists between 1895 and 1905 and in 1966.

The construction of the Manchester Ship Canal not only caused a large part of the Roman site to disappear, but was also responsible for cutting off Greenall's Avenue as a thoroughfare to Chester and it was after the construction of the Ship Canal that this ancient thoroughfare was named Greenall's Avenue.

It is now, of course, the site of Greenall, Whitley and Co. Ltd's Wilderspool Brewery and this company very generously permitted the 1966 re-excavation of the Roman site before the erection of additional premises on the site. The Avenue has been rendered into a pleasing river backwater by the treatment of the bank with grass and shrubs, while a plaque erected by the Warrington Society on the brewery wall commemorates the site as a Roman Station.

## GRAMMAR SCHOOL ROAD

Grammar School Road only received its present name after the building now housing Boteler Grammar School had been erected and opened. The order to alter the name of the street from Grappenhall Road to Grammar. School Road was approved by Warrington Town Council in March, 1942, after a protest had been made by one resident of the street.

Before the construction of the Manchester Ship Canal, Grappenhall Road was a road connecting Knutsford Road, Warrington, with Chester Road, Grappenhall. In doing so it passed Greenbank and Hilltop and the Cheshire portion of this road is now known as Hilltop Road. The original plans of the Manchester Ship Canal also show that a swing bridge was projected to carry Grappenhall Road across the Canal and a further swing bridge was also projected at the end of Wash Lane. These two projected swing bridges, however, were both abandoned in favour of Latchford High Level Bridge.

Thereafter, Grappenhall Road, Warrington, became a pleasing and little used street containing a number of well-situated houses. In 1942, however, 16 acres of land between Grappenhall Road and Wash Lane were purchased by the governors of the Boteler Grammar School as a site for a new school and after the Grammar School came under the control of the local education authority in 1933, plans for the new building were prepared so that the school was opened in September, 1940, by Canon E. Downham.

Before 1940, Boteler Grammar School had been situated for 400 years on School Brow.

The foundation deed which put into effect the intention of the founder of the Grammar School is dated April 16, 1526, but the founder, Sir Thomas Boteler, 15th lord of the manor of Warrington, had died in 1522 having provided in his will a sum of 500 marks in gold to provide lands and tenements to found a free grammar school in Warrington to endure for ever. A house in "Bag Lane" was set aside for the use of the schoolmaster and "Bag" or "Back Lane" and "The Free School" are shown on the 1772 map of Warrington, but later "Back Lane" became known as "School Brow".

Two new school buildings were erected on the School Brow site in the 19th century, one in 1829 and the other, which was occupied until the school moved to Latchford, in 1863.

It was desirable that the School should be situated for so long in close proximity to the Parish Church since the Foundation Deed provided that "the schoolmaster and scholars . . . between Michaelmas and Easter shall be at the Parish Church of Warrington between six and seven of the clock in the morning and there shall say such Prayers as shall be limited and written on a table to be hanged in Boteler's Chapel . . . then immediately after that they shall go to the school house." Between Easter and Michaelmas the scholars had to be at the church between 5 and 6 a.m.!

When the new school in Grammar School Road was planned it was designed for 500 scholars and it accommodated boys from the old School Brow building as well as boys from the Secondary School which then became the High School for Girls.


## GROSVENOR AVENUE

Perhaps the most pleasing housing estate in Warrington is situated on the western side of Bruche Park and consists of a small number of avenues all taking their names from titled families, namely Derby Drive, Grosvenor Avenue, Egerton Avenue, Connaught Avenue and Grantham Avenue.

Some of these families have strong links with Warrington and its history but it is possible that a curious incident in the long history of the Grosvenor family will be remembered in Warrington because it became part of the nation's legal history and because, for a few days, Warrington was the scene in the 14th century, of part of this now famous legal struggle.

It was occasioned because in 1385, a Yorkshire knight named Sir Richard Scrope and a Cheshire knight, Sir Robert Grosvenor, both appeared together in Scotland serving in an army of Richard II bearing the same coat of arms consisting of a bend or golden band, upon an azure, or blue background. Both knights claimed the arms as their own and in consequence the dispute came before the Constable of England (Thomas, Duke of Gloucester) who ordered those concerned to appear at a sitting of the Court of Chivalry at Newcastle-on-Tyne on August 20, 1385.

Eventually the Constable issued orders for evidence to be taken in the country. It was to be gathered by a number of commissioners, 18 being appointed to take depositions for Grosvenor including Sir John Butler of Warrington, Sir Thomas Gerard, William Bromborough, parson of Aldford in Cheshire, Nicholas de Vernon, John de Rixton and Geoffrey Starkey of Stretton.

Grosvenor's commissioners examined about 200 witnesses in various places concerning their knowledge of the Grosvenor arms. The examinations began in Chester on September 3, 1386, and after further witnesses had been interrogated at Stockport and Knutsford, 35 witnesses were examined at the Warrington Friary between September 12-13, 1386, before Sir John Butler, Nicholas de Verson, Sir Thomas Gerard and William Bromborough.

A painting in the Warrington Museum depicts this scene and shows the four Commissioners with Sir John Butler sitting between Sir Nicholas Vernon on his right and William Bromborough on his left. Sir William Gerard sits on the left of Sir William Bromborough and William de Eltonhede, the prior of the Warrington Friary presides.

The disputed shield of arms is displayed on the table in the foregound and witnesses stated that these arms were painted in colours on Bradley Cross in Appleton. They were also to be seen in Budworth Church, Lymm Church, Norton Priory, Bold Hall and elsewhere in the locality.

Not until 1389, however, were the arms finally awarded to Scrope, and Grosvenor was ordered to pay the largest part of the costs of the trial. An appeal followed and ultimately Sir Robert Grosvenor adopted the single golden sheaf of Cheshire on a blue field as his arms, but the memory of the bend or has been perpetuated by a 19th century member of the Grosvenor family, the first Duke of Westminster, who named three of his racehorses "Bend Or", "Ormonde" and "Orme".

Grosvenor Avenue was first named in May 1927 and soon was chosen as the site of the new Mission Church of St. John which had formerly functioned in Beresford Street. The foundation stone of the new church was laid on May 2, 1936, by Mr J.J. Whitley and the new church was dedicated and opened by Dr A. David, Bishop of Liverpool on Wednesday, September 16, 1936.

A special dedication hymn was written for the occasion by the Rector of Warrington, Canon Spencer H. Elliott and the priest-in-charge of the new church was the Rev J.C. McCormick who had collected some of the money required for the building by working on the site as a labourer.

## HEATHSIDE

The new car parks in the vicinity of Queen Street and Heathside, where the Fire Station was situated until last year, were formerly part of Warrington Heath, a large open space on which was situated a windmill in medieval times and where the inhabitants of the town in the 17th century occasionally watered their flax. The practice of watering flax caused an abominable smell and it was prescribed as an offence in the "Ancient Customs, Statutes and Ordinances" of the town so that one Thomas Bullinge was fined 4d. in 1635 "ffor watering hemp or fflax on Warrington heath".

The windmill on the heath is mentioned several times in the Legh Survey of 1465 and this mill, together with water mills at Sankey and Burtonwood, belonged to the successive lords of the manor who drew a sizeable slice of their income from the corn brought by the inhabitants to these mills to be ground.

Indeed the Victoria County History of Lancashire when describing the mills belonging to manorial overlords says: "no manorial obligation was more rigorously enforced or more jealously guarded than this" and in 1323 the eighth lord of the Manor of Warrington, anxious to please two of his tenants, inserted in a lease of land to them the usual condition that "the lessees were to grind all their corn grown upon the land at the lord's mills in Burtonwood, Sankey and Warrington". He graciously added "that they should be hopper free at his mills and to be served next after those whose corn should be in the hopper when they come to the mill."

A street named "Heath Side" is shown on the 1772 map leading from what is now Kendrick Street to Queen Street and in 1864 in addition to other occupants of the street there appears "National Schools. John Brown, master; Miss Ann Gewster, mistress; infants: Miss Jane Pennington, mistress."

Heathside School had been opened in January 1854 for the instruction of boys, girls and infants at a charge of 2d. per week for each scholar and the school was a Church of England foundation attached to St. Paul's Church in particular. John Brown came as master of the boy's school in 1855 and before he left in 1864 an Inspector had recorded that "This is the largest and most efficient school in the whole of my district: 403 boys present." The land, building and equipment of this school cost little more than £1,000

Sankey Street, Warrington in 1900

when it was erected in 1853.

From 1879 until 1968 the pupils of Heathside School had the excitement of being the next door neighbours of the Warrington Fire Brigade whose headquarters were moved to a site bounded by Heathside and Queen Street in 1879.

Subsequent Directories of Warrington show that houses in Heathside were occupied by firemen of the brigade. When the Brigade moved to the Queen Street Headquarters it possessed six manual engines, a reel cart, and a ladder cart, and the first Merryweather Horsedrawn Steam Fire Engine was purchased in 1880.

The first self-propelled petrol driven fire engine was acquired in 1913 and when the Brigade moved to the present Headquarters in 1968, the Coat of Arms and stone bearing the words "Fire Engine Station" were removed and built into the boundary wall of the new headquarters.

## HORSEMARKET STREET

Market Gate was first named in a lease dated 1363 and a century later was described as "a place called le markethe yate, where four streets of the said town meet together in the form of a cross". One of these four streets was rather vaguely described at the same as "the street which leads . . . towards Longforthe" and a century later, in 1580, the same street was apparently still without a name and was described as "The Strete that goth to the Hethe".

The first record of the street being known as "Horsemarket" only occurs in the year 1645 when the burial of Richard Mullinix, son to "Henry Mullinix of Horse Markett" is recorded in the Parish Church Registers. Later records suggest that at the beginning of the 18th century the street was otherwise known as the "Beast Market" but in 1772 the street appears on a map as "Horsemarket" and the name has not changed since then.

Horsemarket Street, like the other three streets forming the cross at Market Gate, has always been a street containing a mixture of shopkeepers, traders and residential property. The lease of property first mentioning Market Gate in 1363 permitted William le Bakester his wife and son to build on a piece of land "next the Markethyate of Weryngton" and there to trade "with bread, iron and fish and all other saleable articles", whilst the Easter Roll of 1580 shows that among the residents of Horsemarket Street was the wife of Sir Richard Taylor, the first master of the Boteler Grammar School.

In the long history of this street, however, probably no business establishment has earned greater renown for Warrington than the printing press of William Eyres which flourished in the second half of the 18th century. His grandfather, Henry Eires was a Warrington bookseller whose name appears in the imprint of a book published in 1704.

William was born in 1734 and a bookplate described him as "Booksellers, printers and stationer near the Market Gate, in the Horse Market, Warrington". A former librarian of Wigan said that "no printer in Lancashire approached him for artistic excellence of production, and few, if any, outside Lancashire excelled him. His paper was good, his type was beautiful, his display pages were tasteful, and his press-work was beyond reproach. Almost alone among Lancashire printers he eschewed ornaments, with the result that his books are distinctive and easily recognisable".

Copies of these books, which include John Howard's "State of the prisons" and Joseph Priestley's "History of Electricity", are preserved in the Warrington Library. The half-timbered premises formerly occupied by Eyres were destroyed by fire in the early part of the nineteenth century but a few of his printer's wood blocks are still preserved.

A century after the fire which destroyed Eyres' premises, near the Market Gate, the existing shops on the east side of Horsemarket Street were demolished in order that the width of the street, from Market Gate to Town Hill could be extended from 22 feet to 60 feet. New premises with Portland stone columns were erected during 1937 and a third portion of the Market Gate Circus thereby came into being.


## HOLT STREET

The trustees of the newly-founded Warrington Academy held a meeting on October 20, 1757, at which the first two tutors to be appointed produced their plan of tuition and regulations for the government of the Academy. Three days later three students began to receive instruction from the two tutors – both of whom bore the same Christian name – "John".

One of these tutors was Dr John Taylor, Tutor in Divinity who died four years later, and the other was the Rev John Holt who continued to serve as Tutor in Mathematics until his death at Warrington in 1772.

Although John Holt served as Mathematics Tutor in Warrington for 15 years, less is known about him than about any of the remaining 17 tutors who served for varying periods during the 26 years the Academy was open in Warrington.

Anna Laetitia Aikin, the daughter of another tutor, once described him as a sort of "reasoning automaton". That this description was both accurate and justified is exemplified by the curious will he wrote and which is now preserved in the Lancashire County Record Office.

The will begins appropriately with the bequest of his house at Kirkdale, together with some furniture and other effects, to his loving wife, Alice Holt. The remainder of his estate was left to his relatives without one of them being named. Each brother was to receive 64 parts; each nephew 32 parts; each niece 16 parts down to each cousin female, who was to receive one part. The method of achieving this curious division depended on the number of living relatives at the time of his death so that at his decease had he been survived by one brother, one nephew and two nieces, the residue of his estate would have been added into 128 parts and divided amongst these relatives according to their degree of kindred as specified in the will.

The task of establishing the number of relatives alive at the time of his death must have proved quite a formidable task for his widow, who was named as an executor, and who survived him by many years on a trifling income.

Another illustration of Holt's curious personality is afforded by the report that when he was a student at Glasgow, in order to visit his brother, he walked during one vacation from Scotland to Rivington Pike above Bolton. Here he asked a messenger to tell his brother, who lived in Bolton, that he would like to see him. After his brother had duly climbed the Pike and talked to him, Holt then turned around and walked back to Scotland.

In 1762, the Academy moved from Bridge Foot to Academy Place and parts of this second home of this distinguished seat of learning still remains in Academy Street. One part of this building, situated on the western side of Academy Street at the junction with Holt Street is now due for demolition and the street sign "Holt Street" at present fixed to this building will disappear at the same time.

Holt Street, like Academy Street, was created long after the Academy had ceased to function and only appeared for the first time in the Burgess List for 1901, and in a Directory of 1908 three houses in Holt Street were listed. The Warrington Motor Company Ltd., is shown under Holt Street in the 1935 Directory and this Company, usually associated with Bank Street, was formed in 1919 by the late Mr Ethelbert Foster. It has been well known, therefore, for 50 years in Warrington for the sale and service of Ford cars and this 20th century enterprise at one end of Holt Street affords a complete contrast to the decaying remains of 18th century learning at the other.


## KENDRICK STREET

It is appropriate that the street in which the Warrington Infirmary is now situated should be called Kendrick Street, for the name of Kendrick was the name of two distinguished Warrington medical practitioners (father and son) who between them practised medicine in the town from 1793 until 1882.

The Warrington Infirmary and Dispensary was built in 1876 and officially opened on January 24, 1877 in a street bounding Bank Park and then known as Heath Lane. A year after the opening of this new building, however, the Town Council decided to rename this street in which the Infirmary was

111

situated, and the resolution of the Council, dated May 9, 1878, reads: "Resolved that the street from Legh Street and Froghall Lane passing the Infirmary be called Kendrick Street."

When the Warrington Dispensary was originally founded in 1810 there was no hospital attached and the institution was conducted on an out-patients basis for the relief of the sick poor. Two surgeons, two physicians and a Resident Apothecary were appointed and one of the two physicians was the elder Dr Kendrick.

At this time Dr James Kendrick lived in a house at the corner of Orford Street and Buttermarket Street opposite the building which was the home of the Dispensary from 1819. When an outbreak of Asiatic cholera caused a rapid increase in the death rate throughout England in 1831-2, Dr Kendrick was actively concerned in the treatment accorded to local victims of the epidemic and published a pamphlet entitled "Cursory remarks on the present epidemic" in 1832. On the titlepage of this pamphlet he described himself as "Senior Physician to the Dispensary, and Infirmary, and consulting Physician to the Ladies Charity, Warrington."

His son, also named James, was born in the Buttermarket Street house in 1809 and served an apprenticeship in the Buttermarket Street Dispensary before taking the degree of M.D. at Edinburgh about 1830.

Apart from his medical practice Dr Kendrick Junior was actively concerned with local history and antiquities. In particular he collected many Roman remains from the Roman Station at Wilderspool and later presented them to the Warrington Museum, of which he was an Honorary Curator. He also gave many local books to the Warrington Library and wrote extensively on matters of local interest.

For a number of years Dr Kendrick Junior held the honorary office of Medical Examiner of the Children attending the Warrington Bluecoat School, an office he resigned in 1866 owing to a disagreement with the Trustees.

Dr Kendrick was deeply concerned about the health and living condition of the children at the school and when he discovered that the diet sheet he had prescribed was not being followed, decided to attempt to improve conditions by correspondence in which he levelled a number of charges against the administration. Subsequently he published a pamphlet entitled "The Warrington Blue-Coat School Exposure and its beneficial results" as he claimed that his criticisms resulted in the faults of administration being rectified.

Dr Kendrick died in 1882 at his home, 27, Bold Street. It is of particular significance that the two men who have written the most extensively on the subject of local history – James Kendrick and William Beamont – should have two adjacent streets in their native town bearing their names.

# KNUTSFORD ROAD

Knutsford Road now extends from Warrington Bridge to the Swing Bridge across the Manchester Ship Canal and yet it just fails to qualify as the longest road within the Borough boundaries.

While the road has been part of the highway leading from Warrington Bridge to Knutsford from the time when the first bridge was erected, various names have been attached to parts of its between Warrington and Grappenhall at different times over a period of nearly seven centuries as circumstances have changed and buildings along the road have risen and disappeared.

Since the road extended for nearly a mile side by side with the River Mersey it was subject to frequent flooding for a long period of time, and this nuisance was such a hindrance to the free movement of traffic that eventually the Earl of Derby decided to construct two causeways leading from Warrington Bridge into Cheshire. One of these causeways is still known as Wilderspool Causeway and the other was originally known as Latchford Causeway.

A legal opinion concerning a claim for the repair of these causeways dated July 29, 1891, states "that these Causeways' were constructed by one of the Earls of Derby in troublesome times for the purpose of affording a safe and reliable access for military forces to Warrington Bridge, the approaches to which before the Causeways were constructed being liable to be submerged by the ride of the River Mersey". It also states that "Latchford Causeway extends from the foot of St. James Street which is a continuation of the Bridge approach for a distance of 1380 lineal yards to the Brook Inn near the Mersey and Irwell Canal now adjoining Black Bear Bridge".

St. James Street is shown on maps of Warrington from 1851 to 1896 extending from the Bridge for a distance of about 400 yards and on the 1826 map is shown as "Chapel Street". The names "Chapel Street" and "St. James Street" for this part of Knutsford Road denote the siting in Knutsford Road of St. James's Church from June 22, 1777 until a new church was erected on Wilderspool Causeway in 1829.

The 1908 Directory of Warrington shows that Knutsford Road was then lined with factories, dwelling houses and shops from Warrington Bridge to the Ship Canal. No. 1 Knutsford Road, next to Warrington Bridge, was occupied by James Fairclough and Sons Ltd., corn millers and the occupation of dwelling houses on both sides of the road by tram conductors and tram drivers serves as a reminder that the first electric tram car ran along Knutsford Road on April 21, 1902. Thomas Domville was a pawnbroker and jeweller at 16, Knutsford Road; Daniel Johnson manufactured hampers next to Black Bear Bridge; the Broadbent family lived at The Hollies and near the Ship Canal, William Wareing, master mariner and Canal Superintendent, lived at Latchford House.

The widening of Knutsford Road began with the demolition of houses on the north side in 1965 so that the river embankment visualised in 1900 by Alderman Arthur Bennett now makes the Knutsford Road approach to the centre of Warrington as pleasant as can be expected in any ancient industrial town.

## LEGH STREET

Legh Street and Lyme Street are two Warrington streets denoting the considerable connection of the Legh family with Warrington and the surrounding district.

In her book entitled "The House of Lyme", Lady Newton said: "At Bradley House, Lancashire, the Leghs continued for many generations, adding to their estates by marriages with successive heiresses, which resulted in a great portion of Cheshire and Lancashire being owned by the family."

Nowadays fortunes are sometimes won by astute speculation in a variety of ways but in medieval times a fortune was often acquired or retained by following three simple rules: 1. Marry an heiress; 2. avoid minorities; 3. always support the winning side of a battle. The Legh family were particularly fortunate in marriage with heiresses and one third of the town of Warrington, or more precisely of the Boteler estates in Warrington, Bradley, Burtonwood and Sankey, passed to the Legh family through a marriage settlement.

In the year 1338 Richard le Boteler, son of Sir William fitz William Boteler (9th Lord of the Manor of Warrington), had married Joan, the daughter of Thomas de Dutton and a marriage settlement was made providing that one-third of the Boteler estates was settled upon the couple and their issue.

Richard died without issue and his wife Joan, survived him to marry a second husband, John de Haydock who claimed her estates after she died in 1387. Eventually the estates passed to his eldest son, Gilbert, although the matter was contested by the Boteler family.

Gilbert's daughter, named Joanna, married Sir Peter Legh of Lyme (who died in 1422 from wounds received at Agincourt) and the claims of the Boteler and Legh families to the estates were only finally settled in 1505 in a hearing before Thomas Wolsey, Archbishop of York and others, when the estates were finally awarded to Sir Piers Legh of Lyme, great grandson of the above Sir Peter.

Thus the Legh family came to possess one-third of Warrington and through another marriage settlement also came into possesion of one-half of the Manor of Grappenhall, so that by the year 1883 the Legh family estates consisted of 7,100 acres in Cheshire and 6,700 acres in Lancashire being worth £45,000 a year at that time.

Legh Street, one of the older streets in the town centre, is first shown on the map of Warrington dated 1826. Development of the street took place in the mid-19th century when, the Warrington Baths Company Limited erected the Legh Street Baths, the foundation stone of which was laid in 1865. This Company continued to operate this early swimming bath until 1873 when the affairs of the Company were placed in voluntary liquidation and the property purchased by the Town Council for £1,100.

The Baths have been subsequently considerably estended and expanded so that the annual attendance has risen from 10,000 during the first year the baths were owned by the Council to 418,000 at the present time.

A primitive Methodist Chapel was erected in 1869 but this chapel is now used for other purposes, while a Strict Baptist Chapel erected in 1870 still flourishes.

In 1924, about 2,000 Warrington girls attended a meeting in the Parr Hall organised by the YWCA when an unanimous "Yes" was given to a proposal to establish a centre in Warrington. Temporary premises, described as "Make-shift" had been secured in Legh Street and today the centre is still situated in a building in Legh Street which bears on the entrance the legend "Sale Rooms 1834". This building also housed an early Warrington motor dealer so that the words "Ireland's Motors" can still be seen on both sides of this building. This building originally housed the firm and salerooms of Thomas Sutton and Sons, auctioneers, valuers and estate agents.

## LOVELY LANE

Lovely Lane is a thoroughfare of some antiquity and is shown on an Estate Plan dated 1775 although it obviously existed long before this since it connected Sankey Green (near to which was Sankey Hall and an ancient water mill) with Bewsey Lane.

In the middle of the 19th century the 1851 Ordnance Survey Map of Warrington shows that only 11 buildings were situated in Lovely Lane. Four of these were on the East side and seven (including Clap Gate Farm and Bewsey Lodge) on the West side.

Housing and other developments in Lovely Lane did not occur before the end of the century and many older Warringtonians often comment that when they were young, Lovely Lane was indeed a lovely country lane. In recent years one aged resident of the locality remembered three thatched cottages standing near to Green Street named the Salt Box, The Mouse Trap and The Bird Cage, and that the entrances to these cottages were covered with a profusion of roses.

It was from the Green Street end of Lovely Lane that terraced housing development began, slowly extending towards Bewsey Road and gradually the older buildings were either demolished or converted. The Brooklands, now a public house, was once a private residence and a letter published in the Warrington Guardian in March 1887 and purporting to be written in a local dialect refers to: "the seekloodid, harestokratik and palashial rejuns of Luvloy Lane".

One of the oldest properties in Lovely Lane was Clap Gate Farm which was only demolished in 1949 and the site of this ancient farm is now marked by Clapgates Road and Clapgates Crescent.

Most residents of the Warrington District, however, will know Lovely Lane today because the main entrance of the Warrington General Hospital is now situated there. Originally this hospital had been a Union Infirmary and was successively known as "Whitecross Hospital" and the "Borough General Hospital".

In 1939, extensions to the Hospital comprising a new ward block, clinics, operating theatres, stores, nurses' home, and a reorganisation of the existing maternity block, were opened by the Duke and Duchess of Kent and to perform this ceremony the royal couple passed along Lovely Lane on July 6, 1939.

Subsequently the hospital passed from the control of the Local Authority to the Liverpool Regional Hospital Board who have begun to extend the Hospital, the first phase of which became operational in June 1968.

The ecclesiastical parish of St. Barnabas was formed in 1884 from St. Paul's and the church was originally erected as a chapel of ease to St. Paul's on land in Lovely Lane given by the Hon. Leopold W.H. Powys. It was designed by William Owen of Warrington and the church register dates from 1881 when the church was in course of erection.

Corporation motor buses first purchased in 1913 operated via Lovely Lane on the Bewsey circular route from July 3, 1913.

## LIVERPOOL ROAD

The part of Liverpool Road which is at present situated within the boundaries of the County Borough of Warrington and which now extends from Bank Quay Bridge to Sankey Bridges has not always been known by its present name. Indeed, different names have been assigned to parts of this road in the past, and these changes in name only appear to be recorded on maps and plans made during the 19th and early 20th centuries.

Originally the road was a street or way leading from Warrington to Sankey and a White Cross stood in this road near to the junction with Green Street. As recently as 1851 the part of the road between the site of the White Cross and Sankey Bridges was known as "Sankey Road" and that from the White Cross to Bank Quay Bridge as "Bank Quay Road".

It was only after an Act of Parliament, passed on April 17, 1753, that a

Latchford High Level Railway Bridge
Manchester Ship Canal Excavations
in Progress Below

Boteler Grammar School

road link with Liverpool was firmly established. This Act authorised a 10-mile extension from Prescot to Warrington (Market Gate), of the existing Liverpool and Prescot Turnpike Road and on the 1851 Ordnance Survey Map of Warrington this road is shown as "Liverpool, Prescot, Ashton and Warrington Trust". The Minute Books of the Trustees show that in 1786 the repair of the Prescot-Warrington road became the responsibility of William Pickavance of Rainhill, "a known good workman and an experienced Paver" who was instructed that the "copper slag" used on the Warrington Road must be broken small. A writer in 1795 describes this copper slag as "the refuse of the Copper-works of Warrington and Liverpool . . . a hard, durable material, and makes the very best road possible". This Turnpike Road with a toll gate at Sankey Bridges continued until November 1, 1871.

As the Western approach to Warrington, Liverpool Road was fortified during the Civil War when earthworks were thrown up near to the house of Edward Bridgeman (now the Black Horse Inn). This was early in 1643 when the town was the Headquarters of Royalist forces under the command of the Earl of Derby.

The earthworks, according to William Beamont, were erected on the north side at Longford; on the south near Mersey Mills; to the east beyond the Church and "on the west near Mr Bridgeman's House at Sankey".

These hastily constructed earthworks did not prevent the capture of Mr Edward Bridgeman's house by parliamentarians under the command of Sir William Brereton and it was not long afterwards that the town was surrendered to the Parliamentarians.

The narrow strip of land between Liverpool Road and the River Mersey was developed during the 18th and 19th centuries for industrial purposes and the construction of the Whitecross to Runcorn Gap Railway in 1852 has prevented the widening of the road in recent years to accommodate the heavy volume of traffic now passing along it each day.

This railway originally had a station at Whitecross at the end of Factory Lane and the 1905 Ordnance Survey Map of Warrington shows the railway as Warrington and Garston Line, L. and N.W.R:, with a railway station at Sankey Bridges.

An entirely new dual carriageway road has now been constructed from Bank Quay to Sankey and is nearing completion so that new scars, including the site of the ancient bowling green near to Crosfield's Centenary Theatre, are apparent as the future development of this much ravaged area is proceeding.


## LONG LANE

For more than a century Long Lane has been more familiar to children and young people than it has been to adults and the number of schools now situated in Long Lane, together with the new Technical College, will certainly ensure that young people residing in all parts of Warrington will continue to be familiar with this ancient highway.

Long Lane appears on early 19th century maps of Lancashire and an early village school was established at Orford in the second half of the 18th century.

This school was eventually restored about 1825 through the support of voluntary subscribers until, in 1861, the existing Orford Village School in Long Lane was erected by William Beamont and endowed by him for religious services as there was no church in Orford until 1908.

Records show that this village school attracted children from a wide area extending from Warrington to Winwick and at the beginning of the 20th century children residing in the Padgate Lane area of Warrington were still attending the Orford school. At this time Long Lane was an undeveloped country lane with tall hedgerows on either side and extended from Winwick Road to Orford Village.

The quiet peace of Long Lane remained more or less undisturbed until it became part of the Kingsway by-pass, after the opening of Kingsway Bridge in December, 1934.

A list of chaplains who conducted services in the Orford School and ministered to the needs of Orford extends from 1833 until the church was consecrated in 1908, and includes a nephew of the inventor of the miner's safety lamp, the Rev E.J. Wilcocks who subsequently became headmaster of the Boteler Grammar School.

Many Warringtonians remember with awe the man who was head teacher of Orford from 1885 until 1920. His name was John Cann and there are many testimonies to his pioneering methods at Orford as well as many certificates still in the possession of Warringtonians signed by this well respected teacher.

The south side of Long Lane is now lined with schools from the Beamont and Oakwood Secondary Technical Schools, to the new Technical College at the junction of Winwick Road, so that no greater concentration of educational buildings exists anywhere else in the Warrington area. The Long Lane County Primary Schools were opened in 1954 and the earliest phase of the new Technical College was first opened in 1956.

On the north side of Long Lane, apart from a much extended village school, there now stands a Social Club for the employees of Tetley-Walker Ltd., while Long Lane itself carries a heavy volume of through traffic from north and south.

# LOUSHERS LANE

Although a resolution of the Warrington Town Council, dated August 10th, 1906, states that "the new road leading from Wilderspool to the Bridge over the Runcorn and Latchford Canal be called Loushers Lane," this resolution can only have been caused by the making into a roadway of part of a thoroughfare that had existed for centuries and which is shown and named on earlier 19th century maps.

The discovery in 1930 of Roman remains in Loushers Lane tended to confirm what many people had previously suspected namely that it was by way of a route along Loushers Lane and Wash Lane that the Roman Station at Wilderspool was connected to the Ford at Latchford and the Roman Road to the North.

It was as a result of the laying of a water pipe in Loushers Lane in March 1930 that the remains of a Roman house were discovered a few hundred yards from Wilderspool Causeway.

An interesting feature of this house was that it was evidently equipped with central heating since the remains of hypocaust pillars were discovered together with hollow tiles. The Romans raised the floors of their dwellings on sandstone pillars so that heat from a furnace could then pass under the floor and through hollow wall tiles into the various rooms. The remains of the Loushers Lane house are now in the Warrington Museum.

Just as Long Lane has developed into a centre of educational activity Loushers Lane has developed into a centre for clubs covering a wide variety of recreational activities.

Possibly the earliest club to appear in Loushers Lane was the Scout hut belonging to the 1st Warrington Scout Troop and this is listed in the 1935 Directory next to "Rugby Union Football Ground". In this same directory the residents of Loushers Lane included three police sergeants and the houses occupied by these members of the Borough Police Force were conveniently situated to the entrance to the Police Athletic Club. Additional facilities at this Club were provided in 1951 and the club was also used for recreational facilities by members of the Warrington Branch of NALGO.

Members of the Warrington Air Training Corp were meeting in a hut in Loushers Lane in 1951 and this hut is now the Headquarters of the Warrington Judo Society. Nearby is a hut used by the Girl Guides' Association and in close proximity, in September 1968 Lord Rhodes officially opened a new headquarters of the Warrington Silver Band.

Probably the most elaborate centre in Loushers Lane, however, is the junior training centre for the mentally handicapped which cost £54,000 and which was opened in September 1965.

Industrial activity in Loushers Lane is represented by the spacious premises of Gilbert and John Greenall's new gin distillery. The foundation stone of these premises, which were estimated to cost £350,000, was laid on Thursday December 21, 1961 by Peter Gilbert Greenall, the eight-year-old son of the Hon Edward and Mrs Greenall. On the opposite side of the Lane are premises occupied by Lion Emulsion Ltd., and these premises appeared in the 1935 Directory as "Dussek Bitumen and Taroleum Ltd., bitumen product manufacturers". Nearby is still another club — The Alliance Box Recreation Club.

At the other end of Loushers Lane is situated the oldest building in the Lane, the Latchford Baptist Church, which has an inscription over the doorway "Bethel Baptist Church 1860".


## MARKET STREET

An open space in which goods and provisions were offered for sale, or a market place, preceded the existing covered markets in Warrington by several centuries and the Market Place in consequence is considerably older than Market Street. Old prints of the Market Place show an open space with a lamp post in the centre and two public houses, the Barley Mow and the Legh Arms, in the background.

It was not until the Legh Arms was demolished about the year 1840 that Market Street came into being and it appears for the first time on a map of Warrington in the year 1851.

This map, the first Ordnance Survey Map of Warrington, shows Market Street connecting the Market Place with Riding Street which in turn led from Queen Street to Horsemarket Street. At the Market Place end of the street, on opposite sides, the map shows the Barley Mow and The Vine Tavern, while on the same side as the Barley Mow is shown the "Police Office" and "Post Office" and half-way between Peter Street and Lime Street, "Post Office Street" connected Market Street to Cheshyres Lane.

Between Peter Street and Riding Street stood the "Market Street File and Tool Manufactory", a grim reminder of the way in which industrial processes of all kinds were conducted in the town centre throughout the 19th century.

In the mid-19th century, before the present covered market was built, Market Street was evidentaly the administrative centre of the town following the Incorporation of Warrington in 1847. Apart from the Police Office and Post Office shown on the 1851 map, a Directory of 1871 states that "The Town Hall is in Market Street, and contains the Borough Surveyor's, Borough Treasurer's, and Poor Rate Collector's Offices, Council chamber, Committee rooms, and Fire Engine house." In this Directory, however the Post Office was located in Sankey Street, and the Police Station in Irlam Street.

About the year 1878 the old Town Hall and Fire Station was removed to make way for an extension of the market so that afterwards Market Street began to assume its present appearance with a covered market situated near to the Barley Mow.

Built in 1561, the Barley Mow was described in the Victoria County History of Lancashire as "the finest specimen of timber work" in Warrington containing "a good chimney piece of Jacobean style, and the staircase has good turned balusters and newels of seventeenth century date". This ancient public house was skilfully restored in recent years and is the oldest building in the Town Centre.

For the past century, therefore, Market Street traders have attended primarily to the needs of the inner man. Butchers, grocers and hostelries standing side by side whilst throughout this period a firm of wholesale tea and coffee merchants, J. Geddes and Son Ltd., provided blends of coffee not readily available elsewhere but regrettably this firm closed down in March this year.

## MERSEY STREET

As the thoroughfare which connects Church Street to Warrington Bridge, Mersey Street must have existed soon after the first bridge was constructed at the beginning of the 14th century. Few dwellings or other buildings were erected in Mersey Street, however, until the end of the 18th century and apart from a few buildings at the bridge end, only one building, opposite to the end of Lower Bank Street, is shown on the 1772 Map of Warrington so that for three-quarters of its length Mersey Street was then fringed with open fields on the eastern side.

The unfortunate juxtaposition of houses and industrial establishments common to all industrial towns soon began to transform the Mersey Street scene and the 1826 Map shows a Tan Yard as well as two gasometers on opposite sides of the street.

Before tanning and gas were established in Mersey Street, however, the western side of the street had been a centre for the production of sail cloth and in that part of Mersey Street once known as the Running Pump, a name derived from the presence of a spring which is mentioned in the Legh Manuscript of 1465, hemp was spun, steeped and bleached.

The tanyard shown on the 1826 map was that laid down by George Furnival and this is shown assessed at £78 under the name of John Furnival in the Assessment Book of 1828. This tannery was destroyed by fire in 1838 and after rebuilding was divided between John and James Tinsley and Pilling and Shaw.

The Warrington Gas Light and Coke Co., were formed in 1821 and the original works was built in Mersey Street. This undertaking was purchased by Warrington Corporation in 1877 and at the turn of the century, after the

Winwick Road About 1830

Knutsford Road Victoria Bridge, Warrington

production of gas had been transferred to Longford, part of the Mersey Street premises were sold to the Tramways Department so that the first Warrington Trams rattled into the Mersey Street sheds from Bridge Foot and Academy Street.

While trams have given way to buses, a number of Mersey Street traders have continued to appear at the same address in various directories of Warrington. The 1908 Directory lists "T. Allen and Sons, plumbers and painters" at No. 18 and so does the latest telephone directory, while at No. 46, William Gandy was listed as a "boot, shoe and clog maker" in 1908 and the name of Gandy still appears there today.

Gradually, however, Mersey Street has been cleared of much old property in recent years to make way for the alarming increase in road traffic and new buildings have appeared on a new and wider building line.

Following the demolition of 69 old houses, new blocks of maisonnettes were constructed and named John Morris House and Brandwood House. These were officially opened in 1963.

Nearby a new public house, The Mersey Hotel has replaced an older house, whilst at the junction of Mersey Street and Church Street property has been cleared to make way for a traffic island.

It is, of course, a road plan for Mersey Street that threatens the demolition of the Old Academy building at Bridge Foot.

## MUSEUM STREET

In the middle of the 19th century large parts of the present central area of Warrington consisted of open fields and gardens. The whole of the area now bounded by Bold Street, Sankey Street, Parker Street and Wilson Patten Street was almost entirely devoid of buildings in 1851 and although a lane is shown on the 1851 map, on the opposite side of Bold Street to St. Austin's Lane, it bears no name and does not even lead to anywhere in particular.

This unnamed lane is now known as Museum Street, a name that cannot have been applied to the lane before the Library and Museum was transferred from Friar's Green to a new building erected on the corner of Bold Street and Museum Street in 1857.

The foundation stone of this new building – a square structure with the main entrance in Bold Street – was laid by William Beamont on September 29, 1855. An extension along Museum Street in 1877 added an Art Gallery with the Reference Library below and changed the building into an "L" shaped structure. A further extension took place in 1930-31 so that the "L" shape became a rectangle with a separate entrance for the Library in Museum Street. Another extension along Museum Street, which involved the demolition of a dwelling house, was opened in October 1965.

Provision was made in the first Library and Museum building in Museum Street to house the Warrington School of Art, and Art School classes continued to be held in the Museum from 1857 until 1883 when a new Art School was opened on the South side of Museum Street.

This building was opened by Councillor John Crosfield on the last day of his Mayoralty, November 10, 1883. Councillor Crosfield had given £1,000 towards the total cost of this building, which was £4,500, and the building was designed by William Owen. The School was transferred to the Warrington Corporation in 1892.

A number of eminent Warrington artists, including Sir Luke Fildes, Henry Woods, John Warrington Wood and Oswald Garside, received their training at the Warrington School of Art which became a College of Art and Design in 1968.

Housing development in Museum Street slightly preceded the erection of the new Art School and the houses on both sides of Museum Street, which are now used by a variety of professional men dentists, accountants, opticians and architects were erected between 1876 and 1882.

At either end of the south side of Museum Street, between Bold Street and Winmarleigh Street are situated buildings housing offices of the Warrington Rural District Council. Of these buildings, the one at the junction of Museum Street and Winmarleigh Street was purpose built as office accommodation in 1923. It is now shared by the Warrington Rural District Council and the Warrington Corporation and is perhaps best known nowadays as the offices of the Registration Department.

The large building next to these offices was formerly the Empire Skating Rink, opened by Lady Greenall and Mr H. Roberts on October 12, 1909. This building was used for a number of exhibitions because of the large floor area inside contained under one roof; it is now used by the Co-operative Wholesale Service as a bread vans department.

Nearby is an old school building — erected as Holy Trinity School in 1884 — that has similarly been converted to industrial use.

Beyond the Arpley Street junction the firm of Edward Greenhalgh and Son Ltd., faces one side of the Arpley Street Police Station while at the west end of Museum Street, the Patten Arms Hotel has stood since it moved from Bank Quay Bridge to the present site soon after Bank Quay Station was also moved from Bank Quay Bridge in 1868.


## MANCHESTER ROAD

The high road from Warrington to Manchester is one of the oldest roads in Lancashire — providing that one discounts the Roman Roads which gradually disappeared after the Romans withdrew from the county in the fifth century.

Only four roads are shown in Lancashire in Ogilby's "Britannia" which was published in 1675; the road from Warrington to Manchester was one of the four. Strangely it did not become one of the earliest Lancashire

125

"Turnpike Roads" and the date of this Warrington to Salford Turnpike, via Lower Irlam, was 1752. As in the case of the Warrington to Prescot Turnpike, slag from the Warrington copper works was used in its construction.

Manchester Road is a continuation of Church Street which is one of the oldest thoroughfares in Warrington. Streets leading to the Church both from the centre of Warrington as well as from the eastern side of the Parish must be as old as the Parish Church itself, so that worshippers from the ancient manor of Bruche as well as the Township of Woolston must have travelled along Manchester Road to the Parish Church for more than 1,000 years.

Manchester Road, Warrington, begins with the house next to the Church graveyard, No. 1, Manchester Road, which has been occupied from 1905 by medical practitioners whose names have become household words in Fairfield and Howley, the first occupant being the late Dr Anderson. Nearby is the entrance to the Training College which was destroyed by fire on December 28, 1923, and this entrance now forms the western boundary of St. Elphin's Park which first became a park of two acres in 1907 and now embraces 14½ acres.

Almost opposite to this entrance a number of terraced houses which have recently been demolished were interesting in so far as they were erected with a second storey as a workroom in which a domestic trade (fustian cutting) was practised. Also now demolished in the same vicinity is the 18th century mansion known as Fairfield Hall, originally the home of Miss Anna Blackburne and later used as a residence for students of the Training College. The site of this house is now occupied by offices of the Ministry of Social Security.

An extensive area along the southern side of Manchester Road, however, has been the Warrington Cemetery since 1857 when 12½ acres provided for burial purposes were consecrated by the Bishop of Chester. Additional land was procured in 1871 and 1940 making the present acreage 35½. The control of the Cemetery passed to the Corporation Parks Department in 1961.

Near to the Cemetery, monumental masons have practised their trade for a century and in the 1871 Directory the names of Edwin Hewitt and William Savage and Son are listed as monumental masons in Manchester Road. Names that are more familiar to the present generation of Warringtonians in this connection, however, are John Wood and Alex Roughley.

Although the Passenger Transport Authority had the necessary powers to construct a tramway along Manchester Road as far as Bruche Bridge from 1900, the tramway opened along Manchester Road in November 1902 only extended from the Central Station to the main entrance of the Cemetery. And before 1935 the tramway had been abandoned in favour of buses.

A twiggery and twiggery farm are shown in the 1864 Directory of Warrington in Manchester Road and as early as 1824 one Richard Swift was engaged in the craft of basket-making in Manchester Road.

Near to the junction of Kingsway and Manchester Road the very pleasant and commodious premises known as Alford Hall were opened on April 11, 1958 by the then Mayor of Warrington (Councillor H.G. Brandwood), as a Social Centre for the employees of Thames Board Mills Ltd., Mersey Works and as a memorial to the late Mr W.J. Alford, founder of the Company.

## MONKS STREET

Monks Street is almost a cul-de-sac on the east-side of Lovely Lane with hospital grounds at one end and a Recreation ground extending along its northern side.It was first named by the Warrington Town Council in 1885 and on the 1888 map of Warrington there were open fields on three sides of the street.

The street was named by the Town Council very soon after Mr F. Monks had ceased to be a member of the Council having served as Councillor for 17 years, and it is very appropriate that the name of this public-spirited Warringtonian should be commemorated in his native town.

It is doubtful whether any Warringtonian has provided employment for more of its townsmen and women than Frederick Monks, since three large organisations for which he was initially responsible still flourish and have been large employers of labour for a century – namely The Whitecross Wire Co. Ltd., Monks Hall and Co. Ltd., and The Warrington Co-operative Society.

Born in Winwick Street in 1834, Frederick Monks was first apprenticed by Rylands Bros., Ltd., Church Street and while employed there was primarily responsible for founding the Warrington Co-operative Society, becoming its first Secretary in 1860. Four years later, imbued with ideas of Christian Socialism and hopes of achieving co-operative industry amongst workmen, he founded the Whitecross Wire Company in 1864 and became manager of the Manufacturing Department. When he found that his idealistic views were not acceptable to others Mr Monks retired from Whitecross in order to found another concern with his brother-on-law. Mr T. Hall, 1874, and this concern is now Monks, Hall and Co. Ltd.

On his retirement from Whitecross a number of wireworkers employed by the Whitecross Wire and Iron Company Limited, met in Cairo Street School to present Mr Monks with a testimonial, a skeleton clock in a glass shade, with an inscribed silver plate which read: "Presented to Mr F. Monks, by the workmen of the wire department of the Whitecross Wire and Iron Company, Limited, as a token of respect and esteem, on his retiring from active management in connection with the company, July 1874."

The Warrington Town Council twice honoured Frederick Monks, the first occasion being when they named Monks Street in 1885 and the second when they made him an Honorary Freeman of the Borough in 1897. This honour has only been accorded to date to 20 men since Warrington first became a Municipal Borough in 1847.

Two donations made to his native town are seen daily by all who pass through the centre of Warrington. The first gift was the Town Hall Gates which were offered to the Council in December, 1893 and opened on Walking Day, 1895. The gates were originally exhibited by the Coalbrook Dale Company at the International Exhibition in London in 1862 as a masterpiece of industrial art, and are still much admired by all who see them.

The second gift, however, has always been the subject of controversy. This was the statue of Oliver Cromwell, now standing at Bridge Foot, which was accepted by the Council in February 1899 to commemorate the ter-centenary of Cromwell's birth. The siting of the statue was the immediate subject of intense controversy and similar controversy has arisen in recent months concerning its re-siting.

When Frederick Monks died in September 1912, a newspaper obituary referred to the passing of a "grand old man" and certainly the bearded figure of this Warringtonian befits that description which is often applied to another bearded figure well known as the "grand old man" of the cricketing world.


## ORFORD LANE

Orford Lane is mentioned in the Survey made by Peter Legh in 1465 where he describes "nine acres of arable and meadow land lying on the south of Overforthe Lane", the said land being tenanted by Richard Bruche.

From the centre of Warrington it is possible to travel today to Orford via Orford Street, Crown Street, Winwick Street, Pinners Brow, Orford Lane, Orford Avenue, Norris Street, Hallfields Road to Orford Road, and apart from the obvious connections that most of these street names have with Orford, three of them are also associated with the old Warrington industry of glass making.

Glass works are shown on the 1826 map of Warrington in Orford Street and Orford Lane as well as at Bank Quay. The familiar conical buildings of these glass works are described on this map as the "Cockhedge Glass Works", the "Crown Glass Works" and the "Bank Quay Glass Works". The "Cockhedge" and "Crown" Glass Works were situated in Orford Street and the name of one of them undoubtedly gave its name to Crown Street, while the Orford Lane Glass Works was situated behind Oliver Street.

Although glass had first been made in Warrington by the Romans, glass making in Warrington as a modern industry began in the 17th century when there is a record of the manufacture of window glass in 1696. A local innkeeper named Peter Seaman was the leading spirit in the erection of a glass house for making flint glass and bottles in 1757 and this glass house is thought to have been the Orford Lane Glass Works. Flint glass, bottle glass and crown glass were made in Warrington and the last surviving glass works in Warrington was situated at Bank Quay until 1935.

Orford Lane now extends from Pinners Brow to Orford Avenue but the part extending from Longford Street to Orford Avenue was originally known as Conies Corner where, until 1890, there stood a large stone obelisk facing the end of Orford Avenue. This obelisk had been erected as a monument to a former resident of Orford Hall, John Blackburne who died in 1786, so that his successors, as they drove from the Hall to Warrington along Orford Avenue, would be faced with the prospect of this splendid obelisk, standing throughout the greater part of the 19th century in open country.

In the mid-19th century, houses in Orford Lane were few and scattered. Between Orford Avenue and Jockey Lane (now Longford Street) there stood Orford Farm with Orford Villas on the other side of Jockey Lane. Mid-way between Pinners Brow and Jockey Lane stood Orford Lodge, the residence of John Rylands, and the 1864 Directory shows the only inhabitants of Orford Lane to be: "John Rylands, Esq., J.P., (Orford Lodge); Robinson and Bolton, flint glass manfr; Thomas Lawton, beer retailer; Joseph Grounds, shopkeeper; John Warburton, farmer; Mrs Rose (Orford Villa); Mrs Hutchings (Orford Cottage) and Thomas Houghton, boot and shoe man."

By 1895 houses and shops had been erected on both sides of the Lane and one of them was James Grounds, shopkeeper, whose premises stood on the corner of Grounds Street. "St. Benedict's Roman Catholic School" was situated between No. 82 and No. 104 while "James Robinson, farmer" tenanted the Avenue Farm.

Although Orford Lodge was evidently still a private residence, in 1895 this building had become the Junior Conservative Club, with Herbert Hayes as Secretary, by 1908. The 1908 Directory also shows, between Nos. 12 and 18, the "Alliance Box Co. Ltd., manufacturers of every variety of plain and fancy card board boxes for all purposes, patent collapsible and metal edges boxes, F. Magin, manager."

At the other end of Orford Lane, the Queen's Cinema was not opened until 1914 and this cinema, which provided entertainment for a large number of Warringtonians flourished until 1960. It was demolished in 1962 to make way for a petrol filling station.

## O'LEARY STREET

Only four public statues have been erected in Warrington to commemorate the association of particular individuals with the locality and only two of these statues are situated in open surroundings namedly the statue of Oliver Cromwell at Bridge Foot and the statue of Lieutenant-Colonel W. McCarthy

Warrington Parish Church

O'Leary in Queen's Gardens. The other statues are of Joseph Priestley in the entrance hall of the Technical College, Long Lane and of Mrs Macaulay in the Warrington Reference Library.

The initial reasons for erecting public statues are soon forgotten and the statues acquire a variety of associations in the minds of those who see them daily, being regarded by some with affection and by others with hatred. There can be little doubt, however, that the statue of Colonel O'Leary is regarded only with affection and in its present setting is probably the most pleasing statue in the town.

It was unveiled on February 21, 1907, only a few years after a street situated appropriately along one side of the Peninsula Barracks had been named O'Leary Street. While the naming of the street was an honour paid to Colonel O'Leary alone, the statue was also erected as a war memorial to those Warrington and Lancashire men who died with him and other soldiers of the Prince of Wales's Volunteers in the South African War.

The action in which Colonel O'Leary and many local men were killed took place on February 27, 1900, when, in order to clear the way for the relief of Ladysmith, an enemy position on Pieter's Hill had to be attacked and the task of taking the central height was allotted to the Lancashire Brigade. This hill was scaled under heavy enemy fire and finally Colonel O'Leary led a bayonet charge to dislodge the enemy. The Colonel was killed with a number of his men but on March 3 the Lancashire Brigade marched through Ladysmith.

The statue of Colonel O'Leary in Queen's Gardens was cast in bronze from the model of Alfred Drury, A.R.A. and was cleaned recently for the visit to Warrington of the Queen.

O'Leary Street had been named by 1901 and is situated alongside the former home of the South Lancashire Regiment. Peninsula Barracks were completed in 1878 and replaced the old Militia Barracks in Crown Street. Until 1958, the South Lancashire Regiment had many strong local ties but in April 1958, the Regiment marched from the Town Hall to the Parish Church for the last time before they were amalgamated with the East Lancashire Regiment. The colours of the Regiment are kept in the Regimental Chapel in the Parish Church while a Regimental Museum was maintained at the Barracks after the amalgamation.

On the opposite side of O'Leary Street from the Barracks is situated Beamont Council School, which was opened on March 21, 1907, by Alderman Arthur Bennett. The first headmaster of this school was Mr William Mason and his first assistant, Mr D. Morgan James, became the second headmaster in 1925. The school catered for both boys and girls and in the first year the headmistress, Miss Mary Taylor, had 400 girls in her department. Miss Taylor retired in 1929 and was succeeded by Miss S. Smith.

One former scholar of Beamont has recorded that the voices of command from the Barracks could be heard in the School and that on the outbreak of war in 1914 an appeal was made to the children of the school to ask their parents for food to feed the stream of recruits arriving at the Barracks!

Today, of course, the voices of command are no longer heard in O'Leary Street and Beamont School has been a school for infants and juniors only since the new Beamont Secondary Technical School was opened in Long Lane.

## PERCIVAL STREET

The Warrington Town Council named Percival Street in 1896 and this small street in Howley never appears to have contained more than eight houses. Nevertheless it is named after one of Warrington's greatest citizens and one whose name was known in many countries of the world in his own lifetime — Dr Thomas Percival.

Dr Percival was the grandson of a Warrington surgeon, Peter Percival, who belonged to a Thelwall family and who is named in a deed hanging in The Cottage Hotel at Thelwall. Thomas Percival was born at a house in Sankey Street, Warrington in 1740 and after attending the Boteler Grammar School for seven years, had the distinction of becoming the first student of the Warrington Academy when it opened in 1757.

Four years later he proceeded to Edinburgh University to begin his study of medicine and at the age of 25, as a result of his friendship with Lord Willoughby de Parham, Percival was elected as a Fellow of the Royal Society of London, the youngest member ever to be elected to that august body. He next moved to Leyden where he obtained his M.D. After returning to Warrington, he married and in 1767 decided to settle in Manchester to practise medicine and there he also actively concerned himself with social problems.

As a doctor he was deeply concerned with the lack of accurate records concerning mortality and in connection with his "Proposals for establishing more accurate and Comprehensive Bills of Mortality in Manchester", Percival corresponded with Benjamin Franklin with whom he had long been acquainted. His sympathies with the poor and growing working population of Manchester led him to form a committee to enforce proper sanitation and also to advocate the establishment of public baths, as well as to advocate factory legislation so that his views were quoted in the House of Commons when an early Factory Act was being debated.

The Manchester Literary and Philosophical Society was founded at Percival's home in Manchester in 1781 and from 1782 until his death, he was the President of that Society, which distinguished service is commemorated by a mural tablet over the chair of the President in the meeting hall of the Society. In 1786, Percival also helped to form the Manchester Academy

132

which still flourishes as Manchester College, Oxford and where he is depicted in a stained glass window in the Library.

Of the many books written and published by Thomas Percival, perhaps the most distinguished is his "Medical ethics, 1803" which was republished in 1827 and 1849 and was the first attempt to codify medical ethics since Hipocrates and it was stated by Professor John F. Fulton, of Yale University Medical School, in 1933 to be "the greatest book on medical ethics that has ever appeared in English". In 1787 Thomas Percival was elected a Member of the American Philosophical Society of Philadelphia and his friends and correspondents included many distinguished Americans and Europeans.

Percival died in 1804 and was buried at Warrington Parish Church were a memorial to him was erected within the Church.

## PADGATE LANE

A much prized map of Lancashire, published by Henry Teesdale and Co., Holborn, on May 1, 1830, shows a minor road proceeding eastwards from Winwick Road, via Jockey Lane and Marsh House Lane to Fearnhead, Leigh and Bolton. Part of this road is now known as Padgate Lane and it was originally known as the "Padyate", which is a combination of two ancient words "Pad" and "Yate" both meaning a path, road or track.

Situated on this road in Fearnhead, Teesdale's map shows "Padyate stocks" but no village named Padgate is shown on this map because it was not until 1838 that an ecclesiastical parish was formed from the civil parish of Warrington and given the name of Padgate. Thus the name of the road was given to the parish.

By 1849 a tiny part of Padgate Lane extending from "Finger Post Farm" to Marsh House Lane was shown on an Ordnance Survey Map as lying within the Warrington Borough Boundary. Finger Post Farm was situated on Manchester Road and the site of this farm now lies at the main entrance to the Warrington Cemetery.

On the opposite side of Manchester Road to the farm, the 1849 map shows a Finger Post which apparently indicated that at this point the mileages to Warrington, Manchester, Bolton and Leigh were 1, 17, 17 and 10 respectively.

A Directory of 1908 shows a Mrs Mary Ann Andrews as the occupant of Finger Post Farm, which, however, is not shown on the Ordanance Survey Map of 1909, though this map shows that Padgate Lane was then fairly well developed from the Cemetary Hotel to Padgate Bridge and beyond. The 1909 map also shows "Fairfield Bakery" on the opposite side of Padgate Lane from a Post Office and the Directory shows that the occupant of the Bakery was John Eckersley, who had a house and Sub-Post Office at Nos. 34-36.

To many of those who spent part of their lives at RAF Padgate, Padgate Lane began with the Cemetery Hotel and ended near to "The Stocks". Older Warringtonians, however, will remember with affection that both the "Cemetery Hotel" and the "King and Queen" both once provided excellent bowling facilities and that Padgate Lane, apart from providing good residential accommodation, was also a road leading to attractive country either by way of Bruche Drive to Manchester Road, or by pathways across the fields to Orford Road.

Today the Lane is fully developed from the Cemetery to well beyond The Stocks, and as part of the development, new shops, churches and other facilities have also appeared. A well used shopping area has grown near to "The King and Queen" where, for a short distance Padgate Lane is part of the Kingsway by-pass, and where the Warrington Co-operative Society opened a butchery in 1932 and subsequently developed a large store.

A little way beyond the present Borough boundary a site was chosen for the erection of a new Roman Catholic Church, the foundation stone of which was laid on May 29, 1927, and where in 1965 a new and larger St. Oswald's was opened when Dr G.A. Beck, Archbishop of Liverpool blessed the new church.

Although the development of RAF Padgate cut off many pleasant field paths leading from Padgate Lane to Orford, the future development of this former RAF camp site will open the area in an entirely new way to provide pleasing living conditions and at the same time will create new streets and roads where once only footpaths existed.


## PRIESTLEY STREET

Four tutors of the Warrington Academy have streets named after them in the Whitecross area, and three of these streets (Aikin, Enfield and Wakefield Streets) are connected by Priestley Street which runs from Froghall Bridge to Green Street where considerable re-development is taking place at the present time.

Of all the men who were connected with the Academy the name of Dr Joseph Priestley is probably the best known among Warringtonians. A statue depicting Priestley performing an experiment connected with the discovery of oxygen was unveiled in the Technical School, Palmyra Square, on April 2, 1913, and this statue has been removed this year to the entrance hall of the new Technical College in Long Lane.

Two plaques commemorating Priestley's association with the town have also been erected by the Warrington Society. One of these was placed upon his former residence in Academy Street and the other is situated in Warrington Reference Library to commemorate his association with

Church of The Ascention, Wooston, 1970

Warrington Circulating Library.

Priestley has been described as a saint and also as a bore but while it is easy to be bored by the virtues of Saintliness, which abounded in the character of this 18th century divine who regarded himself primarily as a student of theology, it is also apparent to all who study the many facets of this great man's life that everything he studied was transformed thereafter as a result of the original perception he brought to bear upon the subjects he considered.

It is chiefly as a man of science that Priestley is now remembered although his scientific discoveries, which sprang from his extraordinary quickness and keenness of imagination, were really his recreation. His lack of scientific training caused him to fail to apprehend the true value of his work with the consequence that he attributed most of his discoveries to chance and so he has been called "the father of modern chemistry . . . who never acknowledged his daughter".

His originality and keen perceptiveness is equally apparent in his theological and education writing, and his revolutionary work in the field of education was at its peak while he was a tutor at Warrington Academy from 1762 until 1767.

It was in Warrington that he published his outline "Syllabus of a course of lectures on the study of history" in 1765 and thus introduced the teaching of history to the world at large. His lectures on history were published in full in 1788 and became models recommended at Cambridge by John Symonds, Professor of Modern History. Also while at Warrington, Priestley published his "Course of Lectures on the Theory of Language and Universal Grammar" in 1762 and his "Chart of Biography" which procured for him the Degree of Doctor of Laws of the University of Edinburgh.

One of his major scientific works "The History and Present State of Electricity", was published in Warrington in 1767 so that it is perhaps fitting that the street named after him in Warrington should contain part of the Whitecross Wire Co's works and that the street itself should have been the home of so many wire-workers, for the original experiments of Priestley on electricity must have led to some of the wide variety of electrical uses to which wire was applied in the 19th and 20th centuries.

## POPLARS AVENUE

Although Poplars Avenue appears to be a very pleasant post-war avenue where history is very much in the making, it was first named in 1936 and the names of eight residents are shown in four houses in Poplars Avenue in the 1936 Burgess List.

A Poplars Farm is shown on the north side of Orford Green near to the beginning of Poplars Avenue on the 1937 revision of the Ordnance Survey

Map and it would appear that the avenue was named as a result of the existence of this farm.

To-day Poplars Avenue is the main thoroughfare of the Orford Housing Estate. It is fully developed for a distance of more than one and a quarter miles from Orford Green to Cotswold Road, and is a principal bus route for those who live on the Orford Estate. It is a pleasing avenue, with strips of grass, trees and a variety of modern dwellings all with gardens that make it well above the standard of municipal housing estates in other towns. And north of the roundabout junction with Capesthorne Road there has been considerable development of the services necessary to such a large residential area.

The development of these services in the post-war years has resulted in a number of opening ceremonies performed by eminent people that have included a member of the Royal Family, a Cardinal Archbishop, a Bishop and a Minister of State.

When Cardinal Heenan visited Poplars Avenue he was then Archbishop of Liverpool and he came on March 3, 1960 to open the English Martyrs' Secondary Modern R.C. School which had cost about £170,000. This building was planned to accommodate 360 boys but at the time of opening it housed 580 boys and girls so that the building of a secondary modern school for girls on an adjoining site was contemplated. Work on this was in progress in 1965 and the school was opened in September 1966.

Immediately before The English Martyrs' School in Poplars Avenue, is situated an Infant and Junior School, opened in 1959, belonging to the new Church of England parish, St. Andrew's, an offshoot of the existing parish of St. Margaret's, Orford.

This new parish had the distinction of building the first new C of E parish church to be built in the Warrington area in this century, and on St. Andrew's Day 1963, the Princess Royal visited Poplars Avenue to attend the consecration service at St. Andrew's Church. The church was consecrated by the Bishop of Liverpool (Dr Clifford A. Martin) and the Princess Royal was accompanied by the Earl and Countess of Derby. This delightful new church, which cost £43,000, made history in a number of ways because it is believed to be the first with a fibre-glass spire and to have most of the interior woodwork of chipboard.

Situated at the roundabout junction of Poplar Avenue and Capesthorne Road is one of the shopping areas of the estate. Next to these essential services is situated a branch of the Warrington Municipal Library. This Orford Branch Library, which cost about £21,000, was opened on October 13, 1965 by Mr Dennis Howell, Joint Under Parliamentary Secretary for Education and Minister reponsible for Sport.

Guests attending the opening ceremonies mentioned above have often commented on the obvious pride shown by residents of the avenue in their gardens and homes and it is clear that this pride is a real and continuing human characteristic in this very pleasant thoroughfare.

## RYLANDS STREET

Constant change seems to have been the keynote of many of the buildings erected in Rylands Street since it was first created in 1861.

The street is a continuation of Suez Street and connects Cairo Street at one end with Bridge Street at the other. Two brothers, Peter Rylands and Thomas Glazebrook Rylands, were both Aldermen of the Town Council when the street was named and it is appropriate that the association of these brothers should be commemorated in Warrington for they were also associated with a third brother, John Rylands, in the firm of Rylands brothers which they had re-shaped in 1843.

Alderman Peter Rylands was elected as a member of the Borough Council at the first municipal election held on June 1, 1847 and was Mayor of Warrington in 1853-4, and his brother Thomas Glazebrook Rylands, was Mayor in 1858-9. In 1868 Peter Rylands was elected as Member of Parliament for Warrington after a closely-contested struggle with Gilbert Greenall, the seat being thereby secured for the Liberal party for the first time in 33 years.

The first building − a handsome stone hall − to be erected in the new street was known as "The Public Hall" and was built by a Limited Liability Company at a cost of £3,460. The foundation stone was laid by Gilbert Greenall, MP, on October 10, 1861, only seven days after the street had been named. This Hall is shown in the 1864 Directory with a Mr John White as Secretary and was situated with four houses and a public house, "The Black Boy", as the only buildings then in the street. Three years later, on May 2, 1867 the Hall was packed to capacity and, as reported in the Warrington Guardian: "Every man of note in the town seemed to be present" when Charles Dickens visited Warrington to give readings from his works. On this occasion the readings were "Doctor Marigold" and "The Trial Scene from Pickwick".

A licence for the performance of stage plays was granted to William Johnson and others at the Hall in 1890 and when this licence was renewed in June 1892 the name of the Hall had been changed to "Royal Court Theatre". This change of name had occurred, in the first half of 1892 since the Council Minutes refer to the Public Hall Co. Ltd., in December 1891.

In December 1906 The Royal Court Theatre was destroyed by fire and was rebuilt an reopened on August 5, 1907. The theatre was ultimately demolished in 1960 to make way for the present supermarket now situated on this site.

Buildings have been erected on both sides of Rylands Street by the time the Public Hall was destroyed by fire and the 1907 Directory shows that at the junction of Cairo Street and Rylands Street, Doctors Edward Austin Fox and his son Dr Edward J. Fox were in partnership. Dr Edward J. Fox was born in Warrington and was a pupil of the Boteler Grammar School. He converted his residence in Rylands Street into a Private Nursing Home in 1914. He also installed the first X-ray plant in his Warrington Home and was responsible for securing the first X-ray installation at the Infirmary where he was appointed as radiologist. Dr Fox became a member of the Warrington Town Council in 1914 and served until 1921. His Nursing Home was ultimately occupied by the Warrington Corporation and converted into the offices of the Corporation's Housing Department in December 1946.

At the opposite end of the street, the building now occupied by Martins Bank was formerly occupied by Ralph Johnson, furniture dealer and cabinet maker. Immediately opposite to these premises the latest development in the street is now taking place as a new shop and office development is rising on the site of the Royal Court Hotel which closed in February 1969.


## SANKEY STREET

Now extending from Bank Quay Bridge to Market Gate, Sankey Street is a centuries-old thoroughfare from Warrington to Sankey. The earliest mention of this street by the name of Sankey Gate, or Street, occurs in a deed dated 1390 recording the purchase by Sir John le Botiler from John Perusson, the smith, of dwellings in the street.

At the eastern end of the street on both sides, the messuages (or dwellings) from the 14th to the 17th century were surrounded with gardens, barns, stables and orchards. A number of these holdings are described in the Legh Survey of 1465. One of these messuages held by John Fulshagh was complete "with barn, stable, and small garden . . . situate . . . on the south side of Sankeygate"; and another, held by John Hardewar, consisted of one barn "with gardens and crofts inclosed by hedges and ditches and containing three acres of arable land" extending from Sankey-gate to Warrington Heath.

Even after the eastern end of Sankey Street had been more fully developed, the western end from Legh Street to Bank Quay simply passed through open fields so that when Thomas Patten erected Bank Hall as his residence in 1750 it stood in open fields with nothing to obscure the view to the south and this is how the situation remained until the middle of the 19th century.

After Bank Hall had been purchased in 1872 and converted into the Town Hall, Park and offices, other residences in the immediate neighbourhood were also acquired and transformed to form a block of municipal office accommodation.

The present Education Office was originally Holy Trinity Vicarage and the Health Office was the former residence of the Garven family. The 1891 Directory shows Thomas Birtles, a photographer, as the occupant of Legh House with the Rev E.C.E. Carleton next door at The Vicarage. Next to the Vicarage at No. 78 is shown the Rev Edward D. Garven, while Bank House (now the Borough Treasurer's Office) was occupied by "C.N. Spinks, surgeon" and "C. and J.R. Garland, school". Bank House was first acquired for corporation office use in 1894 followed by the Education Office in 1904 and the new Health Office in 1905.

Holy Trinity Church replaced an earlier chapel on the same site in 1760. This spendid church is considered to have been the work of the architect James Gibbs who is also credited with the design of Bank Hall. The church contains a number of interesting features including a picture over the altar painted by a Warrington artist, James Cranke, in 1776 and a candelabra that once hung in the House of Commons. The base of the clock tower belongs to the Church, but the iron structure, which houses the Town Clock, belongs to the Town.

Near to Holy Trinity Church, the building now occupied by Woolworths was originally used as the showrooms of the Warrington cabinet manufacturers, Robert Garnett and Sons, who displayed furniture suitable for "The baronial hall, the country mansion, or the unpretentious villa".

The Northern Printing Works of Messrs Mackie and Co. Ltd., were opened by Lord Winmarleigh in 1880 and nearby stood the General Post Office which later became the Labour Exchange after the Post Office had been· re-housed in .Springfield Street. Facing the Town Hall, the Conservative Club was erected in 1884.

So many well known Warrington enterprises have stood in Sankey Street that it is impossible to enumerate them all in the space of a short article but it is quite certain that Sankey Street will always conjure pleasant memories in the minds of all Warringtonians — possibly for a photograph taken by Birtles; a ring bought from Bakers or Eustances; a book purchased from Percival Pearse or W.H. Smith; a tomato sausage from Bayly Isaac or a meal in the Winmarleigh Cafe. Although the street is narrow and considered by many to be dangerous it nevertheless has an intimacy that is possessed by no other street in Warrington.


## ST. AUSTIN'S LANE

St. Austin's Lane, which now connects Barbauld Street with Bold Street, has been transformed in recent years both in appearance and use, by the erection of the Post Office Automatic Telephone Exchange and the introduction of a one-way traffic system in Barbauld Street.

Although it is not named, the Lane is shown on the 1826 map of Warrington connecting Friar's Green (later Barbauld Street) with Ashton's Lane (later Bold Street). The first record of the name of this Lane occurs on the 1851 Ordnance Survey Map, while in a Directory of 1864, Benjamin Pierpoint, J.P. is shown as the only resident of St. Austin's Lane, at the house originally known as "The Stone House".

The name of the Lane is a reminder that nearby in medieval times, stood the Church and Friary of the Hermit Friars of St. Augustine. The Friars wore black habits and were known for short as "Austin" Friars to distinguish them from a contemporary Order known as the Black Friars. The Church of the local Austin Friars stood in Friars Gate and the various buildings belonging to the Friars, according to a deed of conveyance drawn up after the dissolution of the establishment in 1536 included:-"Messuages, houses, buyldings, barns, stabuls, duff housses, orchards, gardens, lands, and grounds." Some of these buildings may have stood on either side of St. Austin's Lane but when the foundations of the Post Office Telephone Exchange were being dug despite a very careful examination of the site, no trace of these Friary buildings was encountered.

Possibly the oldest building still standing in St. Austin's Lane is the house originally known as "The Stone House", now used by the British Legion and known as "St. Austin's Club". This building is shown on the 1826 map and was also the subject of a pen sketch by a local artist named Robert Booth about the year 1820. The house sketched by Robert Booth, however, had been extended by the time it was given to the British Legion by a former occupant of the house, Mr Robert Pierpoint, who was a native of Warrington and who represented Warrington in Parliament from 1892 until 1906. The Club was opened as "The Comrades of the Great War Club, St. Austin', Warrington" on September 7, 1918 by the famous blind V.C. Captain Towse, late of the Gordon Highlanders, and the objects of the club included care of the widows and dependants of those who had fallen, as well as to perpetuate a spirit of comradeship among discharged men.

Almost opposite to the Club stands a building now occupied by R. Spann and Co., Motor Body Builders, but this building known as the Old Vane Lodge, was previously occupied by a well known local antiquary and local historian, Mr Henry Stuart Page, who conducted a business as an antique dealer in this building for 35 years. Mr Page had been vice-president of the British Antique Dealers Association, he was a connoisseur of china and pottery and was a founder member of the Warrington Society.

Until the building of the Post Office Telephone Exchange commenced in 1952 St. Austin's Lane was narrow and little used and on part of the site of the Exchange stood buildings that in 1907 housed The Priory High School for Girls where the Misses Williams were the principals. A brick wall separated the grounds of this school from the Lane and outside stood a stone block to assist

St. Oswald's, Padgate, 1965

those wishing to mount a horse. This Stone block is now preserved at The Museum.

The Post Office Automatic Exchange was estimated to cost £212,000 exclusive of equipment and dispensed with two other Warrington Exchanges. The opening of the Exchanges meant that local phones were converted to automatic dialling and in 1961 Warrington became the fourth town in the North West to have STD.

## SCOTLAND ROAD

Originally known as Scotland Bank, Scotland Road is one of the oldest streets in the town centre and on the 1772 map of Warrington it appears with buildings on both the north and south sides.

Its name has been attributed to the final surrender of the large army of Scots which entered England under the Duke of Hamilton in 1648. This army had been pursued by Oliver Cromwell in a great running fight from Preston to Warrington. A final stand at Winwick had resulted in about 1,000 Scots being killed and 2,000 taken prisoner. The tattered remnants of this army struggled as far as Warrington Bridge and William Beamont states that the final surrender took place on Scotland Bank. The fate of the prisoners taken was hard; many were sent as slaves to Virginia and Barbados and others to Venice to be galley slaves.

On February 5, 1802, Peter Stubs, the landlord of the White Bear Inn, Bridge Street, who had been conducting a file-making industry on a domestic basis since 1773, obtained a lease for 500 years of a piece of land in Cockhedge Fields which was bound on one side by Scotland Bank. Workshops were erected on this land and thus the enterprise was transformed from the old domestic pattern to a factory system. The firm remained at the Scotland Road works until 1963 when a new factory was opened in Wilderspool Causeway as an initial phase of a long term development programme which left part of the enterprise on the old site in Scotland Road.

Five years before the partial movement of this historic industrial enterprise had taken place, a great surprise had confronted a queue of people waiting for admission to the Regent Cinema which is situated in close proximity to the file works. Films had been shown in the cinema on Saturday, September 22, 1958, but the following day, without prior warning, barred doors and a large notice saying that the premises had been closed confronted those queuing for admission.

This news injected a note of sadness into theatre lovers as well as cinema patrons, for the Regent Cinema had originally opened in December 1818 as the "New Theatre" and many famous actors and actresses had performed there during the 19th and 20th centuries including Henry Irving, Dan Leno

143

and Marie Lloyd.

This theatre became the Mechanics Institute in 1836 and reopened as the "Theatre Royal" 10 years later. It was enlarged in 1883 and after 1907 became known as the "Royal Theatre of Varieties". It became a cinema, known as "The Futurist", shortly after World War I and later was re-named "The Regent". A "Theatre Tavern" is shown next door to this theatre in Directories from 1864 to 1907.

Besides Peter Stubs, other enterprises concerned with iron and steel seem to have favoured Scotland Road at different times. Caldwells Ltd., spade manufacturers, are shown as having workshops in Scotland Road in the 1907 Directory and at the opposite end of the road "John Chorley, iron and steel Merchant" appears in the 1935 Directory, while the 1864 Directory lists at No. 21 a "John Needham, engineer and millwright, and manufacturer of horizontal steam engines of all sizes".

A timber yard is shown in Scotland Bank on the 1772 map and many Warringtonians will remember a spectacular fire which occurred in 1940 at the timber yard of Tilling and Gray, which was also situated in Scotland Road. This fire which occurred at night in the war-time blackout, attracted many inquisitive people from as far away as Wigan and also brought unwelcome attention from German bombers.


## TANNERS LANE

The trade of tanner is an ancient one and in early times was often associated with farming, the tanning of hides being a subsidiary of the large farms.

This would probably explain why the list of items on which a toll was charged if they were brought over Warrington Bridge for sale in 1310 included the following:— "Every hundred pelts of sheep, goats, stags, hinds, deer, does, hares, rabbits, foxes, cats and squirrels, a halfpenny." But for "Every hide, either fresh, salted or tanned, a farthing". The single tanned hide, therefore, was taxed as much as 50 pelts.

The trade of currier (or leather dresser) was an occupation in Warrington in the 17th century since the Parish Church Registers record the burial of Edward Wallis, Currier, on August 26, 1634, and one tanner is listed in the Warrington portion of Bayley's Northern Directory for 1781.

Before the end of the 19th century tanning had become a major industry in Warrington and the growth of this industry was sustained throughout the first half of the 20th century until it began to suffer severe competition from plastics, rubber and other causes which caused the industry to decline rapidly and many local tanneries to close.

It is fitting, therefore, that an industry which featured so largely in the life

144

of Warrington for nearly two centuries should have given its name to a local street that was at one time almost surrounded by tanneries.

Tanners Lane appears on the 1772 map of Warrington and it is fairly clear that the Tanyard marked in Tanners Lane on the 1826 map was in existence in 1772. Certainly it was being worked in 1813 by John Leigh Brint and was responsible for the name of Tanners Lane. It was next purchased by John Guest who had been working a tannery at Preston Brook, and on the 1851 map the Tanners Lane premises are shown as "Guest's Tannery". These premises stood on the south side of Tanners Lane at the Winwick Street end. Guests later moved to the opposite side of Winwick Street in order to convert a pin factory into a tannery and the yard in Tanners Lane by 1903 had become the "Tanners Lane Tanning Co.".

The 1851 map shows, besides "Guest's Tannery" in Tanners Lane, an Engine House, Townsend Brewery, and the Three Pigeons Public House. It has often been stated that The Three Pigeons was the original booking office for passengers on the Warrington to Newton Railway which had its Warrington terminal in Dallam Lane from 1831 until 1837. Some doubt has recently been expressed, however, concerning this supposed use in a recent book on the Crewe to Carlisle Railway by Brian Reed, who considers that passengers would have approached the terminal from the town end via Foundry Lane or Bewsey Street, and not from Tanners Lane. This early railway, nevertheless, crossed Tanners Lane at its junction with Dallam Lane and in so doing passed immediately to one side of the public house which will always be associated with this historic railway whether or not it served as the original booking office.

By 1935 a petrol filling station stood on part of the site of the old tanyard and other more sophisticated and less unpleasant trades than tanning were standing nearby, including a firm of shirt manufacturers and a firm dealing in wines and spirits.

Opposite to the petrol filling station now stands the Winwick Street branch of the Warrington Co-operative Society and it is interesting to notice in the 1891 Directory that on this site stood a "Co-operative Hall News Room".

## THELWALL LANE

Thelwall Lane now extends for about three quarters of a mile from Knutsford Road to Latchford Locks and before the construction of the Manchester Ship Canal was known as Thelwall Road because it was the road leading to Thelwall from Warrington.

Until the County Boundary between Lancashire and Cheshire was altered in 1888 and again in 1896, Thelwall Lane was a pleasant country road situated in the County of Cheshire, and some slight indication of its former state may be gained from the small number of cottages that still remain in the lane in spite of the considerable development that has taken place since the Canal was opened in 1894.

From its junction with Kingsway South, Thelwall Lane is now a thoroughfare leading to a number of large industrial undertakings in the vicinity of Latchford Locks as well as to the Locks themselves and the Canal Company's Hydraulic Installation and Latchford Workshop of the Mechanical Engineer's Department. This hydraulic pumping station is necessary for the operation of the locks and also of the three swing bridges in the Warrington area. A brick tower houses an accumulator, and two miles of hydraulic main connects the hydraulic pumping station to the Knutsford Road, Stockton Heath and Stag Inn, swing bridges.

Near to the junction with Knutsford Road, the Latchford Tannery is shown on an Ordnance Survey Map of 1889 and "Latchford Tannery Ltd" appears in the Directories of 1907 and 1951, but the site of the tannery is now occupied by a tyre depot and a firm of haulage contractors. One firm of tanners, however, still remains in Thelwall Lane. This firm, Pierpoint and Bryant Ltd., was founded in 1874 and is listed in Thelwall Lane in the 1907 Directory as "Hide curers, tanners etc" and is now also known for the manufacture of high speed grinding wheels.

At the junction of Knutsford Road is situated the Latchford Methodist Church which was erected after 1907 and extended in 1932, while at the other end of the lane the considerable industrial undertakings of the Richmond Gas Stove Company Ltd., and the British Aluminium Co. Ltd., cause a heavy daily traffic along a road that has become almost a cul-de-sac as a result of the canal being cut.

The first section of Richmonds Works at Grappenhall opposite Latchford Locks was completed in 1906 and the foundry with pattern stores and dressing shops started production of cooker castings. By 1947, one million gas cookers had been manufactured at the Grappenhall works as well as a considerable contribution to the manufacture of armaments during the war.

The adjacent factory of the British aluminium Co. Ltd., came into production in 1943 and was operated initially for the Government as a shadow factory for the recovery of secondary aluminium alloy ingot from aircraft and other scrap as well as for the production of large quantities of granulated aluminium powder for explosives. The factory was subsequently acquired by British Aluminium for commercial purposes.

It is scarcely surprising, therefore, that residents of Thelwall Lane listed in the 1935 Directory of Warrington should have included blacksmiths, moulders, tanners, furnace men, engineers, metal polishers, forge hands, boiler men, range fitters and labourers, as well as canal workers and boatmen. What is a little surprising perhaps, is to find that the 1935 residents also

146

included one miner.

## WILLIS STREET

Willis Street is possibly more widely known to residents of the Warrington area nowadays because it is situated in close proximity to the starting point of thousands of Ministry of Transport driving tests. As such Willis Street became a favourite practice ground for learner drivers and because it runs parallel to Manchester Road from Fairfield Street to Fothergill Street, it is also used as an alternative to the A57 whenever road works close this part of Manchester Road.

It was not until 1897 that Willis Street first appeared in a local Burgess List and this was three years after Fairfield School had been opened. This school was one of a large number of school and mission churches opened -during the long period during which the Rev Frederic W. Willis was Rector of Warrington and his name is undoubtedly perpetuated in the Street.

Coming to Warringtin 1888 from Wellingborough at the age of 46, the Rev F.W. Willis remained as Rector until 1920 when he was succeeded by his son, the Rev F.E. d'Anyers Willis, who remained for 13 years so that father and son were Rectors of Warrington for 45 years. As both were held in high regard by the people of Warrington, it is fitting that their names should be commemorated in a street situated in the heart of their Parish.

The list of building and other works associated with the Parish Church and erected as a result of the energy of the elder Willis is impressive: St. George's Mission 1891; Ellesmere Street School, 1892; Fairfield School 1893; St. Clement's Mission 1897; Repairs, improvement and Memorial Screens in the Parish Church, 1901-3, 1909 and 1912 apart from extensions to Missions and schools in 1905, 1909 and 1912.

When this venerable Rector retired it was said that someone once asked the Bishop of Liverpool why he had "made Willis a Canon". The prompt answer was "Because of his saintliness" and it is obvious from the local tributes paid to this man at the time of his retirement that this was an opinion held by many people in Warrington belonging to a wide variety of trades and professions as well as to different religious denominations.

The Rev Frederic Earle d'Anyers Willis was also made an Honorary Canon of Liverpool in 1925, and was no less well esteemed.

Fairfield School, which stands as a memorial to the elder Willis in Fairfield Street and Willis Street was opened in 1894. The site of the school had been given by Mr Richard Ireland Blackburne and the foundation stone was laid by Lord Cross on December 2, 1893. The school provided accommodation for 832 boys and girls and was erected to replace the Mount School which had been used for the dual purpose of relieving congestion at the National School in Church Street and also for providing a practicing school for students of the Training College.

At the opposite end of Willis Street from the School stands a branch of the Warrington Co-operative Society; this shop was opened during the first World War

Residents of Willis Street have always included wiredrawers, owing to the close proximity of Rylands Brothers Ltd., but have also included school teachers, clerks, insurance agents, joiners and three men closely connected with the Labour Movement in Warrington, namely the late Alderman D. Plinston, Councillor G. Hindle and Mr Benjamin Parkes.

## WINWICK ROAD

There has been a highway from Warrington to Winwick since the Romans conquered the North of England but the Roman road followed a different line from the present road. The Romans crossed the Mersey by way of the ford at Latchford and the old Roman Road proceeded northwards from Howley, crossing Battersby Lane, Orford Lane and Longford Bridge to the junction with Mill Lane where it continued in a northerly direction to the west of the present road.

The present line of Winwick Road and Winwick Street was determined after a bridge had been built across the Mersey about 900 years after the Romans had left England forever, and an 18th century traveller, Arthur Young, describes the state of this road in scathing terms in his "Six months' tour through the North of England" published in 1770.

He says of the road from Wigan to Warrington: "This is a paved road, and most infamously bad. Any person would imagine the boobies of the country had made it with a view to immediate destruction; for the breadth is only sufficient for one carriage; consequently it is cut at once into rutts."

This was nearly half-a-century after an Act of Parliament had authorised the construction of a turnpike road from Warrington to Wigan with toll gates for the collection of tolls for the maintenance of the road. One of these toll gates was situated at Hulme, nearly half-a-mile north of Long Lane, and although about £1,100 was collected annually at the toll gates on this road in the 1830s, very little was spent on road repair, most of the money being used to pay interest on debts accumulated by the Turnpike Trustees.

This very inefficient method of road maintenance continued throughout the 19th century until the Trust was abolished in 1877 following a campaign conducted by a local newspaper proprietor, Mr George Powlson, who was presented by the Mayor of Warrington with a purse of 100 guineas in acknowledgment of his important public service in securing the abolition of the Trust.

Part of Stained Glass Window in
All Saints Church, Thelwall, A Memorial
To Sir Peter Rylands

149

Winwick Road has now been transformed from its narrow and twisting state to a modern dual carriageway and is the longest road within the present Borough boundaries. In recent years new industrial enterprises have been attracted to Winwick Road and the Warrington Corporation has also erected a new Fire Station and Technical College in the same area.

The Warrington Corporation purchased 16 acres of land at Longford for the erection of an additional gas works in 1879 and from 1897 all local gas was manufactured at this station. The undertaking passed into the control of the North Western Gas Board in 1949 and in 1967 a new plant, stated to be the most modern gas-producing plant in Britain, became operational. This plant produces gas from oil instead of coal and was described as "The Cassius Clay of a gasworks – the greatest and even the prettiest – costing more than £10,000,000."

Two of the brand new enterprises to settle in Winwick Road are the Fiat Service Centre for the servicing of new Fiat Cars and the District Bank's Computer Centre which was opened in 1967 by Lord Bowden, principal of the University of Manchester Institute of Science and Technology. This centre deals with accounts of branches from Preston to the Potteries and in 1967 was handling the accounts of 75,000 customers.

Nearer to town, St. Ann's Church is one of the older buildings in Winwick Road. It was originally consecrated on February 27, 1869 and when the Bishop of Liverpool (the Rt Rev Stuart Blanche) visited the Parish on the Centenary Day 1969, he paid a visit to the nearby Tetley Walker Brewery which supplies the church with heating. Steam from the brewery is fed into the church to heat its low pressure water system and the Vicar considers St. Ann's to be the warmest church in the whole town.

Just as this happy conjunction of industry and a church has transformed the atmosphere of the church, so has Winwick Road itself been transformed in recent years by the conjunction of new industrial buildings and road development.


## YOUR CHURCH ST. ELPHIN

Standing on the northern bank of the River Mersey and on one side of Roman Road which passed from north to south, the Parish Church of St. Elphin is dedicated to a Saint whose name implies that this church most probably bears the oldest dedication in Lancashire.

It is a reasonable assumption that a church has stood on the same site as the present Parish Church from the seventh century onwards and when the name of Saint Elfin was recorded at Warrington in the Domesday Survey in 1086 there were only nine other churches recorded as existing in the area between the Ribble and the Mersey.

150

Rising to a height of 281 feet above the ground, the spire of the present church can be seen from most parts of the ancient and extensive parish which formerly stretched along the Mersey from Burtonwood to Hollinfare, but which now only covers an area from Orford to Bridge Foot and from the church itself to Market Gate.

Excluding the spires of the Cathedral Churches at Salisbury, Coventry and Norwich, which vary from 404 to 313 feet in height, Warrington has the third highest parish church apire – Louth being 300 feet and St. Mary, Redcliffe, Bristol, 292 feet in height. Crowned with a weathercock gilded with golden sovereigns, the spire was erected about 1860 after Rector William Quekett had successfully appealed for funds to restore the Church and devised a slogan: "a guinea for a golden cock" to provide for the weathercock.

Today the Church stands in a pleasantly green oasis in the midst of an industrial area and both the green area of the Churchyard and the exterior fabric of the Church give an instant impression of the intense love and care that has been bestowed upon this ancient church in recent years by the present rector, the Rev Canon J. C. Longbottom.

The same love and devotion are apparent when the interior of the church is seen.

The former Boteler Chapel has been transformed by beautiful oak panelling into a Regimental Chapel dedicated to the South Lancashire Regiment while the ancient tomb of Sir John Boteler and his wife, a table inscribed with the name of Sir Thomas Boteler, founder of the Grammar School, and an effigy of the wife of the founder of the chapel, Alicia Boteler, all remain within this ancient church.

It was stated in 1956 that £10,000 had been spent on the Regimental Chapel while more recently, the Warrington Parish Church branch of the Mothers' Union have subscribed about £2,000 to provide a new chapel dedicated to St. Anne. This chapel was originally built by Thomas Massey and later passed to the Wilson Patten family. The recent restoration has provided further examples of pleasing woodwork and when the new chapel was rededicated by the Bishop of Liverpool (Dr Clifford Martin) in 1963 he said the chapel was now "a thing of beauty".

Even a casual inspection of the memorial plaques and tablets on the interior walls of the Parish Church shows that a considerable slice of Warrington's long history is preserved in this venerable building. There are memorials of doctors, schoolmaster, industrialists, civic dignitaries and clergymen besides a museum of relics from some of the churches that have stood on this same site.

One memorial tablet records that: "The Bells of this Church were recast and a New Clock given by Rylands Brothers Limited In memory of William Peter Rylands . . . Born 23rd October 1868, Died 22nd October 1948." The new bells and clock were dedicated in 1950 when the bells were heard at a service which was broadcast by the BBC.

## ST. OSWALD'S WINWICK

Winwick Church is dedicated to Saint Oswald, the Christian King of Northumbria who was slain in battle against the heathen King Penda of Mercia in the year AD 642 at Maserfeld. Although it is attractive to many to suppose that this battle took place at Winwick, Maserfeld is generally located at Oswestry and the Church cannot be older than the date of Oswald's death.

The fragments of a sculptured Anglo-Saxon cross were discovered in the churchyard in 1843, and this important piece of archaeological evidence of early Christian settlement in Lancashire is now preserved in the Church. The dismemberment of St. Oswald is possibly the subject of the sculpture and the fragment of this cross – which measures 4 ft. 11 in. and which represents the cross arms only – shows that the cross was very large, one writer having stated that he knew of only one larger in England.

When St. Oswald's Church was recorded in the Domesday Survey by the Normans it had the same endowment as St. Mary's of Whalley. These two churches were then the most highly endowed in Lancashire, each having a glebe assessed at about 240 arable acres and each took the fines for all crimes and offences committed within their limits while the land was excempt from the Danegeld.

Because the present church was built from a local sandstone, considerable repair work has obscured much of the early history of the building although the spire and tower and southern arcade date from about 1358. The chancel was entirely rebuilt in the mid-19th century in 14th century style by the architect A.W.N. Pugin who is well known for his work on the House of Commons and especially the Clock Tower of "Big Ben".

A carving of a pig on the west front of the Church preserves an ancient legend that the church was originally intended to have occupied another site and that it was removed stone by stone to the place where it now stands. According to this legend the stones were carried by the pig from one place to the other.

A more rational explanation of the Winwick Pig, however, is that it was the stone mason's method of placing the initials of St. Oswald's, Winwick, or SOW, on the church.

That the external outline of Winwick Church has remained for many centuries very much as it appears today is shown from a drawing on an estate plan dated about 1580. And situated as it is on an elevated site about 120 feet above sea level, the church has been a landmark for centuries as well as the focal point for many historic events.

During the early stages of the Civil War in Lancashire, for example, a

WYCLIFFE CONGREGATIONAL CHURCH, WARRINGTON.

Wycliffe Congregational Church

153

contemporary writer has recorded that while people were taking refuge in the steeple of Winwick Church "God sent a deadly messenger out of a fowling piece to one of them" and in 1854 when a grave was being dug near to the steeple, confirmation of this Civil War event was found by the discovery of a skeleton with an iron bullet embedded in the thigh bone.

Seven Rectors of Winwick have been members of the Stanely family and others have been related to the family through marriage. James Stanley, Rector in 1493 became Bishop of Ely and was also Warden of the Collegiate Church at Manchester where he is buried.

Early in the 19th century Winwick Parish covered 26,502 acres and the value of the benefice in 1835 was stated to be £7,000 a year of which £3,000 came from tithes. It was due to the Rev J.J. Hornby, Rector of Winwick from 1812 to 1855, however, that two Acts of Parliament were passed in 1841 and 1845 which resulted in the division of this great Parish into eight separate Parishes and Chapelries.

## ST. WILFRID'S GRAPPENHALL

Grappenhall Parish Church, which is dedicated to St. Wilfrid, Bishop of the Mercians at Lichfield at the end of the seventh century, is situated in one of the most pleasing of Cheshire villages and the surrounds of this church have been compared by one writer to the churchyard in which Gray wrote his famous elegy. Certainly the beauty and antiquity of this church provide a theme worthy of the pen of any major poet.

The modern visitor to this church, having passed the stocks at the gate, may still read insciptions on tombstones placed in the churchyard in the early 17th century and reflect, as Roger Lowe from Ashton-in-Makerfield reflected in April, 1664: "We went to Gropenall church . . . and I went into church yard to look at graves, as it is my common custome, and there stayed awhile admiringe the common frailtie of mankind: how silently now they were lyeing in dust."

An ancient font, generally taken to be of Norman origin, that was discovered buried beneath the floor of the nave in 1873, and which is now mounted on a new pedestal and is now in regular use, is thought by some to bear an indication of a Saxon origin, and if this is true it provides evidence of a church in Grappenhall before the Norman Conquest, although no such church is mentioned in the Domesday Survey. It is known, however, that this great Survey did not mention every church existing at the time of its compilation.

The earliest church known to have been erected on this ancient site, was completed by the Normans about the year 1120 and, still intact within the south aisle of the present church, a portion of the corbel table (or projecting ledge) ornamented with five small faces was formerly a part of the original south outside wall of the Norman Church. On the middle part of this original south wall a chapel was added by Sir William Boydell in 1334 and this chapel was made to form part of a new south aisle during alterations to the church that were completed in 1539. During these alterations the original south wall was pierced and divided into arches which left the top portion of this wall inside the church while the addition of a new exterior wall formed the south aisle. The date 1539 has been carved on one of the piers now supporting the ancient Norman corbet table. A porch was added in 1641 when the initials of a churchwarden, John Rycroft, were carved in close proximity.

Further alterations and restoration work took place in 1850 and 1873 and now, one century later, restoration of the exterior fabric is proceeding and the cost, together with other restorations of the last few years, will amount to more than £5,000.

The present south wall contains a number of beautiful stained glass windows one of which is of great antiquity. This window was placed in its present position in 1850 although the glass dates from 1334 and depicts a number of easily recognisable Saints – Peter, Philip, Bartholomew as well as Mary Magdalene and the central figure of John the Baptist. The glass window was re-leaded in 1964, and another piece of medieval glass, formerly set in the door leading to the organ chamber, is now mounted on the interior base of the tower with an electric light behind to enable the visitor to examine this beautiful example of medieval art.

At the eastern end of the south aisle there is now a chapel, dedicated in 1957 by the Archdeacon of Chester to the memory of Leonard Appleton and the Appleton family.

Before the installation of an organ, music in Grappenhall Church had been provided by an orchestra consisting of bassoon, bass viola and clarionet and the present organ was moved into the position of the original musicians' gallery north of the choir stalls about 1855 when the first organ was rebuilt by Kirtland and Jardine.

An ancient parish chest having three locks, one for the priest and one for each of two churchwardens, is preserved in the north aisle. It is hewn from an oak tree and is of Norman origin.

The effigy of another member of the Boydell family, the grandfather of the founder of the Boydell chapel, reposes cross-legged in the sanctuary and other medieval remains preserved in the church include a Norman stoup.

It is suggested that the figure of a cat, carved on the outside wall of the tower, may have been placed there first as a pun in masonry to the "Catterich" (now Cartridge) family of Grappenhall but it is also reasonable to suppose that, as the father of Lewis Carroll was the rector of Daresbury and a frequent visitor to Grappenhall Church, this cat was also the origin of Lewis Carroll's famous Cheshire Cat. Certainly the ancient cat on Grappenhall Church would be well known to the author of "Alice in Wonderland".

The long list of known Rectors of Grappenhall begins with Robert de Gropenhall who officiated in 1189 and ends with John William Roberts, whose care and devotion to this church is apparent to any visitor.


## CAIRO STREET CHAPEL

Two 18th century churches stand in close proximity to each other in the centre of Warrington and the entrance to both of them was originally from Sankey Street. They were originally erected within the first decade of the 18th century and replaced about 50 years later, but in both the question of original building as well as of subsequent replacement, Cairo Street Chapel preceded its neighbour, Holy Trinity Church by a few years.

Cairo Street Chapel, therefore, is the second oldest surviving place of worship in Warrington apart from the Parish Church. It is also an interesting fact that the man responsible for founding the community that ultimately built the first Cairo Street Chapel in 1703 was the Presbyterian Rector of Warrington, Robert Yates. Having been deprived of his living in 1662, Yates ultimately obtained a licence for public worship in the Court House which stood in Market Place.

After Yates's death in 1678 the charge of this new congregation passed to Peter Aspinwall and then, from 1696 to 1746, to Dr Charles Owen, and in a deed dated 1703, between Dr Charles Owen and the Earl of Warrington, the land was secured on which the original Cairo Street Chapel stood.

All that is known of this early chapel is that it was "late erected" in 1703 and that it stood behind a dwelling house in Sankey Street and was approached from that street by a passage "three yard broad". In 1745 this chapel was taken down and the present chapel erected and apart from internal alterations, repairs and decorations this mid-18th century chapel still remains. It is light and spacious but hardly austere as pleasing windows of coloured glass, one stained glass memorial window, and a fair number of memorial plaques give character and interest to this ancient home of non-conformity.

An approach to the main entrance of the chapel through a graveyard and memorial garden gives an immediate impression of the strong ties that linked this chapel to the Warrington Academy. It is said that the southern boundary of the graveyard is denoted by railings that formerly belonged to the Academy although the plate describing these railings was recently stolen, an act of vandalism that unfortunately is causing the doors of many ancient chapels and churches to be locked except at times when services are being held.

Inside the chapel, apart from the memorial plaque to the elder John Aikin

Bethel Baptist Church, Latchford

Christ Church, Padgate

157

who was one of the original tutors and later a Rector of the Warrington Academy, are two 18th century memorials to young men who died in Warrington after coming as students to the Academy namely: Edward Garlick of Bristol who died in 1758 aged 15, and John Galway of Portaferry who died in 1777 aged 17 and who was the subject of an impressive funeral address by William Enfield.

A pleasing Wedgwood medallion depicting Joseph Priestly also hangs inside the chapel near to a memorial to Frederick—Monks, the Warrington industrialist who donated the Town Hall Gates to his native town and who received much of his early inspiration from a former minister of Cairo Street Chapel, the Rev Philip Pearsall Carpenter. A clock presented to Frederick Monks in 1874 by the workers of the Whitecross Wire Co., Ltd., is preserved in the vestry of the chapel.

Many memorials to those associated with this Chapel — Holbrook Gaskell and other members of the Gaskell family, members of the Woodcock family as well as the Broadbent family are to be seen both inside the Chapel as well as in the graveyard.

A copy of the original Court House Licence hangs in the vestry and the philosophy of the present congregation was expressed by a recent minister, the Rev Eric Wild, who wrote: "We do not question what a man believes to be his ultimate truth. Our mode of service follows the Christian pattern, but we affirm the great Unitarian principle that the revelation of God cannot be confined to one place or time in human history. In a world of conflict we seek, not uniformity, but a unifying principle which we believe lies not in dogma but in the common humanity of all God's children."


## HOLY TRINITY

By an Order in Council published in the London Gazette dated February 8, 1870, Holy Trinity became a separate parish embracing a section of the centre of Warrington from Bridge Street as far west as Sankey Brook.

While this change freed the minister from many harassing restrictions, it also meant this beautiful church depended for its support upon residents of the town centre and during the past century much residential property within this parish has been converted to commerical and professional use so that the number of parishioners has declined considerably. Because of its central position the church is used, however, for quiet meditation by many Warringtonians who do not reside in the parish and, as an adornment to the hub of Warrington, it is clearly desirable that support for the upkeep of this graceful example of 18th century architecture should be forthcoming from all who derive pleasure and satisfaction from its existence.

Trinity Chapel was originally founded and endowed by Peter Legh of

Lyme in 1709 to provide for the needs of a population living at too great a distance from the Parish Church. Until a separate parish was created in 1870 the church was very much under the control of the Rector of Warrington in whose parish the new chapel was situated but the needs of the town centre were such that a much bigger church became necessary within 50 years of the original foundation. On July 22, 1758, the Bishop of Chester signed his faculty for taking down the original chapel in order to allow a new church to be built in its stead. Within a year, £2,647 10s. had been collected for the new church and £2,571 12s. 2d. was spent on this new building which was consecrated by the Bishop on July 20, 1760. It is generally believed the architect responsible for this building was James Gibbs who had also designed Bank Hall (now the Town Hall). The Church has survived since then with little change and is thus the oldest complete Anglican church in Warrington. In 1967, the outside stonework of the church was cleaned at a cost of £2,500 but interior re-decoration is now necessary.

A public footpath passes through the base of the tower which is made of stone and which belongs to the Church but the structure on top of the tower housing the Town Clock belongs to the town. As this clock strikes the hours of the day, it does so on a bell which originally hung in the Court House in the Market Place. This bell was given to Warrington by Colonel John Booth as a curfew bell in 1647 and a Latin inscription on the bell records this fact.

In front of the Crucifix window at the east end of the church (a window erected as memorial to the Rev R.A. Mould, a former incumbent) is the altar which is an 18th century table having elaborately carved legs and a marble top and which was probably used in the original chapel. Above the altar is an oil painting by the Warrington artist James Cranke. This painting, dated 1776, is a copy of a picture in the Louvre by Andrea del Sarto and depicts the Holy Family. It was presented to the Church in 1776 by James Hesketh. Side panels were added as part of a War Memorial erected in 1920 and these side panels were the work of a Liverpool artist, Mr E.Carter Preston.

A candelabra hanging in front of the sanctuary was presented to the Church in 1801 and formerly hung in the House of Commons.

The walls of the church are fairly free of memorial plaques that tend to act as a distraction in so many old churches but former incumbents of the Church are commemorated in stained glass windows while the baptistry was adorned in memory of the Rev E.Garvin and his sister, Margaret Garvin, who formerly resided within the parish at 78, Sankey Street in a house which is now the Health Office.

A Friday afternoon service for shoppers has made Holy Trinity Church a quiet haven for many Warringtonians and the doors of this Church, unlike those of many other town churches, seem to be kept open at all times to welcome all who wish to meditate.

159

## ST. JOHN'S WILDERSPOOL

Presbyterianism can claim many strong ties with the town of Warrington from the Civil War to the present day. It was a treaty signed by Charles I in 1647, which provided the Scots would give support to the English monarch on the understanding that Presbyterianism should be the official religion in England for at least three years, that brought the ill-fated Scottish army into England in 1648 under the command of the Duke of Hamilton. This was the army that was finally defeated at Winwick and Warrington Bridge and led to the presence in Warrington of Oliver Cromwell himself.

It was Charles II who granted a licence for worship by those who were Presbyterians at the Court House in Warrington in 1672 and although it is after this point in ecclesiastical history that the Victoria County History of Lancashire refers to "the maze of later Dissenting and Free Church History", the present Presbyterian Church of England situated on Wilderspool Causeway can claim direct descent from those Presbyterians who worshipped in the Court House in 1672.

The origin of a local Presbyterian congregation known as St. John's began in 1806 when Episcopalians from St. James's Church, Presbyterians from Cairo Street Chapel and a few from Stepney Chapel joined forces and hired a public room for worship. Two years later this congregation built and opened St. John's Chapel in Winwick Street with the Rev Alex Hay, who had been educated at the Countess of Huntingdons College at Trevecca, as their pastor.

This congregation were received into the Presbyterian Church of England on March 1, 1854, and remained in Winwick Street until this Chapel was sold in 1908. The building of a new church on Wilderspool Causeway began in 1909 and it was dedicated on May 26, 1910, so that this church is now exactly 60 years old. This church is strangely now the nextdoor neighbour of St. James', Wilderspool Causeway, from which a large part of the earlier Presbyterian Congregation had come in 1806. Built at a total cost of only £1,800, of which about £800 came from the proceeds of the sale of the Winwick Street church, the church on the Causeway has recently been redecorated and refurnished in connection with the Diamond Jubilee of its opening and many of those formerly connected with the Church will be re-united during these celebrations. Few churches are now as inviting as this attractively and brightly decorated home of Presbyterianism and a very active social life surrounds the church which has a strong alliance with the Scottish community in the town.

An old clock from the Winwick Street church is preserved at the entrance and a plaque records the fact that the church was opened on May 26, 1910, by Mrs William Reid and dedicated by the Rev W.M. MacPhail, General Secretary of the Presbyterian Church of England. As at Cairo Street Chapel, a

160

St. John's Walton

copy of the old court house licence is preserved in the vestry and also in the vestry is a painting of the interior of the Winwick Street church.

A pipe organ was purchased in 1920 and new church halls and Sunday School next to the Church were opened on October 26, 1929. The cost of these new buildings was about £3,000. Unfortunately, the organ was completely ruined as a result of a fire in 1946, but was replaced by the gift of an organ from Chalmer's Church, Ardwick.

This Church has been called the "live little church on the Causeway" and this description appears to the writer to be an accurate description of the present church and congregation.


## ST. ALBANS

Built in 1823, St. Alban's, Bewsey Street, was the first Roman Catholic Church built in Warrington after the Reformation. Secret services had been held in various parts of Warrington until in 1776 the Rev Bernard Anselm Bradshaw, O.S.B., was sent from Lamspringe, in Germany, to Warrington, as a resident priest, and in 1778 he opened an old chapel in Bewsey Street, later known as the "League Hall". This chapel continued to be used until St. Alban's was built through the energy of Dr Alban Molyneux, O.S.B., who had come to Warrington in 1816.

It is said that Dr Molyneux saw that every brick in the building was first put into water and that he spent his mornings in mixing and carrying mortar to the bricklayers.

A bronze handle, bearing the form of the "Lamb", which was brought from Lamspringe in 1776, is now fixed to the sacristy door in St. Alban's, and Dr Molyneux, was responsible for bringing from Lampspringe a 16th century document relating to an early episode of Warrington's history. The document is dated June 30, 1524, and relates to the repayment of a debt owing by Thomas Boteler of Bewsey to Henry VIII. The document was taken after the Reformation by English Benedictines to their house at Lamspringe and then brought back to Warrington by Dr Molyneux in the 19th century and donated to the Warrington Municipal Library, where it is now preserved.

Although St Alban's was built in 1823, it was not consecrated until 1951, an interval of 128 years, because the land upon which the church stands did not belong to the church until then. In preparation for this important event the church was renovated and redecorated at a cost of £11,000.

Possibly the most striking feature of this simple, yet elegant church, is the altar, which was built in 1893 from designs by Peter Paul Pugin. In this year the original pews were also removed and replaced by pitch-pine seats and kneelers and the sanctuary was enlarged. The altar then erected has steps of marble with columns of Caen stone and partly polished granite. The altar stone is one slab of polished marble, 10 feet 6 inches long by two feet wide and is supported on marble pillars. A canopy above the tabernacle is of alabaster and polished marble columns.

New windows of stained glass replaced earlier plain glass windows in 1900, and in 1909 an old gallery that extended far into the body of the church was removed and replaced by a smaller gallery for choir and organ only. At the same time the old porch was removed and a large outside porch erected.

Warrington's first war memorial to the memory of those who fell in the First World War of 1914-18 was erected in front of St. Alban's Church and unveiled by the Rev Lane Fox in June, 1919.

Until recent years an ancient vestment was used during the celebration of Mass each year on the Feast Day of St. Alban (June 22). This vestment is one of two discovered in 1825, when repairs were being executed in the Parish Church and a stairway was discovered leading to a crypt.

The vestments were offered by the Rector of Warrington to Dr Molyneux, the Rector of St. Alban's, and after renovation have been preserved in St. Alban's since then. The vestment that was used annually until recent times is coloured red, but the other, which is green, has not been used for many years.

A marble plaque in the church near to the sacristy door commemorates the priest responsible for the building of St. Alban's — the Rev John Alban Molyneux and records that he died October 13, 1860, aged 78.

## FRIENDS MEETING HOUSE

Probably fewer Warringtonians are aware of the existence of the secluded Meeting House, situated between Buttermarket Street and Academy Street, than of any other place of worship in the centre of Warrington. Yet few places of worship in Warrington have been used for a greater length of time and none stand in a situation of such dignity, quietness and peace as befits the neat and well tended garden of rest surrounding this Meeting House of the Warrington Quakers.

The main entrance is through a wrought iron gateway situated in Buttermarket Street and the Meeting House is elevated on a site above the level of this street and surrounded by trees and lawns in which a few stone memorial tablets record details of Friends who once used this place for worship.

A Meeting House was first erected on this site, with the approval of Friends in Penketh during the year 1725. Little is known of this early Meeting House except that it was not larger than 12 yards long, eight yards wide and of a reasonable height. Interments in the Friends' Burial Ground

Workingmen's Mission

Bethesda Chapel, Stockton Heath

surrounding this Meeting House appear to have commenced in the year 1725.

Almost exactly one century later the early Meeting House stood in need of repair and alteration and it was untimately decided to erect a new building in place in 1829 and the building was completed in May 1830 at a cost of about £800.

Memorial tablets in the Garden of Rest include records of members of the Crosfield and Fell families who were associated as grocers in Warrington at the beginning of the nineteenth century. One tablet records the death on February 16th, 1844 of Joseph Crosfield, the founder of Joseph Crosfield and Sons Ltd. Two of Joseph's children, Maria, aged fifteen and Joseph, aged thirteen, died in the same year as their father and the three memorial tablets rest side by side in this old burial ground.

The present Meeting House is pleasingly decorated but is entirely devoid of anything likely to distract the attention of those who gather there for religious meetings.

Meetings in such simple surroundings have been held since George Fox first set the pattern in the middle of the 17th century. Fox himself paid visits to Sankey in 1667 and 1669 and his Journal contains a reference to a large meeting at the house of William Barnes in 1669. In 1684 John Barnes and his wife, John Gibson and others stood at the sessions because they had "riotously, routously and unlawfully at Warrington the twentie-fifth day of May last . . . come together Congregate and assemble under Coulor and pretence of exercise of Religion in other manner than according to the liturgie and practice of the Church of England".

Riot and rout are the last things one would associate with a meeting of this dignified body and the orderliness and well-managed affairs of this religious body are proclaimed in Warrington by the quiet beauty of this venerable Meeting House and its surrounding garden.


## ST. JAMES'S

Although St. James's Church, Latchford, has stood for more than 140 years on its present site on Wilderspool Causeway, the first St. James's Church stood on what is now known at Knutsford Road from 1777 to 1829. Stranger than the re-siting of the church itself has been the changes in the boundaries of the parish assigned to the church.

Originally St. James's was built to serve a populous area of Grappenhall Parish which extended in the 18th century to Warrington Bridge. After a new site had been chosen for re-building on Wilderspool Causeway on land presented by Thomas Lyon in 1829, the church was still a part of the extensive Parish of Grappenhall. The growth of the population of Latchford and the fact that part of Latchford had become part of the Borough of

Warrington from 1847 finally resulted in a legal parish being assigned to St. James's Church from July 1866 although the patronage still belongs to the Rector of Grappenhall.

Then soon after the Manchester Ship Canal had been constructed and the course of the River Mersey had been altered in consequence, St. James's found that it was standing within the boundaries of a Lancashire County Borough and that part of its River Mersey boundary had become a mere line on the map where the river used to flow. This situation has led in recent years to demands that the river boundary between the Diocese of Liverpool and the Diocese of Chester should be made realistic at this point.

The church, erected in 1829, is a substantial structure of stone built by a Warrington builder, Thomas Haddock, to the designs of a Liverpool architect, Samuel Rowland. Commencing with the laying of the foundation stone on March 19, 1829, the Church was consecrated on December 22, the same year before the tower and paintwork had been completed and the church was closed immediately after the consecration until February 1830.

Originally it was equipped with a gallery but this was removed in 1896 after the Vicar, the Rev F. Slater, had explained in his Parish Magazine that the bequest of Charles Middleton to erect a clock and a stained glass window in memory of his parents could not be fulfilled until the whole length of a window were to be exposed by the removal of the galleries. "Perhaps Mr Middleton's gift and especially the difficulty about the window" wrote the Vicar "will help us to bestir ourselves and see if we cannot get rid of some of the very ugly features of the church, which in spite of its ugliness we love so well."

At the same time an appeal was being made for money to pay for a series of paintings by Alfred O. Hemming and a series of six paintings by this artist depicted "The Nativity", "The Transfiguration" and other aspects of the life of Christ now adorn the walls of the church.

Once the galleries had been removed, the Middleton Memorial Window depicting The Good Shepherd was erected and a more recent stained glass window has been erected as a memorial to William Henry Stansfield who was Headmaster of St. James's School for 40 years and who died April 22, 1933.

It is perhaps because there is not too much stained glass in the windows that the interior of this church is light and attractive and from whatever aspect the interior is viewed the aspect is pleasing.

The oak panelling of the sanctuary is particularly attractive. That on the north side was completed last year at a cost of £1,500 and on the south side the Lady Chapel has been extended so that it now provides 60 seats. This work is still proceeding to conform with current liturgical practice and a new altar table has already been purchased and the transformation effected is indicative of the energy and good taste displayed by the present Vicar, the Rev G.A. Pare.

166

Shields of arms erected on the inside walls of the tower add colour and were designed and executed by students of the College of Art in 1955. These shields represent St. James, Chester and the Provinces of Canterbury and York.

The burial ground was closed in July, 1854, but some interments have taken place since then including that of a former minister, the Rev James Wright who was the incumbent of the church from 1834-1867. This burial ground has been made attractive since it was taken over by the Parks Department in 1958 under the Open Spaces Act of 1906 and as a memorial to Fred Bailey the tower clock faces were illuminated and first switched on by his widow on November 15, 1964.

In spite of the unpreposing exterior of this church it is obviously well loved by those who worship there and the interior affords a complete contrast to the stark and unimaginative exterior architecture.


## ST. PAUL'S

On a map of Warrington dated 1826 in the midst of the open fields on either side of Bewsey Road is an outline of a building marked "intended scite (sic) of new church". This site was provided by Colonel Wilson-Patten and consisted of one acre on which a church was to be built.

At this time Warrington, like towns in many other industrial areas, was growing rapidly and a Church Building Commission had been appointed in 1818 to provide areas having fast-growing populations with new churches. Throughout England more than 200 new churches were erected between 1818 and 1833 from funds provided by this new body and these churches became known as Commissioners' Churches because most of them were built for less than £10,000 resulting, according to one modern writer, "in a medley of drab uninspired buildings" and the same writer refers to this period as "the dreariest of all periods of church building".

Two churches were erected in Warrington in this period, St. James's and St. Paul's, and the latter was built in the year 1830 from Commission funds at a cost of only £4,239 and consecrated on October 31, 1831. It was built from Hill Cliffe red stone to the designs of Edward Blore but this stone has proved to be so inferior as a building material that extensive and costly repairs were necessary before the church was 70 years old. Blore was a leading exponent of Gothic architecture in the early 19th century and was responsible for the completion of Buckingham Palace after Nash had been dismissed.

Both churches were built with galleries in order to accommodate as many people as possible, but while the galleries have been removed in St. James's so that the interior aspect of the church has been improved tremendously, those in St. Paul's still remain and the whole internal aspect of

this church is especially sad at present as dry rot is in process of being removed by a costly building operation.

It was the recent discovery of dry rot in the church which has temporarily halted a scheme for improving both the external and internal appearance of the church so that after the exterior had been partially cleaned the funds raised for these improvements had to be diverted to eradicating the rot. Already £18,000 has been spent on these recent improvements and the outside appearance of this church is now pleasantly attractive when viewed from the extensive and exceptionally well maintained burial ground on the south side of the church.

Alterations to the design of the church took place first with an addition to the vestry in 1894 and later by a new clergy vestry in 1906 when foundation stones were laid respectively by Mrs John Chorley and Mrs Jane Smethurst.

More recently, in November, 1934, a memorial chapel was installed under the gallery in the northeast corner of the church to commemorate Mrs Ada Emily Downham, wife of the Vicar (Rev E. Downham). Earlier adornments to the interior of the church have included a pulpit given by the Rev W.Bracecamp and family after World War I; an oak choir screen, erected as a war memorial; and a white Sicilian marble font, the gift of the GFS Branch and placed in the northwest corner of the church in 1920, also a war memorial.

There is hardly any stained glass in this church but one window at the East end was erected in November, 1860, as a memorial to Anne, the wife of William Beamont. Before the first Mayor of Warrington took up residence at Orford Hall, he had lived in Bewsey Street and had, therefore, lived within the Parish of St. Paul's which was created a separate parish on January 25, 1841. Since then the parish boundaries have been reduced as a result of·the creation of separate parishes of Holy Trinity, St. Ann, St. Peter and St. Barnabas.

Probably the most attractive feature of this church is the large burial ground surrounding the church which was only closed in 1963. This attractively planted open space is beautifully maintained and should be an inspiration and example to others responsible for burial grounds surrounding other local churches.


## DARESBURY

Henry, who was second Prior of Norton from 1159 until 1190, first caused a church to be built in Daresbury which was then an outlying part of the Parish of Runcorn. This early church evidently consisted of a wooden frame filled in with plaster and painted white because it became known as the "White Church of Cheshire".

Little else is known of this church, however, except that it was succeeded by a stone structure at a date unknown. Some rebuilting of this stone church took place in 1773 and finally in the year 1870 the whole of this church, except the tower, was taken down to be rebuilt. Fortunately in 1873, a man who must have known the old church well, William Beamont, published a description of this church in his "History of the Castle of Halton . . . Abbey of Norton . . . and Daresbury Church," while notes taken at Daresbury Church in 1572 and 1670 and describing coats of arms in the Church are preserved in a British Museum manuscript.

The rebuilding took place in 1871-2 and the sixteenth century tower (the oldest part of the existing church) was retained and restored. A date carved on this tower was almost certainly altered by stonemasons in the 17th century so that 1550 was changed to 1110. Within the church a beautifully carved Jacobean pulpit, possibly the most elaborate of its kind in Cheshire, is still in use, and the highly successful restoration which took place in 1871-72 together with the many ancient monuments and tombstones both inside and surrounding the church now give this ancient foundation an air of venerable antiquity highly suited to the delightful village in which it is situated.

The old bells of the church were re-tuned and two new ones were added in 1914 when the clock was also cleaned and equipped with Westminster chimes so that the sound of melodies bells in Daresbury adds further charm on whatever day a visit is paid to this church which proudly proclaims on its notice board that it is "The Lewis Carroll Church".

A window in memory of Lewis Carroll was dedicated by the Bishop of Warrington (Rt Rev Dr H. Gresford Jones) in 1935 and this window is one of a large number of stained glass memorial windows installed during the past century. These windows and many other memorial tablets in the church commemorate local families including:— Greenall, Whitley, Chadwick, Byrom, Stubs, Moore, Hatton and others. Vicars of Daresbury are also commemorated including a plaque in memory of Henry Taprell Clark, Vicar 1896-1901, which states that the sanctuary floor was laid in marble in memory of the man.

Lewis Carroll, of course, was born in Daresbury on January 27th, 1832 while his father, the Rev Charles Dodson, was the Vicar of Daresbury. The association of the author of "Alice in Wonderland" with Daresbury attracts many visitors from all parts of the country — and indeed the world — to this comparatively unspoilt Cheshire village. Certainly the window, which is situated in the chapel — formerly the Chadwick and later the Greenall chapel — is worthy of its subject. It depicts the Nativity and the Adoration of the Shepherds and in one panel Lewis Carroll himself is to be seen in company with "Alice". Other figures from "Wonderland" are also represented as well as the arms of Rugby School and Christ Church College. The window was designed by Mr Geoffrey Webb and a book stands nearby recording the names of all those who subscribed to the cost of the window.

In the ringers' chamber in the belfry is painted a rhyme in which the initial letters of each line form the word Daresbury as follows: —

" **D**are not to come into this sacred Place
**A**ll you good Ringers, But in Awfull grace
**R**ing not with Hatt nor Spurs nor Insolence
**E**ach one that does, for every such offence
**S**hall forfeit Hatt or Spurs or Twelve Pence
**B**ut who disturbs a peal, the same offender
**U**nto the Box his Sixpence shall down tender
**R**ules such no doubt in every church are Used
**Y**our and your Bells that may not be Abused . . .

Peter Lowton
John Okell. Wardens, 1730."

An old parish account book shows that the tower contained a peal of four bells in 1684 and the present bells are not the least attraction of this pleasing and dignified church.

## ST. MARY'S BUTTERMARKET

Sir Nikolaus Pevsner, in his "Buildings of England: South Lancashire" refers to "St. Mary' s (RC), Buttermarket by Pugin and Pugin, 1877" as "one of their best works".

The design for the Church in the early decorated style was the work of E.W. Pugin, the son of Augustus Welby Pugin, but owing to the death of the architect in 1875 the work was finished by Messrs C. and P. Pugin. The foundation stone was laid in May 1875 and the church was opened on August 30, 1877. When first opened it lacked the tower which was added in 1906 and most of the interior embellisment was also added after the opening.

St. Mary's was erected on the site of an old cotton factory and this graceful building has stood for nearly a century since then surrounded by factories in the heart of an industrial town. The site of Allen's Cotton Factory was purchased by Father A. Bury, O.S.B. in 1871 from Mr Holbrook Gaskell and first a school was constructed on this site, partly from materials saved from the ruins of the factory.

Various. legacies and contributions, especially the handsome benefaction of Mr John Ashton, and the hard work of two incumbents of St. Albans (Father P. Hall, O.S.B. and Father A. Bury, O.S.B.) made the building of the church possible. In 1877 Father Bury was also able to purchase the Old Dispensary to add to the building surrounding the church, with the result that more than £24,000 was expended upon the church and other buildings so that a school, presbytery and church were created on the Buttermarket site.

Holy Trinity, Warrington
during widening of Bridge Street, 1907

Father Austin Bury became the first incumbent of St. Mary's in September 1877 and a year later was made Provincial of the Northern District of the English Benedictine Congregation and a Titular Abbot. He remained at St. Mary's until 1882 and both he and his successor, Father Wilfred Sumner O.S.B. were responsible for the internal embellishment of the church.

Marble altar rails were erected in March 1882, and in 1884 the pulpit designed by Pugin Bros. was made in marble and alabaster by Messrs Williams and Clay of Warrington. Father Sumner was responsible for the erection of the manificent reredos, the statuary, the choir stalls and screens, the two side chapels, the organ and the Stations of the Cross.

The whole of this internal beautification was executed so as to achieve a very satisfying unity, with the result that the various sculptures and other ornamentations all mould themselves into the design of the church. The reredos in Caen stone reaches to a rose window in stained glass while the stalls on either side of the sanctuary are in carved oak behind which are carved stone screens dividing the sanctuary from the side chapels.

Both of these chapels conform to the general original concept of the internal embellishment, except that some recent additions tend to distract the eye from the inherent interest of the original embellishment. It also seems a great pity that the clean lines of the beautiful columns of this church should have been partially obscured in one or two instances by modern additions (including loudspeakers) which do not seem to the writer to accord with an already satisfying example of architectural achievement.

In the nave of the church carved heads and shields are to be seen above the arches. The shields represent the Twelve Apostles and the carved heads represent Saints Gregory, Winefrid, Cuthbert, Mildred, Wilfred, Augustine of Canterbury, Hilda, Thomas of Canterbury, Walburga and Bede. Two statues appropriate to a Benedictine church are situated in the columns that carry the chancel archway and represent St. Benedict, Patriarch of Western Monasticism and his sister, St. Scholastica, the foundress of the Benedictine nuns.

A window was placed in the Sacred Heart Chapel by Father T.A. Hind, Rector from 1915-1929, and an additional chapel at the northeast end of the church was also the work of Father Hind. This chapel is a War memorial Chapel and was created in perfect harmony with the rest of this church. Near to this chapel there has also been erected a statue of Our Lady of Lourdes by Philip Lindsey Clark who was responsible for sculpture in wood, stone and bronze in Westminster Cathedral. This statue is in stone and was erected as a memorial to the Rectors of St. Mary's from Father Bury to Father Hind. It was Blessed by the Right Rev J.E. Mathews, O.S.B. Abbot of Ampleforth on December 11th, 1932.

A writer who described this Church in 1910 said: "The Church is quite one of the architectural features of the town, and to lovers of church architecture its interior is well worth a visit." Nothing has occurred since then to render the advice given in 1910 less appropriate in 1970.


## BOLD STREET METHODIST

When Warrington became a municipal borough in 1847 no public building had been erected in a new street that had been named Bold Street only seven years earlier. There was not much longer to wait for this deficiency to be remedied, however, for with admirable foresight the Trustees of the Weslyan Methodist Chapel in Bank Street recognised that changes in the development of Warrington would move the centre of Warrington's activities from east of Market Gate to the west.

Faced with the problem of the extensive enlargement of the Bank Street Chapel, the Trustees met in February, 1849, and promptly invited an architect to report on the respective merits of enlarging the existing chapel or building another church on a new site.

The architect chosen was Mr James Simpson, of Leeds. and following his report it was quickly decided to erect a new church on a plot of land known as Bold Street Spring Gardens. Very quickly indeed the Trustees then raised enough money to secure the site and quickly went to inspect churches in various places to decide the style of building likely to be most suitable in Warrington. A chapel at Burnley was chosen as the model and James Simpson was appointed as architect.

The early Victorians did not seem to waste a great deal of time once they had made up their minds to act and within six months of the first meeting to discuss the possible enlargement of the Bank Street Chapel, the foundation stone of the new church in Bold Street was laid.

This historic occasion took place on July 9, 1849-when, after a procession from Bank Street to the new site, the foundation stone was laid by the Rev Robert Newton, of Stockport. A document placed in a cavity in the stone records the name of the architect James Simpson, and the builder, Messrs J. Gibson and Son of Latchford.

Hill Cliffe stone was used with brickwork and the late Classical design is seen to good advantage from the pleasant gardens situated on the south side of the church. The total cost of building and furnishing was £4,723 15s. 7d. and the church was opened on April 12, 1850. A modern writer on architecture, Peter Fleetwood-Hesketh describes the church as a "good brick building . . . (magnificent interior)".

Vestries were added to the Church in 1854 and two Minister's houses were built in 1856.

Special pride always seems to have been taken by the Bold Street Congregation in the quality of the music in the church and apart from such well-known musical names associated with the choir as Mr T.J. Down,

Mr Frank Hickman and Mr John N. Padmore, two successive organs were installed in the church within 60 years of the opening of the church as well as an orchestra having been used even after the first organ was installed in 1856. This first organ was replaced in 1907 by a magnificent instrument supplied by Brindley and Foster of Sheffield.

The present rostrum, which incorporates part of an old double-decker pulpit, was designed by Mr S.P. Silcock and the woodwork was executed by G. and J. Weaver of Warrington

In recent years the closing of Bewsey Road Methodist Church, together with the closing of Legh Street and Ellesmere Street Churches has led to a new congregation developing at Bold Street with plans for a new church.

These plans have been the subject of careful thought recently in view of impending changes connected with proposals for the future development of Warrington so that the present Minister, the Rev Alan P. Horner, wrote in the Newsletter in June, 1970: "Initiative regarding the site rests with us, and what we are planning is for a new set of premises more economical to run, and more useful in terms of the role of a centre of Christian worship, witness and service as we are coming to understand it.

It is expected that the capital cost of whatever scheme is finally agreed will be met by using the site for "mixed development", with office accommodation for rent or sale.


## ST. THOMAS'S STOCKTON HEATH

Since a separate ecclesiastical parish was created at Stockton Heath from the parishes of Great Budworth and Runcorn in 1838, two churches have been built to serve the new parish. Both were built in the reign of Queen Victoria and the second of these is a very pleasing example, both internally and externally, of Victorian church building.

The first church, dedicated to St. Thomas, was rerected originally as a national school but was consecreated on October 12, 1838 by the Bishop of Chester after a new school had been erected to replace the one converted into a church. The growth of population soon meant that a new church was necessary and a faculty was obtained to take down the old converted school. Then the present church, built from the designs of Mr E.G. Paley of Lancaster in the geometrical style of Gothic architecture was erected in its stead and consecreated on July 31, 1868.

Originally the present church was built without a tower which was added later and the church, which cost £13,000 now consists of a chancel, a nave of five bays, a south aisle and an embattled tower.

A particularly fine harmony of wood, stone and brickwork has been achieved and the archbraced timber roof of the nave is especially pleasing.

In 1877 the interior was decorated and a handsome reredos erected to the memory of the Rev William Hayes, Vicar from 1852 until 1875. This beautiful reredos includes Devonshire marble, agates from Frankfurt -on-Maine, onyx from Mexico, serpentine from the Lizard, alabaster from Derbyshire and marble from Torquay. As part of the decoration of the chancel the angles on the roof were painted with life-size figures of angels bearing the faces of church women of the time. The tile work on the walls of the chancel is very attractive and that on the south wall contains a threequarter-length figure of St. Thomas, painted on the tiles and burnt in.

The large east window, by Clayton and Bell, was the gift of Mrs Greenall, of Walton Hall, and two smaller chancel windows by the same artists were donated by Miss Forde of Stockton Heath Parsonage.

One stained glass window in the south aisle was erected to the memory of Horace Goad Crosfield, the six-year-old son 'of John and Elizabeth Crosfield in memory of his wife. Other stained glass windows commemorate Richard Greenall, Archdeacon of Chester and Robert Davies and one fine window at the west end of the nave by Heaton, Butler and Bayne was presented by the firm of Messrs Greenall and Whitley of Wilderspool.

In 1920 a chancel screen was erected by public subscription, at a cost of £350, to the 103 men of the parish who lost their lives in the Great War 1914-18 and on October 12, 1952 the Chapel in the south aisle was dedicated by the Bishop of Chester as a memorial to the dead of the last war.

The burial ground surrounding the church, although fairly extensive, became full in August 1957 but is well maintained so that the external appearance of the church is enhanced.

There are many attractive features of this church only to be noticed after a careful scrutiny, but the over-riding impression is one of pleasant harmony, dignity and unostentatious charm denoting the love and care bestowed by both the vicar and his parishioners.


## WYCLIFFE CONGREGATIONAL


The present Wycliffe Church can be seen from many parts of Warrington because of its high tower. Indeed Sir N. Pevsner's description of this church is that it is: "Big, of brick, with round-arched windows and a square NW tower with pyramid roof." He goes on to express a fear that a matching tower on the SW corner might be intended, but since the cost of renovating the tower in 1951 was felt to be burdensome and the tower was only included originally after strong difference of opinion among members of the original building Sub-Committee, it seems doubtful whether a second tower has ever been projected at any time.

Congregationalism in Warrington was first established in Warrington at

Stepney Chapel, Flag Lane, in 1797 as the result of a secession from Cairo Street Chapel in 1779 during Dr Enfield's Ministry. A later secession from Stepney Chapel in 1811 led to the foundation of Salem Congregational Chapel, Golborne Street, but both of these early Congregational Chapels had ceased to be used by Congregationalists before the mid-19th century. The Lancashire Congregational Union, dissatisfied with the cause of Congregationalism in Warrington, made efforts to re-establish the cause in the town with the result that the first Wycliffe Church was opened on October 23, 1851.

This chapel, in the Anglo-Norman style of architecture cost about £1,200 and was graced with a figure of John Wycliffe from the studio of Mr J.A. McBride of Liverpool over the entrance of the porch. There seems little doubt that the most energetic worker for this new church was the Rev Dr R. Vaughan, the Principal of the Lancashire Independent College, Manchester, who solicited subscriptions to such affect that the church was opened nearly free of debt.

In 1866, Sunday Schools were erected by the side of the church at a cost of £1,700 and signatories to the appeal for this development were headed by Samuel Rigby who became an outstanding supporter of the Congregational cause in Warrington.

Extensions to the church property were made to accommodate the growing congregation until in 1871 it was resolved to take down the old church and erect a new one in its stead.

A General Committee with the Rev G.S. Reaney as president Mr Z. Armitage, secretary; and Messrs W. Ashton, R.W. Murray and S. Rigby as treasurers concerned itself with the building proposals which ultimately resulted in the opening of the present building on September 4, 1873. Contributions were received from various parts of Lancashire as well as many handsome contributions from local church members, notably: Samuel Rigby, R.W. Murray, Mr McMinnies and members of the Rylands and Crosfield families, so that total receipts amounted to £9,488 while the expenditure on building amounted to £9,433.

The architect was George Woodhouse, of Bolton, who modelled the church on the design of Hope Chapel, Oldham and the resulting structure, mainly of brickwork, accommodates 1,100 people, the seating being almost equally divided between the body of the church and a gallery, supported upon pillars.

The pulpit was given special mention in a booklet, printed when the church was opened, as: "A remarkable feature in the structure. It is designed in the Norman Gothic style of architecture, and constructed of Dantzic oak. It is notable for a certain massive simplicity, although by no means free from ornament . . ." The panels of the pulpit were carved by Mr G.F. Armitage, brother of Mr Z. Armitage, whilst a carved Communion Table was made in

Friends Meeting House Warrington

Grappen Hall Church over 100 years ago

1877 from wood brought from the Holy Land by Henry Lee and presented to the Congregation by William Armitage.

Mr Ziba Armitage was organist of Wycliffe Church from 1870-9 and other notable musicians who have served at Wycliffe have included Mr W.H. Payton, Mr George Newall and the present organist Mr J. Gordon Fletcher. The organ was renovated fairly recently at a cost of £2,500.

To celebrate the Jublilee of Wycliffe in 1901, the foundation stones of the Rigby Memorial Building adjoining the church, were laid by the Mayoress of Mrs Warrington (Mrs Henry Roberts), Mrs Jesse Haworth, Mrs Ziba Armitage and Mrs Yonge (wife of the Rev John Yonge who was the Minister of Wycliffe from 1876 to 1912).

During the past 20 years, during the pastorate of the Rev B.H. Sackett, the internal and external renovation of the church including the tower, has been undertaken and by the joint efforts of Wycliffe and Elmwood Avenue Congregational churches a new church has been opened at Orford.

## ST. MARGARET AND ALL HALLOWS, ORFORD

Early in the 19th century, Orford, was a very small village situated at a remote distance from the town of Warrington which barely extended to the north beyond Tanners Lane. Nevertheless a small village school had existed there during the latter part of the 18th century and the idea of a church for Orford was suggested in 1832 by Mrs Hornby, widow of the Rector of Winwick.

After subscriptions had been collected, however, the villagers were disappointed when the church was built at Padgate instead of Orford so that church worship for residents of Orford became no easier.

An appeal was made to the Vicar of Padgate, therefore, for a curate who should officiate in the Orford School, but it was not until 1855 that Orford's church-school was licensed for regular observance of divine worship, and threequarters of a century had passed from the time when Mrs Hornby first suggested a church of Orford, to the moment when the two corner stones of the present church were laid on October 18, 1907. One of these stones was laid with Masonic rites by the Earl of Lathom in memory of William Sharp, solicitor, and the other stone, to the memory of Letitia Beamont, was laid by Mrs Margaret Stapylton, a principal donor to the building.

The church was built to the design of Mr Albert Warburton of Warrington by John Dolan and Son, builders of Warrington and is mainly of brick with a green slate roof.

The total cost was £4,500 and the church was consecrated on October 31, 1908 when the ecclesiastical parish was formed from Padgate. Comprising a nave with an open timber roof seating 251, a south aisle arcade of six arches and piers, a chancel with a timber vaulted ceiling, a tower which is 48 feet high containing organ chamber, ringing chamber and belfry, and vestries the church presents an attractive internal and external appearance.

Internally the church has changed considerably since it was consecrated through the addition of memorial windows, and many other adornments.

The West window is a memorial to William Mortimer and family and was erected in 1924 whilst two windows in the chancel commemorate the architect, Mr Albert Warburton, and the Rev George Vale Owen the first vicar. Another memorial to the Rev G. Vale Owen is the carved reredos on the old altar, but current liturgical practice has necessitated a new altar situated in front of a chancel screen of carved oak that was erected as a War Memorial. Carved wood figures were added to this chancel screen in 1938 as a memorial to Mr Henry Hankinson and the chancel, which had been re-floored in quarzite in 1939, has now been carpeted in connection with the liturgical changes recently effected.

The ministry of the Rev C.T. Allwork from 1928-56 has been commemorated by placing 16 statues of saints in pairs near the windows of the nave and aisle and also by hanging framed embroidery Stations of the Cross on the walls. These were placed in the church in 1958 and dedicated by the Bishop of Wangaratta, the Rev T.M. Armour, who was Vicar of Orford from 1922-27.

Recent redecoration has added attractive colour to the interior of the church and particularly by the colouring of the frieze in the nave with heraldic shields representing the progression of the Church of England in history.

The shields depict the See of Canterbury, 601; See of York, 627; See of Lichfield, 920; See of Chester, 1542; See of Liverpool, 1880; Pascal Lamb, 1908; the dedication of the church. Also the crests of families associated with Warrington and District are depicted.

Many other memorials, including the church gates and the carved oak altar front of the old altar, denote the love felt for this church by its parishioners and the devotion of the four incumbents from the Rev G. Vale Owen to the Rev N. Carter.

## ST. BENEDICT'S

Perhaps the noblest brick-built church in Warrington is the present St. Benedict's which is the second church to serve this particular parish: both churches were erected during the 20th century.

As in several other Warrington parishes, a school preceded a church and St. Benedict's school in Orford Lane commences as an overflow from St. Alban's, King Street School on January 10, 1881.

In 1896 Father Wilfred Baines, O.S.B. took charge of the district and the school became a Mass centre. Father Baines next took up residence in St. Benedict's Place, Orford Lane, in 1902; the new parish was placed under the patronage of St. Benedict and on June 19th, 1904, a temporary "tin" church was opened in the playground of St. Benedict's School near Watkin Street. This "tin mission" was capable of seating 500 persons but quickly proved to be too small for the growing parish so that in 1912 work began on the present church in Rhodes Street.

Father Baines had been succeeded by Father Oswald Swarbreck, O.S.B., and the foundation stone of the new church was laid by the Abbot of Ampleforth, Abbot Oswald Smith, on July 12, 1914. Almost exactly one year later the church was opened by Cardinal Bourne, Archbishop of Westminster, on July 11, 1915.

Erected to the designs of Matthew Henan, A.R.I.B.A., of Liverpool, the church is in the Byzantine style of architecture with a campanile at the west end, a nave measuring 70 feet by 40 feet, passage aisles, a large sanctuary, a Lady Chapel and a Chapel of the Blessed Sacrement. There are also three confessionals, a baptistry and a choir gallery. Large arches together with vaulting and panelled ceilings give an attractive spacious appearance to the nave and sanctuary, while the Lady Chapel possesses a most intimately appealing atmosphere that contrasts strikingly with the spaciousness of the main body of the church. The contractor was Mr James Pilkington of Rainford, and the cost of the building was about £6,000.

Subsequent additions have beautified the interior of this church. A marble communion rail as a memorial to Father Swarbreck was dedicated in March 1921 and was designed in Sicilian and Siena marble to harmonise with the Byzantine character of the church.

The High Altar erected in 1927 was the gift of the congregation as a memorial to those who lost their lives in the first World War and the mosaic above this altar depicts the Crucifixion and is stated to be the largest single mosaic in Britain.

Following recent liturgical changes, however, a new altar has been placed in the sanctuary and this is a simple portable altar in wood and metal made by the men of the parish to the design of Father J. Carbery. It is simple and effective and incorporates the Benedictine Crest. A fine Venetian sanctuary lamp was purchased about 1955 together with an early 17th century thurible, while the Stations of the Cross were erected to the memory of those killed in the Second World War.

In 1935 a new baptistry was opened to the memory of Father J.V. Corbishley, Parish Priest for 17 years.

Father Corbishley had been responsible for the erection of the Bell Hall at a cost of £6,500 and this hall is now used mainly as a Youth Club, while a new social club costing £50,000 was opened in May 1967 due largely to the efforts of Father D.O. Forbes.

The church is attractively decorated and presents a handsome external appearance suitable marched by an inviting and beautiful interior.

## ST. MARY'S GREAT SANKEY

Very few churches in Warrington and the immediate neighbourhood have survived in buildings that have remained substantially unchanged for more than two centuries.

St. Mary's, Great Sankey was consecreated on July 11, 1769 and at that time this attractive structure replaced two earlier chapels in the same place, the first of which was built about 1640.

A sketch made about the year 1825 by Robert Booth shows the present church easily recognisable in spite of additions and alterations effected during the 19th century. The embattled south wall and diminutive tower and belfry present very much the same appearance as the present church which is still situated on the main highway to Prescot and Liverpool and enclosed with the trees concerning which William Beamont wrote in 1882: "It was a piece of excellent taste which led the re-builders of the chapel to enclose it on three sides with its wall of clipped green lime trees, so fitting and so natural as an ornament of a country churchyard, and which, it is hoped, will be preserved with the care as it has been hitherto."

Beamont's hope concerning the churchyard has been partly fulfilled for the present churchyard on the south side of the church is beautifully maintained. A burial ground on the north side of the church, however, was described by the Vicar in 1967 as a "virtual wilderness" and he expressed a hope that has not yet been fulfilled that it would soon be transformed into a garden of rest. This burial ground was first consecrated in 1833.

The tower of the church which is at present "in splints" was rebuilt about a century ago after the tender of Short and Domville in the sum of £220 had been accepted for this purpose and an enlargement to the church consisting of a new chancel, organ chamber and vestry finally shaped the existing building and was consecrated on August 13, 1883. It was at this time that a new parish was formed and the former Chapel which had been situated within the Parish of Prescot became the Church of St. Mary, Great Sankey. A choir vestry was added to the church in 1930 and in 1969, when the church celebrated its bi-centenary, an excellently detailed history of the church by Ronald Graham was published to mark the occasion.

Internally the church is attractive and full of interest.

A timber roof possesses especially pleasing timber supports and there are a large number of stained glass windows and other memorials recording the long history of the church and those who have lived and worshipped in the parish.

An Austrian oak reredos together with a matching Communion Table was erected in 1935-6 and were the gifts of the Tinsley and Warburton families. On the south wall a marble tablet is erected to the memory of the Rev James Simpson who was the Vicar for 57 years and was buried aged 84 in the Chapel yard. Soon after the death of the Rev James Simpson in 1871, William Beamont commented that there had only been two incumbents of the Chapel in 97 years and during the century that has followed there have only been another seven vicars.

Appropriately the memorials and windows of the church reflect the variety of interests and pursuits followed by those who have worshipped and served this church. The East Window was presented by employees of the Widnes Alkali Company as a memorial to Edward Bolton while one memorial tablet was erected to the memory of Captain George Webster Owen who was killed in 1913 at Gallipoli, and another tablet was erected to the memory of a family doctor of the parish, Thomas Alexander Murray, by his friends of the medical profession.

Other windows and tablets are memorials to past Vicars of the Parish as well as parishioners and one of them was the gift of a relative resident in Toronto, Canada.

The churchyard too reflects the long history of this parish and this has all been appropriately documented.


## CHRIST CHURCH PADGATE

Christ Church, Padgate, is a place of special significance to all who are interested in the history of Warrington, for two of Warrington's most devoted citizens and historians – William Beamont and Dr James Kendrick – are buried in the pleasant churchyard surrounding this attractive church.

Both William Beamont and his wife Letitia are described on a tablet fixed on the outside of the church as "munificent benefactors" of the parish and the extension of the churchyard from the memorial tablet to the road was carried out by public subscription as a memorial to Warrington's first Mayor and his wife. The tablet was unveiled and the extension consecrated by the Bishop of Liverpool on April 4, 1908.

Christ Church was originally erected in 1838 after efforts made by Mrs Hornby, the widow of a former Rector of Winwick, to raise subscriptions for a new church at Orford. The new church, however, was built instead at Padgate after the Rev Horace Powys, Rector of Warrington, had consented to the formation of a new district comprising the townships of Poulton-with-Fearnhead, Woolston-with-Martinscroft and the hamlet of Orford.

A site was provided for the church and graveyard through the generosity of the Hatton family and a stone tablet has recently been placed in the floor of the chancel commemorating the Rev Horace Powys as the founder of the church.

Within five years of the building of the church, a school costing £543 and a vicarage costing £1,366 were erected to the designs of the Clerk of Works who was engaged upon the building of the Clergy Daughters' School near to the Warrington Parish Church.

After the Rev William Henry Williams had become Vicar of Padgate, the church was extended and re-designed internally. A new chancel was built, the interior was re-seated, new vestries were added and a new organ was purchased. The total cost of this restoration was £1,345 and the consecration of the new chancel took place on June 15, 1883. Two stained glass windows at the West end of the church were erected as memorials to the Rev W.H. Williams who died in 1889 and his wife who died in 1890.

After this 19th century re-shaping of the church, threequarters of a century passed before any further significant development or change to the interior or exterior of the church was effected and by this time the church was in a poor condition necessitating a full scale restoration plan.

The Vicar, the Rev J.O. Colling, wisely called for the services of a highly qualified archited, Mr George Pace of York, and a plan for the complete restoration of the church was evolved whereby, stage by stage over a period of eight years from 1959 until 1967 at a cost of approximately £16,000, the interior of the church was re-modelled and the exterior renovated.

The result is a delight to the eye. The instant impression of the interior of the church is that it is a modern church presenting a most satisfying unity in concept and execution. Perhaps the most pleasing part of this remodelling is the chancel. This is designed in oak and wrought iron to conform with recent liturgical practice and has the appearance of a complete design instead of an alteration.

Old pitch pine pews were stripped, bleached, waxed and polished to harmonise with the new woodwork of the chancel and while an old font, a memorial to the Rev H. Powys has remained at the West end of the church, a new moveable font of modern design is used. A handsome brass lectern, a memorial to William Beamont, also remains in use.

Christ Church, Padgate, is possibly the most successful and is certainly the most satsifying example of a modern church restoration in the Warrington area, and the situation of the church remains pleasingly rural in aspect in spite of the rapidly developing urban area of which this church is now an active centre.

## ST. ANN'S

The centenary of St. Ann's Church was celebrated in 1969 but the Parish and St. Ann's School had been established for five years before the church was built.

By an Order in Council dated November 1, 1864 there came into being "The District of Saint Ann, Warrington" taken from a district that had previously been part of St. Paul's, and the Bishop of Chester granted a licence for divine worship in the schools that had been built in Dannett Street in 1863. The Rev William J. Melville was licenced to officiate as the Minister of the District and the first issue of a church magazine known as "St. Ann's Chronicle", dated April 1, 1867, shows that the schools were then being used, not only for church services and for Day and Sunday School purposes, but also contained a Reading Room, open every evening from 7 until 10, and a Lending Library from which books were lent for one week for a halfpenny per book.

A piece of land for the erection of a church was given by Lord Winmarleigh and a church to the designs of Mr John Douglas, a Chester architect, was eventually erected. St. Ann's Chronicle, dated June 1868, reported: "The Church is now all but finished, and might if required be made ready for Divine Service in a week" and the Church Building Committee, with William Beamont as Chairman and with the architect (Mr Douglas) as well as the builder (Mr Gibson) present had decided that the outstanding sum of £1,100 should be raised if possible before the building was consecrated.

It was not until February 27, 1869, however, that the consecration took place and this solemn occasion was followed by a congregational tea-party in the school.

The total cost of the Church, which is constructed in brick, was £6,000 and included the provision of an organ. A generous donor to the building fund was William Beamont and at a later stage an endowment was provided by Mr and Mrs Beamont.

Internally the nave of the church is lofty and spacious and the single span of the roof is supported by wooden framework and beams. The chancel, however, has a somewhat unbalanced appearance being rather small in comparison with the nave. Externally the church is far from unattractive although it is dominated by a somewhat massive tower with a pyramid room and one small turret. Sir Nikolaus Pevsner describes it as: "An impressively forceful High Victorian piece, blunt and uncompromising.

As a major part of the centenary celebrations in 1969 the church was re-decorated in attractive pastel colours and, combined with very little stained glass, the inside now presents one of the lightest and brightest church interiors in the locality.

The chancel is dominated by four painted figures of the Evangelists as a reredos and an unexpected touch of modernity has been added by the gift, from Dr May Bourhill, of a circular window in stained glass and of contemporary design. The only other stained glass window is on the south side of the church and is a memorial to Richard Ridyard.

Recently a modern Hammond organ has replaced the old pipe organ and a choir vestry and an occasional room have been added to the west end of the church.

Today the church stands almost surrounded by Tetley Walker's Brewery but an excellent arrangement exists whereby steam from the brewery is fed into the church to heat its low pressure water system. Houses near to the church are being demolished at a high rate and the future of this industrial parish is filled with uncertainty but there is little doubt that the church is loved by its parishioners and well cared for by the present vicar the Rev Harold Sanderson.


## PENKETH METHODIST

George Percival is credited as the father of Methodism in Penketh at the beginning of the 19th century. Together with William Gandy, he headed a list of Trustees when a deed of conveyance was drawn up in 1818 whereby a plot of land at the corner of Stocks Lane and Warrington Road passed into the possession of Trustees who erected a chapel on the land which was complete and open for worship on May 30, 1819. This old chapel remained in use until 1860 when it was sold because it had become unsafe and expensive repairs would have been an unsatisfactory solution to the need for a larger chapel.

Dr Joseph Smith had been Senior Society Steward from 1839-1853 and his offer of a plot of land prompted the decision to build a new chapel in Chapel Road where the foundation stone was laid in July and the Chapel completed in November, 1860. This was probably a most appropriate year so far as the donor of the land was concerned because during that year Dr Joseph Smith was Mayor of Warrington and a number of Warrington's leading public figures contributed to the total cost amounting to £1,300, of building the Chapel and also a school nearby.

These men included Gilbert Greenall, MP, and one man who was not only earning a widespread reputation as a manufacturer of handsome wooden furnishings but who was also closely associated with the Methodist Church in Penketh where he resided, namely Robert Garnet.

Although Garnett's extensive showrooms in Sankey Street and the equally extensive workshop are no longer used by "Cabinetmakers, upholsterers . . . designers and makers in every style of high-class woodwork" as an advertisement of 1908 described the firm of Garnetts' Warrington, much of the furniture made by the firm is still held in high regard by those who possess it. Nor would it be unreasonable to suppose that some of the handsome wooden furnishing of the Chapel came from the first of Garnets'. Certainly the long connection of the Garnett family with this church is well remembered today

186

because there are a number of memorials in the Church to various members of the family.

It was Robert Garnett's son who paid the entire cost of extending the 1860 chapel when his father died in 1877. The enlargement was finished in 1877 and instead of having four windows along each side the enlarged chapel had five and an extra 80 seats.

In the west wall was placed a large high window which incorporates stained glass memorial panels bearing the leged "He, being dead, yet speaketh". Further enlargements took place in 1891 and a new organ was purchased in 1908. Subsequently buttresses have been erected to prevent sagging at the point where the first extension was made and yet, in spite of extensions and buttressing, this church has an attractive appearance and a homely atmosphere.

Another memorial in this intimate church, appropriately carved in wood, is to Charles Edward Parker who died in 1939 and his wife Helen who died in 1941. Helen Parker was the daughter of Mr and Mrs Robert Garnett of Hall Nook, Penketh. Charles Edward Parker was not only a prominent man in the public affairs of Warrington but founded the Penketh Tanning Company Ltd., and resided in Penketh where he possessed a very fine garden and wrote a treatise on "Soils and Crops".

The school next to the Church was originally opened in 1861 and was a Day School. It was extended in 1887 and although it was altered in 1908 it had ceased to be a Day School when Penketh Council School was opened.

As part of the centenary celebration in 1960 a "Centenary Handbook" was published written by Frank E. Bowyer which soberly records the long story of this modest home of the Methodists.

## ALL SAINTS, THELWALL

A mid-seventeenth century manuscript in Warrington Municipal Library relating to chapelries at Thelwall and Daresbury records: "That there is an ancient chapell which stands upon the ground belonging to Thelwall Hall and neare unto the sayd Hall and it is comonly reported belonginge to the sayd Hall where by the leave of the Lord there the Inhabitants ... sometymes procure service and sermon to God." This chapel was apparently built in the time of Queen Elizabeth and having been used by the inhabitants as stated in the manuscript, it was made into a parochial chapel in 1782 when it was repaired with an augmentation from Queen Anne's Bounty and when the incumbent was Thomas Blackburne.

In 1843, when William Nicolson was resident at Thelwall Hall, the present church was built and dedicated to All Saints with William Nicolson as patron: the Nicolson family at a later stage sold the advowson to Keble College, Oxford. The chancel was added 1857 and in 1890-91 the church was further enlarged by the addition of the North West Aisle, vestry and porch and was re-seated throughout when the entire cost of this enlargement was met by Henry Stanton, of Greenfields.

Built in the Early English style of architecture, the church is possibly the most attractive example of Victorian Gothic church building in the locality and as the intention of this style of architecture was to provide the romantic medieval atmosphere considered to be the most suitable for church worship in the reign of Queen Victoria and still possesses many modern adherents, Thelwall Church has proved successful.

Every window in the church is of stained glass which makes the interior rather dark, a circumstance that can only be overcome by artificial lighting. Many of these windows have been erected as memorials to those who have worshipped in this church, most are Victorian and commemorate members of the Pickering, Nicolson, Stanton and Rylands families, but one modern window depicting St. Christopher has been erected in the memory of Sir William Peter Rylands and Lady Nora Mary Rylands his wife. Lady Rylands died in 1946 and Sir Peter Rylands in 1948. This window also contains the Rylands crest and a reproduction of a wiredrawer at his bench. It was unveiled in October 1950.

The reredos which consists of murals depicting Elijah and Saints Michael, George and Werbuga as well as carved representations of the Transfiguration and the raising of Lazarus, was erected in 1874 in memory of the Rev J. Parry Jones Parry and Margaret his wife, the parents of Elizabeth Nicholson, by James and Elizabeth Nicholson.

Once a huge medieval statue of St. Christopher stood at Norton Priory facing the crossing of the River Mersey at Runcorn and this statue has only recently been removed to the Walker Art Gallery.

In Thelwall Church are two representations of St. Christopher, presumably with the proximity of the local ferry in mind. One of these is a painted mural on the North West wall and the other is contained in the memorial window to Sir William Peter Rylands.

On the south wall of the church a tablet, erected to commemorate the Coronation of Edward VII in 1902, records the association of Edward the Elder with Thelwall and contains the appropriate quotation from the Anglo-Saxon Chronicle.

A lych-gate entrance to the churchyard and the well-maintained burial ground was erected as a memorial to John and Ellen Naylor of Cuerden Hall, while more recently the organ was replaced by a modern extension organ. The present vicar, the Rev Derek Smith, has just completed a Stewardship Campaign, the object of which is to place the church finances on a sound long term basis and also to raise money to build a new Parish Hall for which at least £20,000 is required.

# LATCHFORD BAPTIST

In 1952 when the centenary of Latchford Baptist Church was celebrated, the occasion was to mark the anniversary of a meeting and not the erection of a building. This meeting had been preceded by other meetings, held at first in the home of Mr Joseph Wilkinson of Stockton Heath, where a group of people formerly connected with Hill Cliffe Baptist Church met from 1849 until the house was no longer large enough to accommodate the growing group of worshippers, and then in an old barn. This "Old Barn Chapel" became their place of worship in January, 1851, until on February 4, 1852, a church of baptised believers was instituted and Mr Joseph Wilkinson was called to be first pastor with Mr J. Yarwood and Mr Ashbrook as deacons.

Another meeting in 1859 in the house of Mr William Wilkinson was held to consider better equipped church premises and as Mr Wilkinson promised a handsome donation which he later doubled, plans for a new church proceeded forthwith until on July 10, 1860, the foundation stone of the present church, near the junction of Ackers Lane and Loushers Lane, was laid.

This church was completed and opened for worship on Good Friday, March 29, 1861, and has remained substantially unaltered since then. It is a very neat and attractive structure in the Grecian or Doric style and is constructed of brick and sandstone. The architect was Mr Reade and the builder a Mr Warburton. Providing seating for 240 people it was equipped with a gallery for a Sunday School as well as vestries and cost £800.

The gallery over the vestries for a Sunday School continued in use until 1878, when a separate school hall was built at a cost of "over £400" to which classrooms were added in 1902 and a primary hall and ladies' room was built in 1929. An organ and choir seats now occupy the gallery originally used as the Sunday School.

A monument outside the church and a marble table inside the church commemorate the pastorate of the Rev Joseph Wilkinson who died in 1881, and beneath the marble tablet is a smaller bronze plaque in memory of his son, William Thomas Wilkinson who died in 1919 and who had held the post of organist for about 30 years.

The first pipe organ, which replaced a harmonium, was installed in 1902 but was severely damaged as the result of a gale in 1940 when it was replaced by the present handsome pipe organ.

Another marble tablet has been placed in the church to commemorate the pastorate of the Rev Charles Andrew who died on December 28, 1896, and other memorial tablets include a memorial to members of thechurch who died in World War I as well as to the memory of Mr John R. Conway, secretary of the Church 1905-1942, in whose memory the church clocks were also installed.

An extension to the porch was effected in memory of church members who died between 1950-60 and this year the church was attractively decorated after the ceiling had been replaced.

Internally the church is as attractive as it is externally and although it was to a certain degree cut off by the Manchester Ship Canal from the area it was originally intended to serve, modern urban development has placed it again in a useful if somewhat secluded position where it embellishes the neighbourhood.


## WORKINGMEN'S MISSION

Like the Friend's Meeting House in Buttermarket Street, the Chapel of the Workingmen's Mission in Thewlis Street until recently could not easily be seen from the street as it was largely hidden from view by a spacious school erected a few years before the Chapel. The pleasant space in which the chapel stands will be revealed in the immediate future as a result of the recent road works that have taken place at Bank Quay.

The present chapel, however, was preceded by an earlier chapel situated on Liverpool Road which had been erected through the interest and munificence of John Crosfield who had been actively concerned with the Warrington Town Mission from 1862-1869.

One of the missioners of the Town Mission, who visited the sick and conducted prayer meetings in their homes, was John Urmson and with the termination of the Town Mission he became the first missionary, paid by John Crosfield, of a Workingmen's Mission in 1870 when children were gathered in a Sunday School in a fustian-cutting shop opposite the Ship Inn.

So popular was this venture that John Crosfield then erected a chapel near to the Ship Inn and this was opened for public worship on December 24, 1871 and was used at first both as a Sunday School and Chapel open to all denominations and conducted on a non-sectarian basis.

Very quickly a separate Sunday School was built adjoining the Chapel and this opened for Sunday School scholars in 1874 only to be used to accommodate a Day School additionally in the year following. A new Sunday School, also used as a Day School until about 1930, was erected in Thewlis Street in 1899 and four years later, owing to the expansion of Crosfield's works, the foundation stone of a new chapel was laid in Thewlis Street behind the new school.

The foundation stone of this new chapel, which still stand substantially as it was first erected, was laid by Captain G.R. Crosfield on August 15, 1903 and another stone records the opening of the Chapel by Mrs John Crosfield on February 27, 1904.

Much of the furniture from the old chapel – the pews and the pulpit, as

190

well as the organ — were moved to the new chapel and in addition, a marble plaque that had been erected in the old chapel to the memory of Eliza Crosfield, the first wife of John Crosfield, was removed and re-erected at the rear of the new chapel.

A large stained glass window depicting Christ blessing a group of children faces the visitor entering this chapel. Erected as a memorial to John Crosfield, the window was executed in Flemish glass by a London firm and given by Gertrude Crosfield in 1906. Another stained glass window was erected in 1935 to the memory of Thomas Dale, for many years a President of the Mission, and the name of George Dale was added subsequently to this window which depicts the Good Shepherd. The remaining windows of the chapel are fitted with tinted glass.

Other memorials in the chapel include a War Memorial tablet and a new Communion Table and small reading desk in the memory of Alfred Tilling who died in 1962 and who was a former President.

All those who watched the Warrington Walking Day Procession this year will have noted the strength of the youth and other organisations belonging to the Workingmen's Mission, a vigorous element among these organisation being the Scouts, Guides, Cubs and Brownies as well as the Scout Band and there are also thriving women's organisations.

Music plays a prominent part in the life of this Mission as in addition to pianos situated in many school classrooms, a new organ was installed soon after the chapel in Thewlis Street was opened and the organist for the past 50 years has been Mr Thomas Tanner, who is well known in Warrington as a musician and music dealer.

Services in the chapel are often conducted by visiting preachers from the Baptist, Congregational and Methodist College in Manchester as well as by visitors from other Christian bodies. The initial interest of the Crosfield family in this Mission has never ended since not only have endowments been made by John Crosfield, his wife and members of his family, but as recently as 1931 the generosity of the Crosfield family was extended to the gift of the freehold of land in Lovely Lane where a recreation club belonging to the Mission had started in 1919.

The centenary of the Workingmen's Mission is to be celebrated next year and the chapel is shortly to be re-decorated in preparation for this event.


## STOCKTON HEATH METHODIST

On opposite sides of Walton Road Stockton Heath, with their front entrances face to face stand a church and a church hall. The church was erected in 1905 and has the external appearance of a building of that year while the church hall, opened in 1957 looks much more modern and the interior matches the exterior.

A great surprise awaits the visitor to the church, however, because a reconstruction of the interior which took place in 1964 has converted a building which had the internal appearance of a barn into an inviting church, distinctly modern in appearance, and one that gives complete aesthetic satisfaction.

Early Methodist worship in Stockton Heath indeed took place in old "Barn" chapel situated between London Road and Walton Road until a chapel, known as the "Ebenezer" chapel was erected in 1886 on the site of the present church. This early chapel was purchased in 1888 by the Wesleyan Methodist Society of the Warrington Circuit and the rapid growth of membership of this chapel soon led to a decision to take it down and erect a new church on the same site.

Little time was lost after the decision was taken and following the last service in the old chapel on May 14, 1905, the new church was opened for worship on October 26 the same year. The roof timbers and roof supports of this church gave it the appearance of a barn and it is to the great credit of the architect of the recent extension and alteration, Mr S. Cliffe, a former Church Trustee, that the concept of covering the wood roof supports and continuing their line to the floor has provided internal butresses that flow into graceful curved roof supports.

The interior design of the church was also altered to provide extra seating, a new chancel, choir stalls, pulpit, Communion rail and table and while the alterations were taking place in 1964 a Building Committee worked under the direction of Messrs J.R. Ashall, and R.B. Bladen with the Rev D.F. Vickers as chairman. The organ, which had replaced an earlier instrument in 1923, was repositioned and screened and the wooden panelling behind the Communion rail matches effectively with the new pulpit, choir stalls and font. Considerable thought also appears to have been given both to the natural and artificial lighting of the church so that the total effect is that presented by a completely new building of modern design.

The total cost of this scheme was £17,000 and the modernised church was re-opened by Mrs Polly Cliffe, one of the oldest members of the church, on December 5, 1964. This Church is remarkably free from memorial plaques and windows but there is a War Memorial plaque in the porch as well as a small tablet recording the thanks of the Trustees for the generous gift from the Joseph Rank Benevolent Trust towards the Church renovation and extension.

Residents of Stockton Heath cannot fail to notice the tremendous activity associated with this Church. The Church Hall opposite the Church, which cost £22,000 and which was opened on March 16, 1957, is used by groups associated with the Church every day of the week. These groups include a thriving Dramatic Society, a Youth Club, Fellowship meetings, Junior

Adventuerers as well as Guides and Brownies and the week-day activities give way to equally well attended services in the Church on Sundays.

All those associated with this Church have every reason to be proud of the church buildings and the religious and social activities connected with these buildings.

## ST. JOHN'S WALTON

Walton Church has the appearance and the polish of a cathedral in miniature. It was erected at the expense and upon the estate of one man, Sir Gilbert Greenall, and his family and descendants have maintained an active interest in this church ever since it was first dedicated in 1882.

Clearly, in building this church for the parish of Walton, Sir Gilbert Greenall spared no expense because almost the entire interior embellishment of this impressive building – the roof decoration, the magnificent oak reredos, the Devonshire marble font, the religious symbolism contained in the windows and interior stone carvings, the organ and the tiling of the chancel – were all included when the church was originally opened. Small wonder that this delightfully maintained church in such a beautiful setting should have become so desired as the appropriate setting for a wedding of distinction.

What a pity that the beauty of the interior of this church can only be seen at times of divine service, because the recent increase in vandalism and theft has meant that churches like St. John's must be kept locked except when a service is taking place.

Paley and Austin, of Lancaster, were the architects and demonstrated their capacity for interesting variations on medieval styles of architecture.

Cruciform in plan, the church is dominated by the tower which, together with its spire, attains a height of 130 feet. Internally the church roof at the tower crossing is particularly attractive and unusual as rib vaulting springs from the corbels, but the entire barrel-vaulted roof with its painted decorations delights the eye of the beholder. Because of the size of the tower, and crossing, the nave of this church seems strangely small compared with the length of the chancel, an effect which is emphasised by the fact that the roof of the chancel is the same height as the roof of the nave. But any momentary impression of a lack of balance between nave and chancel is quickly counteracted by the pleasing aspects presented when the interior is viewed from the crossing. A most attractive form of interior electric lighting was installed in 1934 by Troughton and Young of London, from Lady Daresbury's suggestions, thus preserving the unity of interior embellishment of this family church.

The woodwork inside the church is of oak throughout and the sole

193

contractor for the building was Mr R. Fairhurst, of Higher Whitley. Window designs were by Shrigley and Hunt of Lancaster and the three-manual organ was built by Hill and Sons, London. The total cost of the building is stated to have been about £17,000.

At present a new chapel is being created in an area formerly occupied by family pews on the north side of the chancel. This memorial chapel is being constructed to the designs of the late Geoffrey Owen and houses a memorial book in which records are maintained of the interments of cremated remains.

The altar of this chapel is a memorial to James Bainbridge; the Communion rails a memorial to Ada Ellen, mother of the present Vicar, the Rev V.G. Davies and donated by the Vicar; and a Clergy stall is in memory of Vera Brown. Embroidery on kneelers in this chapel was the work of a group of ladies taught at the Warrington School of Art by Mrs Fauset.

A marble bust of Sir Gilbert Greenall, the work of the local sculptor J. Warrington Wood, stands in front of the Founder's Window on the south side of the nave and the graves of Sir Gilbert Greenall and his wife, as well as of his son Lord Daresbury and Frances, Lady Daresbury are in the churchyard.

This church was their church in a very real sense and so far it has remained little changed or marked in any way by others associated with the parish. There are memorials and graves of the first vicars; there is also a well executed War Memorial, but unlike many other parish churches that give a strange conspectus of the history of a parish, Walton Church largely records the history of a family and an estate. No doubt time will gradually cause this to change but when it does the pristine freshness of this Victorian creation will vanish. The Parish was formed in May 1885 when the church was consecrated and the parish boundaries were altered slightly in 1965.


## SACRED HEART

Sacred Heart Church was built at Bank Quay to serve the needs of hundreds of working class families at a time when the Whitecross and Bank Quay area of Warrington was at peak of industrial activity and before any real attempt was being made to control the atmospheric pollution created by the concentration of factory chimneys which surrounded the new church.

No rustic churchyard surrounds this church. Instead, it now stands with great dignity in the middle of an area that is just beginning to recover from a redevelopment "blitz", so that the description of this church by Sir Nikolays Pevsner seems particularly appropriate when he writes that it is: "a remarkably strong straightforward design."

Certainly this church has needed strength to withstand the ravages of the factory smoke and heavy use imposed by its industrial setting and now that the new dual carriageway road from the church to Sankey is in use, the tower, which rises to a height of 114 feet, dominates the view of the traveller approaching Warrington along this road from Sankey.

The foundation stone of this church, lain on a Sunday, bears a latin inscription which translated into English means: To the honour of the Holy Trinity and in the name of the Sacred Heart of Jesus, the foundation stone was laid June 3, 1894 by the Most Rev James Canon Carr, Vicar Capitular; Rev Michael Ryan being the Rector. Money for the building of the church, but not for its furnishing or the land on which it was built, was provided by two priests, Fathers John and James Lennon.

Built to the designs of Messrs Sinnot, Sinnot and Powell of Liverpool, the church was constructed in red brick with sandstone edgings to the windows and the builder was Mr Winnard of Wigan. The total cost was around £6,000 and it replaced a smaller chapel on the same site.

Bordering each aisle are three massive pillars and the carving at the top of these was the work of a Mr Essenhigh. Either side of the high altar are chapels to the Sacred Heart and Our Lady, and the organ which was originally installed on the left of the sanctuary, now stands in a gallery constructed over the porch at the rear of the church.

The church was opened for worship on Sunday October 6, 1895 when the Rt Rev Bishop Whiteside, D.D. of Liverpool sang pontifical high mass and the Rt Rev Bishop Bilsborrow of Salford delivered the sermon.

A memorial to those of the parish who lost their lives in the First World War in the form of a carved oak Pieta (a representation of the Virgin Mary holding the dead Christ in her arms) was erected in June 1921.

A new carved oak reredos and High Altar in grey Italian marble were installed in 1951 when the church was renovated and redecorated. The reredos was carved by Messrs J.H. and I. Sankey, of Church Street, and the total cost of improvements carried out at this time to the church and the school was nearly £6,000. A new altar in oak has recently been installed in the front of the sanctuary to conform with liturgical changes.

Certain repairs will have to be effected to the top part of the tower as this has shown signs of movement and a reconstruction of the tower will have to be undertaken in the very near future. It is estimated that this work will cost in the region of £7,000.

Unlike many other churches in the industrial areas of Warrington, Sacred Heart Church was built and used before the school which, standing behind the church, was first opened on April 13, 1896 in premises now used as the Parochial Clubroom. In recent years, of course, the number of parishioners has decreased considerably as a result of the clearance programme in the Whitecross area, but it is anticipated that the members will soon begin to increase as redevelopment takes place.

A new school is in the planning process of development and is included in the Starts Programme of the Department of Education and Science for 1970-71. This school will be situated on a site adjoining the new road close to the end of Wellfield Street. The plans for the school having been approved by the Department of Education and Science it is anticipated that building work will commence in the early months of 1971.

## STRETTON

An ancient chapel of ease at Stretton within the parish of Great Budworth was stated to have been "ruinous and in decay" in the year 1666. How old this ancient chapel was at that time is not stated and similarly there is no information concerning the subsequent repair of this chapel. Before Stretton became a separate civil parish, however, a new church was erected in the years 1826-27, largley from the funds administered by the Church Building Commissioners. The architect was Philip Hardwick and his sketch and plan of Stretton Church appear in a book by M.H. Port, *Six Hundred New Churches: A Study of the Church Building Commission, 1818-1856* . . . S.P.C.K., 1961. Costing £2,986, of which £2,121 was provided by the Commissioners, Hardwick's church provided seating for 250 and was an uninspiring Gothic structure with a tower. The first Vicar of Stretton was the Rev Richard Janion, who died in 1831 at the age of 40 and who is commemorated by a marble tablet in the floor of the present church. He was succeeded by the Rev Richard Greenall, who later became Archdeacon of Chester.

In 1859, Archdeacon Greenall commissioned Mr Gilbert Scott, the eminent architect, to build a chancel at a cost of £1,700, and after the death of Archdeacon Greenall in 1867 it was decided to rebuild the nave as his memorial. This decision was soon amended in view of building difficulties and, with Gilbert Scott as architect, the church was entirely rebuilt except for the chancel, in the years 1870-72. The Archdeacon's widow shared the cost of rebuilding the tower with Mr Lyon and the total cost of rebuilding was £5,000. A font was presented by the Clergy Daughters of St Elphin's School in memory of Archdeacon Greenall.

The wisdom of employing such an eminent architect as Gilbert Scott is apparent to all who now behold this beautiful church. Possessing the most pleasing exterior in the locality, the interior is equally attractive and it is impossible to discern that the Chancel was erected 10 years earlier than the rest of the church. With adequate natural light from the clerestory, the nave is divided into five bays, the pillars of which are alternately circular and octagonal and are surmounted by richly moulded capitals. All the windows in the south and north aisles are now of stained glass, but originally only two windows in the south aisle at the estern end of the church and the large memorial window in the west end of the tower were of stained glass executed by Clayton and Bell of London.

Mr Fairhurst of Higher Whitley was the builder and the sub-contractor for stonework was Mr Holland of Northwich. A Willis organ was the gift of Mr Lyon and the interior beauty of the church was enhanced by a red deal roof, pews of English oak and a pulpit of carved oak supported on marble pillars. The passage tiles were red and black.

Subsequent memorials have been erected in the form of additional stained glass windows to members of the Lyon family while two memorials contained in the chancel are to the memory of James Parkinson, organist for 33 years who died in 1928 and his widow.

A more recent and very beautiful window at the west end of the chancel is to the memory of a much loved Vicar, the Hon. Charles Francis Cross, Canon of Chester, Rural Dean and Vicar from 1897-1937. Below this window an oak reredos was erected in 1957 to the memory of Christopher Stephen Lunt and the carving of this reredos as well as that on the altar now standing in front of the reredos, was the work of the local cabinet makers J.H. and I. Sankey.

A peal of six bells is contained in the tower which also possesses clock faces on the west and south sides. Both of these clock faces are of some interest since instead of numbers they have letters which, beginning at the conventional point of 10 to the hour, read respectively:— "Time is not all" and "Forget not God". A lych-gate was erected by Mrs Henry Lyon.

Standing in a well maintained church yard, Stretton church can be seen to advantage from all sides and is quite obviously held in high regard by all those who now worship there.


## OUR LADY'S

Rising to a height of 50 feet, the roof of the nave of Our Lady's Church, St. Mary Street, Latchford, stands well above the surrounding houses. It can be seen quite easily from the bridge over the Wilderspool Crossings and from this point of view the great mass of the high roof appears to need the compensating balance of a tower and spire. It is no through fault of architecture that such a tower and spire do not exist, for the original designs provided a very beautiful design for this necessary embellishment to what is one of the finest local buildings designed by a Warrington architect. Unfortunately, when the building was erected in 1901-3, the lower part of the tower was erected and the remainder, together with the spire, was left for completion at a later date, presumably on the grounds of economy.

The architect was Robert Curran, who was responsible for many in other churches situated in Blackburn, Colwyn Bay, Manchester, Aberdeen, St. Helens, and Worcester, and who commenced practice in Warrington in 1866.

Our Lady's Church was opened on Sunday, October 19, 1903 by the Bishop of Shrewsbury (Right Rev Dr Allen); and the erection of this beautiful church followed the considerable missionary efforts of a number of priests in Latchford beginning with Father Alcock who first celebrated mass in Latchford in October 1869, in the premises originally used by Roberts, Dale and Co., chemical manufacturers. The following year Father Mulvaney became the first resident priest and on September 3, 1871, a school-chapel in St. Mary Street was opened, with the title of "Our Lady of the Assumption".

It was after the Rev Father McGrath had become parish priest in 1898 that plans were made to build a new church, adjoining the schools and presbytery.

This church is a lasting tribute to the Warrington architect responsible for its design and is an impressive example of what may be fairly described as Victorian Gothic. It consists of nave, two side aisles, sanctuary with two chapels either side as well as a gallery over the main entrance to accommodate choir and organ. The church is 124 feet long, 53 feet wide and 50 feet high. The clerestory is supported by polished granite columns with bosses and caps of Yorkshire stone and the sanctuary is divided from the nave by a white polished marble step. White marble stoups for holy water at each side of the nave commemorate an early benefactor of the church, Mr Thomas Wallington. The cost of the building was £6,000.

For the occasion of the consecration of the Church in May, 1950, a new high altar, reredos and side panelling were built costing £3,000. Portland stone was used for the altar, whilst the reredos and side panelling were carved in English oak. The design of these alterations to the sanctuary was the work of another local firm of architects, Massey and Greaves.

The consecration was by the Bishop of Shrewsbury (Right Rev J. Murphy) who had been curate at Our Lady's for 12 years.

Outside the main entrance stands a memorial to those who lost their lives in the First World War. This memorial, which was blessed in 1920, is a stone reproduction, on a two-tier base, of a crucifix then in the possession of Mr Walter Wallington of Grappenhall.

Internally this church is well maintained and is both beautiful and impressive.


## CHRIST CHURCH, LATCHFORD

Wash Lane, Latchford is one of the ancient thoroughfares of Warrington since it led at one time to the nearby ford across the Mersey. Because of the increasing population in this area in the 19th century, Thomas Greenall, the patron of Grappenhall Church, purchased land in Wash Lane and in 1844 erected a small infants' school thereon with the aid of a grant from the National Society. Members of Thomas Greenall's family subsequently erected

198

a church next to the school and this church was consecrated under the name of Christ Church by D. Graham, Bishop of Chester on July 16, 1861. There is a brass plate in the chancel stating that the church was erected to the memory of Thomas Greenall, of Wilderspool and Grappenhall.

Christ Church is a Gothic structure in a decorated style of architecture and is rather curious insofar as although when viewed from a distance it appears to be a conventional church with tower and spire, the building actually consists of three separate elements that are joined together.

The tower and spire are situated above the porch on the south side of the church and are attached to the nave by short corridor. On the north side of the nave an aisle was an addition to the rest of the church in 1902. The architects were Messrs Kennedy and Rogers of London and Bangor and the builders were Messrs Joseph Gibson and Sons of Warrington. On the south side of the tower the masons carved the likenesses of two popular heroes of the day, Garibaldi and his lieutenant, Colonel Paed. The Italian patriot visited England in 1862 where he was received with great enthusiasm by the public, but was requested to return home by the government.

At first the church was a chapel of ease to Grappenhall Church but was made into a parish church with its own district by an Order in Council dated March 12, 1866.

There are many stained glass windows in the church exhibiting a wide variety of examples of this particular art. Some are memorials to those having strong associations with the church and with Latchford and these include the East window, a thanks offering from Sylvanus and Jane Reynolds and at the opposite end of the church, a large window to the memory of Emma, wife of J. Malin Edelsten. On the south and north sides are windows to the memory of members of the Broadbent family and the most recent addition, dedicated in 1969, is a beautiful example of modern stained glass to the memory of Fanny Louisa Dale, a member of the Mothers' Union. Other memorials in the church have been erected to Egerton Fairclough and Miss E.L. Broadbent as well as to Henry and Mary White.

In 1946 a fire destroyed the organ and damaged the chancel. Subsequent restoration has resulted in the installation of a new organ as well as oak choir pews, pulpit, lectern and screen, together with a restored memorial to those who lost their lives in two world wars.

The North aisle now contains the altar from St. Margaret's Latchford and is used daily as a chapel, while St. Margaret's is used as a parochial hall.

It is a great pity that lamp standards in Wash Lane obsure the view of anyone wishing to photograph this church which otherwise presents a pleasing view and which is situated in an attractive setting elevated from the roadway.

St. Mary's Buttermarket Street

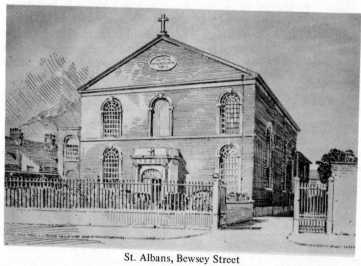

St. Albans, Bewsey Street

# ST. ANDREW'S ORFORD

Beginning as a mission of St. Margaret's and All Hallows, Orford, St. Andrew's Church became the centre of the Conventional District in 1961 with its own priest, the Rev T.S. Stanage, who became responsible for the erection of the present church and parsonage.

The area it serves is largely a postwar Corporation housing estate and the beautiful new church consecrated by the Bishop of Liverpool (Dr Clifford A. Martin) on November 30, 1963, was the first to be completed in the Diocese in response to the Bishop's "Call-to-Build Appeal".

Cruciform in plan it was especially designed to sit comfortably among the dwellings and other buildings of the Orford Housing Estate by the architects, Arthur Farbrother and Partners, of Manchester. It was intended to be dominant, but not domineering, and to this end was provided with low external walls and steeply-pitched roof, the whole being crowned with a tall slender spire of timber clad in fibre glass. From outside, an eye-catching feature is an engraved glass panel over the main entrance depicting St. Andrew, Fisher of Men. The main doorway leads to a foyer separated from the body of the church by a wall of glass and above this entrance hall is a balcony for choir and organ.

An impression of great height is given by the steeply-sloping ceiling supported by timber trusses and the tinted windows provided a pleasing and restful interior light.

The eye, however, is immediately attracted by a large cross suspended over the altar which is set against a wall of silver-grey facing bricks. Beautiful colouring effects are produced by the light from two windows containing stained glass in an abstract pattern and situated on either side of this rear wall. Similar light effects are also produced in the Lady Chapel situated on the left of the simulated crossing. On the right of this crossing is a recess containing a portable baptismal font.

Two stone tablets on either side of the ·chancel record, in a pleasing Anglo-Saxon lettering, the laying of a stone by the Venerable Eric H. Evans, Archdeacon of Warrington, on May 11, 1963 and the consecration of the church by the Lord Bishop of Liverpool in the presence of Her Royal Highness, The Princess Royal, on November 30, 1963.

Pleasing decorations and furniture complete this delightful church and the total cost, which included the organ supplied by Jardine's of Manchester, was £43,000.

A bell in the spire, in keeping with the modern nature of this church, is operated electrically by means of solenoids which control the striking hammer.

The figure of St. Andrew, engraved in glass over the main entrance was from a full-scale cartoon by Mr Brian Nolan; the hanging cross was designed

201

by Mr Edward Blackwell as were the lectern, altar and candlestick; and the main building contractors were Brew Bros. of Cadishead.

This successful church having been consecrated on St. Andrew's Day 1963, quickly became the parish church of a new parish on January 11, 1964. It now stands as the centre of a complex of associated buildings – a school, vicarage and church hall – on a well populated housing estate that will grow still larger by the addition of new dwellings in the next few years.


## ST. OSWALD'S PADGATE

Although the present church of St. Oswald at Padgate is a recent building, the parish is now nearly a half century old.

A pamphlet, published in 1926, announced a sale of work at the Ashton Hall on February 25-27 to be opened by the Bishop of Lancaster in aid of St. Oswald's New Mission and Schools, Padgate Lane. In this pamphlet, Father T.A. Hind, Parish Priest of St. Mary's appealed for funds to establish St. Oswald's which was to be erected upon a site that had been purchased together with Bruche Hall by the Catholic Community of Warrington for educational purposes.

So great was the response to this appeal for funds that the foundation stone of the first church on the site was laid on May 29, 1927 by Dr Keating, Archbishop of Liverpool. When the building was complete it was blessed and opened on June 17, 1928 by Bishop Dobson, Vicar Capitular of the Liverpool Archdiocese and the total cost of this first church, though not of the site, amounting to £3,500 had by then been paid.

The new parish thus created largely through the efforts of Father Hind flourished to such an extent that by the time the present Parish Priest of St. Oswald's, Father D. Ryan arrived, the original presbytery had been taken down and a new one erected nearby to make way for further developments.

After new schools had been built, a new social club was opened in April 1964 and by November of that year the building of a much larger church, costing £60,000 was well advanced, so that a total debt of around £200,000 had been incurred on the various projects undertaken.

On Wednesday, June 16, 1965, the new church was opened by Dr G.A. Beck, Archbishop of Liverpool and the opening ceremony was attended by about 600 people.

Providing seating for about 500 people in the body of the church and for an additional 100 in a gallery over a porch at the main entrance, the new St. Oswald's is a fine example of modern church building.

Cruciform in plan the church has been so designed that the spacious open interior, without supporting pillars, permits the entire seating to be arranged so that worshippers in all parts of the church are close to the sanctuary and high altar, although there are side altars on either side.

The architects were L.A.G. Pritchard, Son and Partners of Liverpool and a local firm of builders, Harper and Finch, erected the church. A steel framework, including a tower rising to a height of 75 feet, was first erected and this was then clad in brickwork.

Occupying an area of 90 feet by 80 feet the church is 46 feet from floor to apex and a suspended timber ceiling of cedar wood is a striking internal feature.

Three large circular windows and other windows contain stained glass in abstract patterns that help to create the beautiful interior atmosphere of this new church and the marble altar rails and floor of the sanctuary are also of great beauty.

Since the church was opened a recessed tabernacle has been made behind the high altar and the construction of this recess, which has involved an external projection with perspex light, was undertaken by Father Ryan and four parishioners. Internally the natural illumination from the perspex light of this recess immediately focusses attention on the altar and on a large crucifix suspended over the tabernacle.

The Stations of the Cross round the walls of the church consist of wooden carvings and externally five mosaics over the main doorway and containing religious symbols were designed by Robin Riley of Liverpool. Provision has also been made on the west exterior wall for a statue to be erected in the future.

When the new church was erected the old church was left standing and it is now used as a school hall.

The future provision of a Youth Club for St. Oswald's is envisaged by Father Ryan, to whose energy and devotion this spacious and loyal church is a striking testimonial.


## BETHESDA CHAPEL STOCKTON HEATH


Almost exactly 200 years after the opening of the Warrington Academy at Bridge Foot, Warrington on October 20, 1757, a new Christian home of worship and study known as Bethesda Chapel, was opened on Saturday, October 1957 at the junction of Lumb Brook Road and Chester Road in Stockton Heath.

While the Warrington Academy was established for those who were prevented by religious tests from pursuing higher educational studies at the established universities, it nevertheless admitted the members of any Christian denomination who cared to attend, and the Academy itself, of course, stood upon the north bank of the River Mersey.

Bethesda Chapel was built to meet the spiritual needs of anyone prepared to practice Christianity and those who worship at Bethesda seek to follow the New Testament pattern of a local church. The site for this new home of Christian worship was literally carved out of the North bank of the Bridgewater Canal, and the chapel is a striking testimony to the energy and enthusiasm of the founders and especially to the dedication of Mr Alfred Jones.

It is a very simple building of brickwork with concrete supports and yet both internally and externally it possesses simplicity without austerity.

Externally the building stands pleasantly on a spacious car-parking area with the bank of the Bridgewater Canal at the rear and is fronted by an attractive low brick wall. Internally the roof supports are gracefully shaped and the internal woodwork is mostly of Japanese oak, so that the doors, the preaching desk and other fittings all harmonise in a very agreeable manner. In front of the preaching desk a baptistry is situated in the floor as baptism in the chapel is by full immersion and special apparatus is provided to heat the water used.

A piano and an organ are situated on either side of the preaching desk; the organ is in memory of Eva Catherine Jones. All the seats are movable and are provided with Dunlopillo cushions while attractive half-dome lights are fixed in the ceiling.

The chapel was designed by Richard C. Symonds, architect, and was built by George Moss and Sons of Leigh and the total cost amounted to about £9,000.

A framed illuminated copy of the Dedication Service hangs in the main entrance porch and at the opening on October 26, 1957, Mr Alfred Jones dedicated the building and presided at a service in which the speaker was Dr F.A. Tatford of London and a trustee of the chapel.

As many groups connected with this chapel meet there for bible studies and a variety of activities the building was erected with a large classroom and other rooms at the south end, but owing to the numbers attracted to this chapel an extension soon became necessary.

Erected across the south end of the building the extension provided an additional classroom in June 1958 and cost about £4,000. The result is that a Sunday School now provides accommodation for Primary and Junior Schools and for boy and girl Convenanters. There is also a Ladies' Fellowship and a Young Wives' Group. A Bible Study group meet one morning each week and there are Ministry meetings on one night each week.

The Chapel supports two Missionaries, Harry and Phyllis Aspinall, in North India so that the influence of this congregation is already felt far beyond the locality in which this chapel is situated.

# WOOLSTON

This series of articles concerning churches in the Warrington area began with an account of St. Elphin's which is the oldest church in Warrington and probably the oldest church in Lancashire. It is appropriate, therefore, that the series should end with an account of the most recent church to be erected in the area and in a part of what was originally the Parish of Warrington.

Long before Padgate had become a separate parish, a Commission, in accordance with an Act of Parliament of 1649, was ordered to survey the parishes and churches of the country and meetings of the Lancashire Commission were held in 1650.

The Commissioners reported that: "the Tyth hempe and fflax in Woulston and Martinscroft wee find belongs to Mr Standish of Woulston . . . And wee Doe present that some part of the said Towneships is aboute two myles distant from Warrington Church, and three myles and a quarter from Hollingfaire Chappell; And wee present that it is fitt that there should be a Church built within Woulston, neare unto the house of John Fearnehead."

Nearly 200 years passed after this recommendation had been made before a new ecclesiastical district which included Woolston was carved from the ancient Parish of Warrington. It was almost another 50 years after Padgate Church had been erected that a mission was built in Woolston.

The Woolston Mission was first opened as a school in 1885; it became licensed as a mission church in 1909 and the school continued until 1951. On May 3, 1970 the last service was held in this Mission Church which has been used as a Parish Hall since the new daughter Church of Padgate, the Church of the Ascension, Woolston, was opened on May 7, 1970.

The Church of the Ascension is situated at the junction of Hillock Lane, Dam Lane and Warren Lane on a plot of ground that had been given for the erection of a church by Mr Edward Gorton in 1917. When it was finally decided to erect a church on this site the act of cutting the first turf to prepare the site for building was performed on May 19, 1968 by Miss C.M. Gorton of Grappenhall, the daughter of the donor of the land and a lady who has become the organist of the new church.

Another ceremony on the site took place on September 15, 1968 when the foundation stone, blessed by the Bishop of Warrington, the Right Rev L.A. Brown, was laid by the Vicar of Padgate, the Rev J.O. Colling. Nearly two years later the new church was complete and was consecrated by the Bishop of Liverpool, The Right Rev Stuart Blanche, on May 7, 1970.

It is very appropriate that the latest church to be erected in the area should also be the most modern in design, incorporating as it does an arrangement of the altar, reading desk and sedilia to permit services to be conducted in conformity with recent liturgical ideas.

The architect was George C. Pace, of York, who is consultant to the

Chapter of Liverpool Cathedral, and the builders were Messrs J. and D. Punshon.

The building is rectangular with a porch and vestries on either side. Within the main building, the altar is situated across one corner so that seating faces this area from two directions at right angles to each other, while in the V-shaped space between the rows of seats, and in front of the altar, is situated a font. The reading desk is placed behind the altar; between the desk and the altar is situated a sedilia. The whole is seen to best advantage from a Lady Chapel which is separated from the church by a wall containing large windows.

Internal fittings are on limed oak and wrought iron, the altars both in the Church and Lady chapel, are of York stone.

An exhibition pipe organ, constructed by Rushworth and Draper was installed and was loaned to Chester Cathedral, before the new church was complete, while the cathedral organ was being re-built. Various musical recitals incorporating the use of the organ have been held in the new church since it was opened.

A tower over the main entrance porch contains a bell which is electrically operated through a device which pulls a bell rope and controls the rate at which the bell is tolled.

The church is built of pleasing brickwork with a copper roof and the total cost, including fittings and organ was about £50,000, part of which was met by the Bishop of Liverpool's "Call to Build Fund".

The first vicar of the Church of the Ascension is the Rev J.R.I. Wikeley and the church is organised as a daughter church of Padgate.

# ALPHABETICAL INDEX OF CONTENTS

## ERRATA

Page 1    — Insert heading THE MID-MERSEY VALLEY.
Page 3    — Line 23 — delete "consists" and insert "consist".
Page 14   — Line 14 — delete "writted" and insert "written".
Page 135  — Caption to Illustration —
             delete "Ascension, Wooston" and insert "Ascension, Woolston".
Page 178  — Caption to Illustration —
             delete "Grappen Hall" and insert "Grappenhall".
Page 201  — Line 11 — delete "Farbrother" and insert "Fairbrother".

# BIBLIOGRAPHY

Accounts of the surveyor of the highways of the township of Grappenhall 1732-1829 *MS.*

An act for making the rivers Mersey and Irwell navigable from Liverpool to Manchester 1721.

The Anglo-Saxon Chronicle. Transl. with an intro. by G.N. Garmonsway *London*, Dent 1953.

ASHTON, T.S. An eighteenth-century industrialist: Peter Stubs of Warrington 1756-1806. *Manchester U.P.,* 1939.

BAGLEY, J.J. *Editor.* A History of Cheshire, *Cheshire Community Council,* Chester 1964 – in progress.

BAGSHAW, S. History, gazeteer, and director of the County Palatine of Chester, *Sheffield, 1850.*

BARKER, T.C. The Sankey navigation. *Historic Society of Lancashire and Cheshire V* 100 1948.

BEAMONT, W. An account of the Cheshire township of Appleton. *Warrington Evening Post* 1877.

BEAMONT, W. Bruche: a monograph. *Warrington Mackie, Brewtnall & Co.* 1878.

BEAMONT, W. A discourse of the warr in Lancashire. *Manchester Chetham Society* vol 62 1864.

BEAMONT, W. Hale and Orford. *Warrington Guardian Steam Printing Works* 1886.

BEAMONT, W. History of the castle of Halton and the Priory or Abbey of Norton. *Warrington, Percival Pearse* 1873.

BEAMONT, W. History of Latchford. *Warrington, Percival Pearse* 1889.

BEAMONT, W. A literal extension and translation of the portion of Domesday Book relating to Cheshire and Lancashire . . . *Chester* 1882.

BEAMONT, W. Warrington Church notes. *Warrington, Percival Pearse* 1876.

BEAMONT, W. Warrington in M.CCCC. LXV as described in a contemporary rent roll of the Legh family. *Manchester Chetham Society* vol 17 1849.

BEAMONT, W. *and* RYLANDS, J.P. An attempt to identify the arms formerly existing in the windows of the Parish Church and Austin Friary at Warrington. *Warrington, Percival Pearse* 1878.

A Book of survey of the Baronry of Warrington . . . parcell of the possessions of . . . Robert Erle of Lecester. 1587. *MS and typed transcript,* (Binders title: Demenes and Tearme land in Bewsey and Warrington).

BOWER, Mary. Memories of Stretton. *Warrington, Guardian Press* (1964).

BOWYER, J.F. Penketh Methodist Church 1860-1960. Centenary Handbook. *Wigan, Murray* 1951.

BOYD, A.W. A country parish: Great Budworth in the county of Chester. *London, Collins* 1951.BROXAP, E. The great civil war in Lancashire (1642-1651) *Manchester U.P.* 1910.

BROXAP, E. The great civil war in Lancashire (1642-1651) *Manchester U.P.* 1910.

CARTER, G.A. Digging up the past in Warrington and District (an essay and a book list) *Warrington, Library and Museum Committee* 1964.

CARTER, G.A. The free borough of Warrington in the thirteenth century. *Historic Soc. Lancs and Cheshire* v 105 1953.

CARTER, G.A. Transcript and translation of the part of the Legh Survey 1465 relating to Grappenhall *MS.*

CARTER, G.A. WARRINGTON HUNDRED: a handbook published by the Corporation of Warrington on the occasion of the centenary of the Incorporation of the Borough. *Warrington pr. Garside & Jolley* 1947.

CARTER, G.A. *editor* The Warrington Academy by Rev William Turner. *Warrington, Library and Museum Committee* 1957.

CARTER, G.A. The Whitecross Company Limited 1864-1964. *Warrington, Pr Pr* 1964.

CHARLESWORTH, Ruth. The history of education in Warrington. 1933. *typewritten.*

CHARLTON, K. James Cropper (1773-1840) and agricultural improvement in the early nineteenth century. *Historic Society of Lancashire and Cheshire* vol 112 1960.

CROPPER, J. Last will and testament of James Cropper. 7th January 1839. *MS.*

CROPPER, J. Some account of an agricultural school for orphans at Fearnhead near Warrington. *Warrington. Thomas Hurst* 1839.

DALLAM, T. The diary of Master Thomas Dallam 1599-1600. In early voyages and travels in The Levant. (*The Hakluyt Society* No. 87. 1893).

DAWN: a monthly magazine vol 4, 1904, p83.

DICTIONARY of National biography. *London, Smith, Elder & Co.* 1885-1900 63 vols and suppls.

DOMESDAY BOOK . . . Facsimile of the part relating to Cheshire. *Ordnance Survey Office,* Southampton, 1861.

EARWAKER, J.P. Ancient charters and deeds at High Legh, Cheshire. *Journal of Chester Archaeological and Historic Society* 1886-7.

EKWALL, E. Concise Oxford dictionary of English Place-Names, *Oxford Clarendon Press* 1960.

EKWALL, E. Place names of Lancashire. *Manchester U.P.* 1922.

ENGLISH PLACE-NAME SOCIETY. The Place-names of Cheshire, by J. McN. Dodgson. *Cambridge U.P.* 1970.

FARRER, W. Lancashire pipe rolls 1130-1216 and early Lancashire Charters. *Liverpool, Henry Young & Son* 1902.

FULTON, J.F. The Warrington Academy (1757-1786) and its influence upon medicine and science. *Repr. from Bulletin of the Inst. of the History of Medicine (Supplement to Bulletin of the John's Hopkins Hospital, vol. LII No. 2 Feb. 1933).*

GARDNER, C.S.B. – Memorials of the family of Sankey, 1207-1880. *Swansea pr. pr.* 1880.

HARRISON, W. Ancient fords, ferries and bridges in Lancashire. *Lancashire and Cheshire Antiquarian Society* vol 12 1894.

HARRISON, W. Development of turnpike system in Lancashire. *(Lancashire and Cheshire Antiquarian Society, 1886 and 1892 vols IV and X).*

HAWTHORN, J. Centenary of Wycliffe Congregational Church, Bewsey Street, Warrington 1851-1951. *Warrington* 1951.

HAWTHORN, J. Diary of a Warrington Mayor (William Beamont). *Warrington Lit. and Phil. Soc.* 1932.

HIGH LEGH ESTATE. Catalogue of sale of High Legh Estate 1919.

HODGKINSON, Archer. The accounts of the surveyors of the highways for the township of Grappenhall 1732-1829. *Lancashire and Cheshire Antiquarian Society,* vol 48 1934.

HODGSON, J.S. History of Penketh School 1834-1907. London, Headley Bros. 1907.

KAY, Derrick M. History of Lymm Grammar School. *Altrincham Sherratt* 1960.

KELLY, E.R. Post Office directory of Cheshire, *2nd ed.* 1865. *London Kelly & Co.* 1865.

KELLY'S DIRECTORIES LTD. Kelly's directory of Cheshire, *4th ed.* 1892 – *13th ed.* 1939. *London, Kelly's Directories Ltd.* 1892-1939 10v.

KELLY'S DIRECTORIES LTD. Kelly's directory of Lancashire 1924. *London, Kelly's Directories Ltd.* 1924.

KENDRICK, James. Profiles of Warrington Worthies. *Warrington, J. Haddock & Son.* 1853.

KENWORTHY, J. History of the Baptist Church at Hill Cliffe. *London, Mackie & Co.* 1889.

LANCASHIRE BIBLIOGRAPHY. Part I, Lancashire Directories 1684-1957. *Manchester* 1968. Part II, Lancashire Acts of Parliament 1266-1957. *Manchester* 1969.

LEGH MANUSCRIPT 1465. Survey of lands, properties and tenements belonging to Sir Peter Legh . . . 1465. Situated in Warrington and other places in Lancashire and Cheshire 1465. *MS photocopy.* •

MANSIONS OF ENGLAND AND WALES: Cheshire. *London, Stovin and Bartlett* 1850 2v.

MARSHALL, C.F. Dendy. Centenary history of the Liverpool and Manchester Railway. *London, Locomotive Pub. Co. Ltd.* 1930.

MAY, T. Warrington's Roman remains . . . *Warrington, Mackie & Co.,* 1904.

MAYES, S. An organ for the sultan. *London, Putnam* 1956.

MEE, A. *editor.* Cheshire (n.d.) (*The King's England*).

"MILLING" Vol CXXVI No. 20, May 19, 1956.

MOUNFIELD, A. A village centenary: the Independent Methodist Church at Stockton Heath, 1806-1906. *Wigan, Independent Methodist Book Room* 1907.

MULLINEUX, F. The Duke of Bridgewater's Canal. *Eccles, Eccles and District Historic Society* 1959.

MUSSON, A.E. Enteprise in soap and chemicals, 1815-1916. *Manchester University Press* 1965.

ORMEROD, G. History of the County Palatine and City of Chester. *London, G. Routledge* 1882 3 vols.

OUGHTRINGTON ESTATE. Catalogue of sale of Oughtrington and Beechwood estates. 1911.

OUGHTRINGTON HOUSE. Sale prospectus c1862.

OWEN, G.V. Life beyond the veil. *London, Thornton Butterworth* 1920-21 4 vols.

PALMER, W.T. The River Mersey. *London, Hale* 1944.

PORT, M.H. Six hundred new churches: a study of the Church Building Commission, 1818-1856. S.P.C.K., 1961.

POTTER, S. Cheshire place names. *Historic Society of Lancashire and Cheshire,* vol 106 1954.

POULTON-WITH-FEARNHEAD. Town's book, 1669-1814. *MS* 2v.

RAINES, F.R. *ed.* The visitation of the county Palatine of Lancaster, 1567 by William Flower. *Manchester Chetham Society* vol 81 1870.

REED, B. Crewe to Carlisle. *London, Ian Allan,* 1969.

RICHARDS, R. Old Cheshire churches. *London, Batsford* 1947.

RICHMOND, I.A. and CRAWFORD, O.G.S. The British section of the Ravenna Cosmography. *Oxford* 1949.

SMITH, A.H. English place name elements. *Cambridge U.P.* 1956 (*English Place-Name Soc.*).

ST. THOMAS' CHURCH, STOCKTON HEATH. 100 years of faith 1868-1968. *Warrington pr pr.* 1968.

STEWART-BROWN, R. The Scrope and Grosvenor controversy *Lancashire & Cheshire Historic Society,* vol 89, 1938.

STRETTON TOWN BOOK. 1791-1834 *MS.*

TEMPEST, *Mrs* A.C. The descent of the Mascys of Rixton 1889.

THOMPSON, F.H. Roman Cheshire, *Chester* 1965 (*Volume Two of A History of Cheshire. General Editor − J.J. Bagley*).

VARLEY, W.J. Cheshire before the Romans. *Chester,* 1964. (*Volume One of a History of Cheshire. General Editor − J.J. Bagley*).

VICTORIA COUNTY HISTORY OF THE COUNTY OF LANCASTER *ed.* by W. Farrer and J. Brownbill. *London,* 1908 8 vols.

WAINWRIGHT, F.T. The Anglian Settlement of Lancashire. *Historic Society of Lancashire & Cheshire,* v 93 1941.

WALTON ESTATE, Cheshire. Sale catalogue of the Walton Estate, Cheshire; by direction of Lord Daresbury 1941.

WARBURTON COW CLUB. Articles to be observed by the Warburton Cow Club . . . *Warrington, Haddock* 1842.

WARRINGTON GUARDIAN. History of the elementary schools of Warrington. *Warrington Guardian* 1933.

WHITAKER, H. Descriptive list of the printed maps of Lancashire 1577-1900 (*Chetham Soc. vol. 101 NS 1938*).

WHITAKER, H. Descriptive list of the printed maps of Cheshire 1577-1900 (*Chetham Soc. vol. 106 NS 1942*).

WINTERBURN, J. An outline of Culcheth's history *Culchet's* 1967 *duplicated.*

WOMENS' INSTITUTE. Cheshire village memories II. *Tilston Court Cheshire Federation of Women's Institutes* (1961).